The American Beast

Also by Jill Lepore

If Then:
How the Simulmatics Corporation Invented the Future

This America:
The Case for the Nation

These Truths:
A History of the United States

Joe Gould's Teeth

The Secret History of Wonder Woman

Book of Ages:
The Life and Opinions of Jane Franklin

The Story of America:
Essays on Origins

The Mansion of Happiness:
A History of Life and Death

The Whites of Their Eyes:
The Tea Party's Revolution and the Battle over American History

New York Burning:
Liberty, Slavery, and Conspiracy in Eighteenth-Century Manhattan

A Is for American:
Letters and Other Characters in the Newly United States

The Name of War:
King Philip's War and the Origins of American Identity

The
American
Beast

Essays, 2012–2022

JILL LEPORE

JOHN MURRAY

First published in Great Britain in 2023 by John Murray (Publishers)

1

A CIP catalogue record for this title is available from the British Library

Hardback ISBN 9781399810173
Trade Paperback ISBN 9781399810180
ebook ISBN 9781399810203

Printed and bound in Great Britain by Clays Ltd, Elcograf S.p.A.

John Murray policy is to use papers that are natural, renewable and
recyclable products and made from wood grown in sustainable forests.
The logging and manufacturing processes are expected to conform to
the environmental regulations of the country of origin.

Carmelite House
50 Victoria Embankment
London EC4Y 0DZ

www.johnmurraypress.co.uk

John Murray Press, part of Hodder & Stoughton Limited
An Hachette UK company

To H.F.

The nation seems to slouch onward into its
uncertain future like some huge inarticulate beast.

—Richard Hofstadter, "The Future of
American Violence," 1970

Contents

Some of these essays were previously published under different titles. All essays originally appeared in *The New Yorker*, and passages from some of them were included in *These Truths*, published by W. W. Norton. The introduction has not previously been published.

Introduction

"This is the year of the ballot or the bullet."
—Malcolm X, 1964

W HAT IF THE PROBLEM OF THE UNITED STATES IN the twenty-first century is not the decline of democracy but the persistence of violence? The two can scarcely be separated— rule by force is what replaces the rule of law—but it has long been the preference of American politicians to decry assaults on democracy, strenuously, and especially while running for office, but merely to fret, vaguely and ineffectively, about acts of violence, about mass shootings and police brutality, about domestic terrorism and armed civilians, about murder and mayhem. Does there come a point in time when a nation founded upon a right to revolution simply loses its bearings and devolves into chaos, an endless fight about the right to fight?

"Democracy never lasts long," the irascible John Adams once wrote. "It soon wastes, exhausts, and murders itself." Adams, at the time, was nearly eighty years old—he had not much longer to last himself—and I had always dismissed this remark as the cantankerous grumblings of a frustrated old man, shaking his fist at younger men, Jacksonian Democrats, fighting for the right to vote. But lately, it's been haunting me. "There never was a Democracy Yet, that did not commit suicide," Adams went on, drawing on his reading of history to predict a violent death. If a democracy begins to waste, exhaust and murder itself, what would be the warning signs? Who would be able stop a seemingly inexorable act of self-murder, and how? Who can halt the corruption of power? "Individuals have conquered themselves, Nations and large Bodies of Men, never," Adams observed. Like every ungoverned person, every democracy, he believed, would descend into "Fraud, Violence, and Cruelty." What force, what restraint, could act as a brake?

Although I didn't quite realize it at the time, these questions animated a series of essays I wrote for *The New Yorker* magazine over ten tumultuous years of American history, from the murder of Trayvon Martin and the start of the Black Lives Matter movement, in 2012, to the report of a congressional committee into the armed insurrection at the U.S. Capitol in 2022. These were years of widening political polarization and rising political violence within the United States, alongside growing fears of the possibility that the nation would descend, once again, into a civil war. As a U.S. political historian, I year after wearying year found those fears wildly overdrawn, a product of polarization, rather than a commentary on it. I still do find those fears overdrawn and, generally, reactionary. But I've also come to believe that the analysis of American democracy can't proceed absence an analysis of American violence.

The United States has the highest rate of gun ownership in the world. Four in five homicides in the United States are gun-related (as opposed to one in twenty-five in the UK). The United States also has the highest murder rate among affluent nations. In Europe, the murder rate has been falling for centuries, a decline historians attribute chiefly to the growing power of a centralizing state to disarm civilians, curtail violence, and enforce law and order—in short, to claim a monopoly on the use of force. In medieval Europe, the murder rate for a long time, as best as can be calculated, hovered around 35 murders for every 100,000 people. By 1500, that rate had fallen to about 20; by 1700, to 5 and by 1900, to about 2. In the UK, and in most of Europe, the murder rate in 2020 was about 1. The American history of homicide looks entirely different. Over the course of the nineteenth century, while Europe's murder rate plummeted, the U.S. rate kept rising. After the Second World War, it briefly dropped to about 5 but then began climbing again, reaching about 11 in 1990. In 2020, it was 7.

Or consider policing. In 2013, police in Finland fired six bullets; on a single encounter on a single day of that year, in a single town in the United States, three policemen fired seventeen bullets when they shot and killed an unarmed thirty-five-year-old orchard worker from

Mexico. The *Guardian* once reported that "in the first 24 days of 2015, police in the US fatally shot more people than did police in England and Wales, combined, over the past 24 years." Or consider incarceration. "By population, by per capita incarceration rates, and by expenditures, the United States exceeds all other nations in how many of its citizens, asylum seekers, and undocumented immigrants are under some form of criminal justice supervision," the historian Khalil Gibran Muhammad has written. "The number of African American and Latinx people in American jails and prisons today exceeds the entire populations of some African, Eastern European, and Caribbean countries."

These divergences suggest a gruesome form of American exceptionalism, a dark backwardness. The essays in this book explore many possible explanations for that exceptionalism. But here's one more. In a book called *The History of Murder*, the comparative historical criminologist Pieter Spierenburg speculated that democracy came too soon to the United States because it came before the establishment of the state. In Europe, people had long since accepted the authority of the state and its monopoly on force by the time European states became democracies over the course of the long nineteenth century. The reverse was true in the United States. Democracy came first, and then came the state. And so, instead of yielding the right to bear arms to a strong central government, eighteenth-century American Revolutionaries preserved that right for themselves. It seemed, to them then, like freedom. It is, to us, a shackle.

THE ESSAYS IN THIS BOOK explore the history of American politics, journalism, and technology. I wrote them in my capacity as a staff writer at *The New Yorker* but I also wrote them in the context of my day job as a professor of American history at Harvard. I wrote these essays during a period of terrible, tragic decline in the United States, short, sharp years, marked by rising political violence, endless, vicious culture war, a series of constitutional crises, catastrophic climate change, and a global pandemic. To essays on these subjects, I mostly bring the vantage of scholarship, and snippets of archival evidence—I have a rule that every piece I write has to have, hidden within it, an archival easter egg—but I also did my best to get out of the classroom and the library and go see what I could see, hoping to offer up some view of what the present looks like by way of the past. I set out, more than once, to report: to interview the head of the NRA, to meet with the Boston chapter of the Tea Party, to attend the New Hampshire primaries, to watch presidential debates from the debate stage, to sit in the halls of nominating conventions. Finally, it needs saying that I wrote these essays during a time when I was also writing, and then revising, a sweeping history of the United States, a book called *These Truths,* published in 2018. I in fact wrote *These Truths* because of these essays, and so many more essays that are not included here, when I came to realize that, without intending to, I was, word by word, writing a very long history of the United States. That means that readers of *These Truths* might find passages in this collection familiar—in writing that book, I raided nearly every piece of political history I've ever written.

A red thread runs through nearly all these essays, an unraveling spool, a worry about rule, every kind of rule, at every scale. Who rules? Do they rule well? Does this species of rule, within a family, a polity, a nation-state, distribute power fairly? Is it just? Can it be just? And what about a written constitution, by which the living are ruled by the dead? And, finally, can a population in which one in three people owns at least one gun even be said to be a democracy?

BATTLEGROUND AMERICA

JUST AFTER SEVEN THIRTY ON THE MORNING OF FEB-
ruary 27, 2012, a seventeen-year-old boy named T. J. Lane
walked into the cafeteria at Chardon High School, about thirty miles
outside Cleveland. It was a Monday, and the cafeteria was filled with
kids, some eating breakfast, some waiting for buses to drive them
to programs at other schools, some packing up for gym class. Lane
sat down at an empty table, reached into a bag, and pulled out a
.22-caliber pistol. He stood up, raised the gun, and fired. He said not
a word.

Russell King, a seventeen-year-old junior, was sitting at a table
with another junior, Nate Mueller. King, shot in the head, fell face
first onto the table, a pool of blood forming. A bullet grazed Mueller's ear. "I could see the flame at the end of the gun," Mueller said
later. Daniel Parmertor, a sixteen-year-old snowboarder, was shot in
the head. Someone screamed "Duck!" Demetrius Hewlin, sixteen,
was also shot in the head, and slid under the table. Joy Rickers, a
senior, tried to run; Lane shot her as she fled. Nickolas Walczak, shot
in his neck, arm, back, and face, fell to the floor. He began crawling
toward the door.

Ever since the shootings at Columbine High School, in a Denver
suburb, in 1999, American schools have been preparing for gunmen.
Chardon started holding drills in 2007, after the Virginia Tech massacre, when twenty-three-year-old Seung-Hui Cho, a college senior,
shot fifty-seven people in Blacksburg.

At Chardon High School, kids ran through the halls screaming
"Lockdown!" Some of them hid in the teachers' lounge; they bar-
ricaded the door with a piano. Someone got on the school's public-
address system and gave instructions, but everyone knew what to do.

Students ran into classrooms and dived under desks; teachers locked the doors and shut off the lights. Joseph Ricci, a math teacher, heard Walczak, who was still crawling, groaning in the hallway. Ricci opened the door and pulled the boy inside. No one knew if the shooter had more guns, or more rounds. Huddled under desks, students called 911 and texted their parents. One tapped out, "Prayforus."

From the cafeteria, Frank Hall, the assistant football coach, chased Lane out of the building, and he ran off into the woods.

Moments later, four ambulances arrived. EMTs raced Rickers and Walczak to Chardon's Hillcrest Hospital. Hewlin, Parmertor, and King were flown by helicopter to a trauma center at MetroHealth Medical Center, in Cleveland. By eight thirty, the high school had been evacuated.

At a quarter to nine, police officers with dogs captured Lane, about a mile from the school.

"I hate to say it, but we trained for exactly this type of thing, a school emergency of this type," Dan McClelland, the county sheriff, said.

Danny Parmertor died that afternoon. That evening, St. Mary's Church opened its doors, and the people of Chardon sank to their knees and keened. At the town square, students gathered to hold a vigil. As night fell, they lit candles. Drew Gittins, sixteen, played a Black Eyed Peas song on his guitar. "People killin', people dyin'," he sang. "People got me, got me questionin', Where is the love?"

Russell King had been too badly wounded. A little after midnight, doctors said that they couldn't save him.

IN 2012, there were nearly three hundred million privately owned firearms in the United States: a hundred and six million handguns, a hundred and five million rifles, and eighty-three million shotguns. That works out to about one gun for every American. The gun that T. J. Lane brought to Chardon High School belonged to his uncle, who had bought it in 2010, at a gun shop. Both of Lane's parents had been arrested on charges of domestic violence over the years. Lane found the gun in his grandfather's barn.

The United States is the country with the highest rate of civilian gun ownership in the world. (The second highest is Yemen, where the rate is nevertheless only half that of the U.S.) No civilian population is more powerfully armed. Most Americans do not, however, own guns, because three-quarters of people with guns own two or more. According to the General Social Survey, conducted by the National Policy Opinion Center at the University of Chicago, the prevalence of gun ownership has declined steadily in the past few decades. In 1973, there were guns in roughly one in two households in the United States; in 2010, one in three. In 1980, nearly one in three Americans owned a gun; in 2010, that figure had dropped to one in five.

Men are far more likely to own guns than women are, but the rate of gun ownership among men fell from one in two in 1980 to one in three in 2010, while, in that same stretch of time, the rate among women remained one in ten. What may have held that rate steady in an age of decline was the aggressive marketing of handguns to women for self-defense, which is how a great many guns are marketed. Gun ownership is higher among whites than among blacks, higher in the country than in the city, and higher among older people than among younger people. One reason that gun ownership was declining, nationwide, might be that high school shooting clubs and rifle ranges at summer camps were no longer common.

Although rates of gun ownership, like rates of violent crime, were falling, the power of the gun lobby was not. Between 1980 and 2012, forty-four states passed some form of law that allows gun owners to carry concealed weapons outside their homes for personal protection. (Five additional states had these laws before 1980. Illinois was the sole holdout.) A federal ban on the possession, transfer, or manufacture of semiautomatic assault weapons, passed in 1994, was allowed to expire in 2004. In 2005, Florida passed the Stand Your Ground law, an extension of the so-called castle doctrine, exonerating from prosecution citizens who use deadly force when confronted by an assailant, even if they could have retreated safely; Stand Your Ground laws expand that protection outside the home to any place that an individual "has a right to be." Twenty-four states soon passed similar laws.

The day before T. J. Lane shot five high school students in Ohio, another high school student was shot in Florida. The *Orlando Sentinel* ran a three-paragraph story. On February 26, seventeen-year-old Trayvon Martin left a house in a town outside Orlando and walked to a store. He was seen by a twenty-eight-year-old man named George Zimmerman, who called 911 to report that Martin, who was black, was "a real suspicious guy." Zimmerman got out of his truck. Zimmerman was carrying a 9 mm pistol; Martin was unarmed. What happened next has not been established, and is much disputed. Zimmerman told the police that Martin attacked him. Martin's family has said that the boy, heard over a cell phone, begged for his life.

Zimmerman shot Martin in the chest. Martin did not survive. Zimmerman was not immediately charged. Outside Orlando, the story was not reported.

THE DAY AFTER THE SHOOTING IN OHIO, I went to a firing range. I'd signed up for a lesson the week before. Once, when I was in Air Force ROTC for a year, I spent an afternoon studying how to defeat a sniper, but I'd never held a gun before.

The American Firearms School sits in an industrial park just north of Providence, in a beige stucco building topped with a roof of mint-green sheet metal. From the road, it looks like a bowling alley, but from the parking lot you can tell that it's not. You can hear the sound of gunfire. It doesn't sound like thunder. It doesn't sound like rain. It sounds like gunfire.

Inside, there's a shop, a pistol range, a rifle range, a couple of class-rooms, a locker room, and a place to clean your gun. The walls are painted police blue up to the wainscoting, and then white to the ceiling, which is painted black. It feels like a clubhouse, except, if you've never been to a gun shop before, that part feels not quite licit, like a porn shop. On the floor, there are gun racks, gun cases, holsters, and gun safes. Rifles hang on a wall behind the counter; handguns are under glass. Most items, including the rifles, come in black or pink:

there are pink handcuffs, a pink pistol grip, a pink gun case, and pink paper targets. Above the pink bull's-eye, which looks unnervingly like a breast, a line of text reads, CANCER SUCKS.

The American Firearms School is run by Matt Medeiros, a Rhode Island firefighter and EMT. Medeiros is also a leader of the Rhode Island chapter of Pink Heals, a nonprofit organization of emergency and rescue workers who drive pink fire trucks and pink police cars to raise money for cancer research and support groups. When Pink Heals opened a women's center in West Warwick, Medeiros held a fundraiser at the Firearms School.

Unlike many firing ranges, which are private clubs, the American Firearms School is open to the public. Most mornings, federal, state, and local law enforcement agencies, as well as private security firms, rent out the ranges for training and target practice. Classes, from beginner to advanced, are held in the afternoons, and are run by certified instructors.

In many states, to purchase a gun from a licensed dealer you need a permit, which requires you to complete firearms safety training, not unlike driver's education. But even if all states required this, not everyone who buys a gun would have to take a class. That's because 40 percent of the guns purchased in the United States are bought from private sellers at gun shows, or through other private exchanges, such as classified ads, which fall under what is known as the "gun show loophole" and are thus unregulated.

At the American Firearms School, the Learn to Shoot program, for novices, costs forty dollars for ninety minutes: a lesson, a gun rental, range time, two targets, and two boxes of bullets. This doesn't constitute sufficient instruction for a gun permit in the state, but the school offers a one-day, ninety-nine-dollar course that does: Basic Firearms Safety includes shooting fundamentals, a discussion of firearms law, and guidance in safe firearms storage.

The idea that every man can be his own policeman, and every woman hers, has necessitated revisions to the curriculum: civilians now receive training once available only to law enforcement officers, or the military. A six-hour class on concealed carrying includes a lesson in "engaging the threat." NRA Basic Personal Protection in the Home teaches "the basic knowledge, skills, and attitude essential to the safe and efficient use of a handgun for protection of self and family" and provides "information on the law-abiding individual's right to self-defense," while NRA Basic Personal Protection Outside the Home is a two-day course. A primer lasting three hours provides "a tactical look at civilian life." This raises the question of just how much civilian life is left.

As I waited for my lesson, I paged through a stack of old magazines while watching Fox News on a flat-screen television. In Michigan and Arizona, Mitt Romney and Rick Santorum were competing in that day's Republican primaries. At the top of the hour came the headlines: in Ohio, Demetrius Hewlin had just died. For a tick, the news announcer fell silent.

I put down *Field and Stream* and picked up *American Rifleman*, a publication of the NRA. The magazine includes a regular column called The Armed Citizen. A feature article introduced David Keene, the NRA's president. Keene is a longtime conservative political strategist. Grover Norquist once called him "a conservative Forrest Gump." The 2012 presidential election, Keene told *American Rifleman*, is "perhaps the most crucial election, from a Second Amendment standpoint, in our lifetimes."

THE SECOND AMENDMENT READS, "A well-regulated militia being necessary to the security of a free State, the right of the people to keep and bear arms shall not be infringed." Arms are military weapons. A firearm is a cannon that you can carry, as opposed to artillery so big and heavy that you need wheels to move it, or people to help you. Cannons that you can carry around didn't exist until the Middle Ages. The first European firearms—essentially, tubes mounted on a pole—date to the end of the fourteenth century and are known as "hand cannons." Then came shoulder arms (that is, guns you can shoulder): muskets, rifles, and shotguns. A pistol is a gun that can be held in one hand. A revolver holds a number of bullets in a revolving chamber, but didn't become common until

Samuel Colt patented his model in 1836. The firearms used by a well-regulated militia, at the time the Second Amendment was written, were mostly long arms that, like a smaller stockpile of pistols, could discharge only once before they had to be reloaded. In size, speed, efficiency, capacity, and sleekness, the difference between an eighteenth-century musket and the gun that George Zimmerman was carrying is roughly the difference between the first laptop computer—which, not counting the external modem and the battery pack, weighed twenty-four pounds—and an iPhone.

A gun is a machine made to fire a missile that can bore through flesh. It can be used to hunt an animal or to commit or prevent a crime. Enough people carrying enough guns, and with the will and the training to use them, can defend a government, or topple one. For centuries before the first English colonists traveled to the New World, Parliament had been regulating the private ownership of firearms. (Generally, ownership was restricted to the wealthy; the principle was that anyone below the rank of gentleman found with a gun was a poacher.) England's 1689 Declaration of Rights made a provision that "subjects which are Protestants may have arms for their defence suitable to their condition and as allowed by law"; the Declaration was an attempt to resolve a struggle between Parliament and the Crown, in which Parliament wrested control of the militia from the Crown.

In the United States, Article VI of the Articles of Confederation, drafted in 1776 and ratified in 1781, required that "every state shall always keep up a well regulated and disciplined militia, sufficiently armed and accoutred, and shall provide and constantly have ready for use, in public stores, a due number of field pieces and tents, and a proper quantity of arms, ammunition and camp equipage." In early America, firearms and ammunition were often kept in public arsenals. In 1775, the British Army marched to Concord with the idea of seizing the arsenal where the colonial militia stored its weapons. In January of 1787, a Massachusetts resident named Daniel Shays led eleven hundred men, many of them disaffected Revolutionary War veterans, in an attempt to capture an arsenal in

Springfield; they had been protesting taxes, but they needed guns and ammunition. Springfield had been an arsenal since 1774. In 1777, George Washington, at the urging of Henry Knox, made it his chief northern arsenal. By 1786, Springfield housed the largest collection of weapons in the United States. In the winter of 1787, the governor of Massachusetts sent the militia to suppress the rebellion; the Springfield arsenal was defended. That spring, the Constitutional Convention met in Philadelphia. Among the matters the delegates were to take up was granting to the federal government the power to suppress insurgencies like Shays's Rebellion. From Boston, Benjamin Franklin's sister Jane wrote to him with some advice for "such a Number of wise men as you are connected with in the Convention": no more weapons, no more war. "I had Rather hear of the Swords being beat into Plow-shares, and the Halters used for Cart Roops, if by that means we may be brought to live Peaceably with won a nother."

The U.S. Constitution, which was signed in Philadelphia in September of 1787, granted Congress the power "to provide for calling forth the Militia to execute the Laws of the Union, suppress Insurrections and repel Invasions," the power "to provide for organizing, arming, and disciplining the Militia, and for governing such Part of them as may be employed in the Service of the United States, reserving to the States respectively, the Appointment of the Officers, and the Authority of training the Militia according to the discipline prescribed by Congress," and the power "to raise and support Armies, but no Appropriation of Money to that Use shall be for a longer Term than two Years."

Ratification was an uphill battle. The Bill of Rights, drafted by James Madison in 1789, offered assurance to Anti-Federalists, who feared that there would be no limit to the powers of the newly constituted federal government. Since one of their worries was the prospect of a standing army—a permanent army—Madison drafted an amendment guaranteeing the people the right to form a militia. In Madison's original version, the amendment read, "The right of the people to keep and bear arms shall not be infringed; a well armed and well regulated militia being the best security of a free country: but no person religiously scrupulous of bearing arms shall be compelled to render military service in person." This provision was made in the same spirit as the Third Amendment, which forbids the government to force you to have troops billeted in your home: "No Soldier shall, in time of peace be quartered in any house, without the consent of the Owner, nor in time of war, but in a manner to be prescribed by law."

None of this had anything to do with hunting. People who owned and used long arms to hunt continued to own and use them; the Second Amendment was not commonly understood as having any relevance to the shooting of animals. As Garry Wills once wrote, "One does not bear arms against a rabbit." Meanwhile, militias continued to muster—the Continental army was disbanded at the end of the Revolutionary War—but the national defense was increasingly assumed by the United States Army; by the middle of the nineteenth century, the United States had a standing army, after all. Harpers Ferry was the U.S. Army's southern armory, Springfield its northern. In 1859, when John Brown and his men raided Harpers Ferry, they went there to get guns.

AT THE AMERICAN FIREARMS SCHOOL, you can either rent a gun or bring your own. It's like an ice-skating rink that way, except that renting skates when you don't know how to skate is different from renting a gun when you don't know how to shoot. The guys who work at the school don't take any chances. In the twelve years since the school opened, there has never been an accident. "You can't do anything here without us watching you," Tom Dietzel told me. "In a swimming pool, there are lifeguards. And this place is a lot more dangerous than a swimming pool."

Dietzel, who is twenty-four and has long dark hair, is one of the few instructors at the school who isn't ex-military, ex-police, or ex-rescue. He led me to a classroom, opened a case, and took out a .22-caliber Mark III Target Rimfire pistol. Dietzel studied history in college, and on weekends he gives tours of the Freedom Trail, in

Boston. We talked about the eighteenth-century portraits in the new wing of the Museum of Fine Arts; we debated the oratory of Joseph Warren. Dietzel owns a flintlock musket; he's a Revolutionary War reenactor, with the Thirteenth Continental Regiment. He showed me a photograph of himself in costume: a cocked hat, a mustard-colored scarf of flax. He could have been painted by Gilbert Stuart.

Dietzel is a skilled and knowledgeable teacher, steady, patient, and calm. He had written safety rules on a whiteboard: Never point your gun at anyone. Keep your finger off the trigger. Don't trust the safety. Assume every gun is loaded.

He explained how to load the magazine. "This is a semiautomatic," he said. "After you fire, it will load the next bullet, but you have to pull the trigger again to fire. We don't have automatics here." Automatic weapons are largely banned by the federal government. "An automatic, you pull the trigger and it keeps shooting." Dietzel shook his head. "Because: Why? Why?"

Gun owners may be more supportive of gun safety regulations than is the leadership of the NRA. According to a 2009 Luntz poll, for instance, requiring mandatory background checks on all purchasers at gun shows is favored not only by 85 percent of gun owners who are not members of the NRA but also by 69 percent of gun owners who are.

Dietzel rose. "Stand like a shortstop about to field a ball," he said. He showed me how to hold the .22.

Every day, Dietzel goes to work and, at some point, has to hand a gun to a perfect stranger who has never used one. He went over the rules again.

We got earplugs and headgear and ammunition and went to the range. I fired a hundred rounds. Then Dietzel told me to go wash my hands, to get the gunpowder off, while he went to clean the gun.

The halls at the American Firearms School are decorated with framed prints: Monet's *Impression, Sunrise*; Van Gogh's *Irises*. A sign on the door of the women's restroom reads EVERY TUESDAY IS LADIES NIGHT. LADIES GET FREE RANGE TIME FROM 5:00 PM TO 9:00 PM.

I opened the door, and turned on the tap. T. J. Lane had used a .22-caliber Mark III Target Rimfire pistol. For a long time, I let the water run.

ON MARCH 8, 2012, Trayvon Martin's father, Tracy Martin, held a press conference in Orlando. "We feel justice has not been served," he said. He demanded the release of recordings of calls to 911. "Family Wants Answers in Teen's Death," the Associated Press reported.

Two days later, the biggest gun show in New England was held in West Springfield, Massachusetts, in an exposition center the size of an airport hangar. (Nationwide, there are about five thousand gun shows annually.) Early in the morning, men with guns lined up to have them inspected at the door: two policemen made sure that every gun was unloaded; a plastic bucket on the floor, half filled with sand, was for dumping ammunition, like the bin at airport security where TSA officers make you chuck your toothpaste. Tickets cost eleven dollars, but there was no charge for children younger than twelve.

Inside was a flea market: hundreds of folding tables draped with felt tablecloths and covered with guns, along with knives, swords, and a great deal of hunting gear. Long guns stood on their stocks, muzzles up. Handguns rested under glass, like jewelry. CASH FOR GUNS, the sign at the Tombstone Trading Company read. Ammunition was sold outdoors, in cartons, as in the fastener aisle of a hardware store. At the NRA booth, membership came with a subscription to one of the NRA's three magazines, an NRA baseball hat, twenty-five hundred dollars of insurance, "and the most important benefit of all—protecting the Constitution."

I stopped at the table of Guns Inc., which advertises itself as the largest firearms dealer in western Massachusetts. Guns Inc. is also an arsenal: a place where people who don't want to keep their guns at home can pay to have them stored.

IN THE NINETEENTH CENTURY, the Springfield Armory grew to become the single biggest supplier of long arms to the U.S. Army. It shut its doors in 1968. A National Historic Site now, it houses about ten thousand weapons, most of which are shoulder arms. A sign on the door warns that no firearms are allowed inside. "People ask about that," Richard Colton, a park ranger and the site's historian, told me when I visited, "but we have plenty of guns here already."

The story of the Springfield Armory illustrates a shift in the manufacture and storage of firearms: from public to private. In 1974, a family in Illinois founded a company devoted to arms manufacturing and import called Springfield Armory Inc. The firm, "the first name in American firearms," is one of the largest of its kind in the United States. Dennis Reese, the current CEO, and his brother Tom have staunchly opposed gun regulation. I asked Brian Pranka, of Guns Inc., if he had any Springfield Armory guns. He said, "You can't buy a Springfield handgun in Springfield." The company does not make handguns that conform to all the gun safety regulations in states like Massachusetts, New York, and California, and in Illinois they have lobbied the legislature, successfully defeating a state ban on assault weapons. In 2008, the Illinois State Rifle Association gave the Reeses the Defenders of Freedom Award.

On the first day of the Springfield gun show, Trayvon Martin's parents appeared on *Good Morning America*. On March 19, the Department of Justice, responding to growing protests, announced that it would conduct an investigation. On March 23, President Obama answered questions about the shooting at a press conference. "If I had a son, he'd look like Trayvon," the president said. Later that day, Rick Santorum spoke outside a firing range in West Monroe, Louisiana, where he'd just shot fourteen rounds from a Colt .45. He told the crowd, "What I was able to exercise was one of those fundamental freedoms that's guaranteed in our Constitution, the right to bear arms."

IN THE TWO CENTURIES FOLLOWING the adoption of the Bill of Rights, in 1791, no amendment received less attention in the courts than the Second, except the Third. As Adam Winkler, a constitutional law scholar at UCLA, demonstrates in a remarkably nuanced book, *Gunfight: The Battle Over the Right to Bear Arms in*

America, firearms have been regulated in the United States from the start. Laws banning the carrying of concealed weapons were passed in Kentucky and Louisiana in 1813, and other states soon followed: Indiana (1820), Tennessee and Virginia (1838), Alabama (1839), and Ohio (1859). Similar laws were passed in Texas, Florida, and Oklahoma. As the governor of Texas explained in 1893, the "mission of the concealed deadly weapon is murder. To check it is the duty of every self-respecting, law-abiding man."

Although these laws were occasionally challenged, they were rarely struck down in state courts; the state's interest in regulating the manufacture, ownership, and storage of firearms was plain enough. Even the West was hardly wild. "Frontier towns handled guns the way a Boston restaurant today handles overcoats in winter," Winkler writes. "New arrivals were required to turn in their guns to authorities in exchange for something like a metal token." In Wichita, Kansas, in 1873, a sign read LEAVE YOUR REVOLVERS AT POLICE HEADQUARTERS, AND GET A CHECK. The first thing the government of Dodge did when founding the city, in 1873, was pass a resolution that "any person or persons found carrying concealed weapons in the city of Dodge or violating the laws of the State shall be dealt with according to law." On the road through town, a wooden billboard read THE CARRYING OF FIREARMS STRICTLY PROHIBITED. The shoot-out at the O.K. Corral, in Tombstone, Arizona, Winkler explains, had to do with a gun control law. In 1880, Tombstone's city council passed an ordinance "to Provide against the Carrying of Deadly Weapons." When Wyatt Earp confronted Tom McLaury on the streets of Tombstone, it was because McLaury had violated that ordinance by failing to leave his gun at the sheriff's office.

The National Rifle Association was founded in 1871 by two men, a lawyer and a former reporter from the *New York Times*. For most of its history, the NRA was chiefly a sporting and hunting association. To the extent that the NRA had a political arm, it opposed some gun control measures and supported many others, lobbying for new state laws in the 1920s and '30s, which introduced waiting periods for handgun buyers and required permits for anyone wishing to carry a concealed weapon. It also supported the 1934 National Firearms Act—the first major federal gun control legislation—and the 1938 Federal Firearms Act, which together created a licensing system for dealers and prohibitively taxed the private ownership of automatic weapons ("machine guns"). The constitutionality of the 1934 act was upheld by the U.S. Supreme Court in 1939, in *United States v. Miller*, in which Franklin Delano Roosevelt's solicitor general, Robert H. Jackson, argued that the Second Amendment is "restricted to the keeping and bearing of arms by the people collectively for their common defense and security." Furthermore, Jackson said, the language of the amendment makes clear that the right "is not one which may be utilized for private purposes but only one which exists where the arms are borne in the militia or some other military organization provided for by law and intended for the protection of the state." The Court agreed, unanimously. In 1957, when the NRA moved into new headquarters, its motto, at the building's entrance, read FIREARMS SAFETY EDUCATION, MARKSMANSHIP TRAINING, SHOOTING FOR RECREATION. It didn't say anything about freedom, or self-defense, or rights.

THE MODERN GUN DEBATE BEGAN with a shooting. In 1963, Lee Harvey Oswald bought a bolt-action rifle—an Italian military surplus weapon—for $19.95 by ordering it from an ad that he found in *American Rifleman*. Five days after Oswald assassinated President Kennedy, Thomas Dodd, a Democratic senator from Connecticut, introduced legislation restricting mail order sales of shotguns and rifles. The NRA's executive vice president, Franklin L. Orth, testified before Congress, "We do not think that any sane American, who calls himself an American, can object to placing into this bill the instrument which killed the president of the United States."

Gun rights arguments have their origins not in eighteenth-century Anti-Federalism but in twentieth-century liberalism. They are the product of what the Harvard law professor Mark Tushnet has called the "rights revolution," the pursuit of rights, especially civil rights, through the courts. In the 1960s, gun ownership as a constitutional right was less the agenda of the NRA than of Black nationalists. In a 1964 speech,

Malcolm X said, "Article number two of the constitutional amendments provides you and me the right to own a rifle or a shotgun." Establishing a constitutional right to carry a gun for the purpose of self-defense was part of the mission of the Black Panther Party for Self-Defense, which was founded in 1966. "Black People can develop Self-Defense Power by arming themselves from house to house, block to block, community to community throughout the nation," Huey Newton said.

In 1968, as Winkler relates, the assassinations of Robert Kennedy and Martin Luther King Jr. gave the issue new urgency. A revised Gun Control Act banned mail order sales, restricted the purchase of guns by certain high-risk people (for example, those with criminal records), and prohibited the importation of military surplus firearms. That law, along with a great deal of subsequent law-and-order legislation, was intended to fight crime, control riots, and solve what was called, at the time, the "Negro problem." The regulations that are part of these laws—firearms restrictions, mandatory sentencing guidelines, abolition of parole, and the "war on drugs"—are now generally understood to be responsible for the dramatic rise in the U.S. incarceration rate.

The NRA supported the 1968 Gun Control Act, with some qualms. Orth was quoted in *American Rifleman* as saying that although some elements of the legislation "appear unduly restrictive and unjustified in their application to law-abiding citizens, the measure as a whole appears to be one that the sportsmen of America can live with."

DAVID KEENE, THE NRA'S PRESIDENT, is the former chairman of the American Conservative Union. In his office in Washington, he has a photograph of Ronald Reagan on the wall and a view of Pennsylvania Avenue out the window. Keene has white hair, blue eyes, and an air of plainspoken geniality. When he was eight or nine, he says, his grandfather taught him how to shoot by aiming a .22 at squirrels and rabbits.

Keene's parents were labor organizers. They never once voted for a Republican. "My first political activity was going door to door passing out pamphlets for JFK in the snows of Wisconsin," Keene told me. In the 1950s, he said, "Lionel Trilling considered conservatism to be a political pathology." Keene became a conservative in high school, when he read *The Constitution of Liberty*, by Friedrich Hayek. In 1960, at the Republican National Convention, Barry Goldwater said, "Let's grow up conservatives, if we want to take this party back, and I think we can someday. Let's get to work." Four years later, Keene volunteered for Goldwater's campaign.

After Goldwater's defeat, Keene finished college and went on to law school. He became the national chairman of the Young Americans for Freedom. "What brought conservatism to dominance was the Great Society," Keene argues, because Johnson's vision represented "the culmination of the thinking that you could solve everything with money, and nothing worked." Keene went to DC to work for Spiro Agnew, and then for Richard Nixon.

On Election Day in 1970, Keene was at the White House. Joseph Tydings, a Democratic senator from Maryland who had introduced a Firearms Registration and Licensing Act, was running for reelection. "The returns were coming in, and someone said, 'What's going on in Maryland?'" Keene recalled. "And someone answered, 'I can tell you this: everywhere except Baltimore, there are long lines of pickup trucks at the polls. He's going down over gun control.'"

IN THE 1970s, the NRA began advancing the argument that the Second Amendment guarantees an individual's right to carry a gun, rather than the people's right to form armed militias to provide for the common defense. Fights over rights are effective at getting out the vote. Describing gun safety legislation as an attack on a constitutional right gave conservatives a power at the polls that, at the time, the movement lacked. Opposing gun control was also consistent with a larger anti-regulation, libertarian, and anti-government conservative agenda. In 1975, the NRA created a lobbying arm, the Institute for Legislative Action, headed by Harlon Bronson Carter, an award-winning marksman and a former chief of the U.S. Border Control. But then the NRA's leadership decided to back out of politics and move the organization's headquarters to Colorado Springs, where a new recreational-shooting facility was to be built. Eighty members of the NRA's staff, including Carter, were ousted. In 1977, the NRA's annual meeting, usually held in Washington, was moved to Cincinnati, in protest of the city's recent gun control laws. Conservatives within the organization, led by Carter, staged what has come to be called the Cincinnati Revolt. The bylaws were rewritten and the old guard was pushed out. Instead of moving to Colorado, the NRA stayed in DC, where a new motto was displayed: "The Right of the People to Keep and Bear Arms Shall Not Be Infringed."

Ronald Reagan was the first presidential candidate whom the NRA had endorsed. David Keene ran Reagan's southern campaign. Reagan's election, in 1980, made it possible for conservatives to begin turning a new interpretation of the Second Amendment into law. As the legal scholar Reva B. Siegel has chronicled, Orrin Hatch became the chair of the Subcommittee on the Constitution, and commissioned a history of the Second Amendment, which resulted in a 1982 report, "The Right to Keep and Bear Arms." The authors of the report claimed to have discovered "clear—and long-lost—proof that the Second Amendment to our Constitution was intended as an individual right of the American citizen to keep and carry arms in a peaceful manner, for protection of himself, his family, and his freedoms."

In March of 1981, John Hinckley Jr. shot Reagan, the White House press secretary, James Brady, a DC policeman, and a Secret Service agent. He used a .22 that he had bought at a pawnshop. A month later, the *Times* reported that Harlon Carter, then the NRA's executive vice president, had been convicted of murder in Laredo, Texas, in 1931, at the age of seventeen. Carter had come home from school to find his mother distressed. She told him that three teenage boys had been loitering nearby all afternoon, and that she suspected them of having been involved in stealing the family's car. Carter left the house with a shotgun, found the boys, and told them that he wanted them to come back to his house to be questioned. According to the trial testimony of twelve-year-old Salvador Peña, Ramón Casiano, fifteen, the oldest of the boys, said to Carter, "We won't go to your house, and you can't make us." Casiano took out a knife and said, "Do you want to fight me?" Carter shot Casiano in the chest. At Carter's trial for murder, the judge, J. F. Mullally, instructed the jury, "There is no evidence that defendant had any lawful authority to require deceased to go to his house for questioning, and if defendant was trying to make deceased go there for that purpose at the time of the killing, he was acting without authority of law, and the law of self-defense does not apply." Two years later, Carter's murder conviction was overturned on appeal; the defense argued that the instructions to the jury had been improper.

When the *Times* broke the Casiano murder story, Carter at first denied it, saying the trial record concerned a different man with a similar name. He later said that he had "nothing to hide" and was "not going to rehash that case or any other that does not relate to the National Rifle Association."

James Brady and his wife, Sarah, went on to become active in the gun control movement, but neither the assassination attempt nor Carter's past derailed the gun rights movement. In 1986, the NRA's interpretation of the Second Amendment achieved new legal authority with the passage of the Firearms Owners Protection Act, which repealed parts of the 1968 Gun Control Act by invoking "the rights of citizens . . . to keep and bear arms under the Second Amendment." This interpretation was supported by a growing body of scholarship, much of it funded by the NRA. According to the constitutional law scholar Carl Bogus, at least sixteen of the twenty-seven law review articles published between 1970 and 1989 that were favorable to the NRA's interpretation of the Second Amendment were "written by lawyers who had been directly employed by or represented the NRA or other gun rights organizations." In an interview, former chief justice Warren Burger said that the new interpretation of the Second Amendment was "one of the greatest pieces of fraud, I repeat the word 'fraud,' on the American public by special interest groups that I have ever seen in my lifetime."

The debate narrowed, and degraded. Political candidates who supported gun control faced opponents whose campaigns were funded by the NRA. In 1991, a poll found that Americans were more familiar with the Second Amendment than they were with the First: the right to speak and to believe, and to write and to publish, freely.

"IF YOU HAD ASKED, IN 1968, will we have the right to do with guns in 2012 what we can do now, no one, on either side, would have believed you," David Keene said.

Between 1968 and 2012, the idea that owning and carrying a gun is both a fundamental American freedom and an act of citizenship gained wide acceptance and, along with it, the principle that this right is absolute and cannot be compromised; gun control legislation was diluted, defeated, overturned, or allowed to expire; the right to carry a concealed handgun became nearly ubiquitous; Stand Your Ground legislation passed in half the states; and, in 2008, in *District of Columbia v. Heller*, the Supreme Court ruled, in a 5–4 decision, that the District's 1975 Firearms Control Regulations Act was unconstitutional. Justice Scalia wrote, "The Second Amendment protects an individual right to possess a firearm unconnected with service in a militia." Two years later, in another 5–4 ruling, *McDonald v. Chicago*, the Court extended *Heller* to the states.

Nevertheless, Keene says that all of these gains are fragile, because President Obama—who in his first term has not only failed to push for gun control but has signed legislation extending gun rights—has been hiding his true convictions. (From 1994 to 2002, Obama served on the board of the Chicago-based Joyce Foundation, which funds pro-gun-control advocacy and research.) "If this president gets a second term, he will appoint one to three Supreme Court justices," Keene says. "If he does, he could reverse *Heller* and *McDonald*, which is unlikely, but, more likely, they will restrict those decisions."

This issue has been delivering voters to the polls since 1970. Conservatives hope that it will continue to deliver them in 2012. Keene, in his lifetime, has witnessed a revolution. "It's not just the conservative political victories, the capture of the Republican Party, the creation of a conservative intellectual elite," he said, "but the whole change in the way Americans look at government." No conservative victories will last longer than the rulings of this Supreme Court.

One in three Americans knows someone who has been shot. As long as a candid discussion of guns is impossible, unfettered debate about the causes of violence is unimaginable. Gun control advocates say the answer to gun violence is fewer guns. Gun rights advocates say that the answer is more guns: things would have gone better, they suggest, if the faculty at Columbine, Virginia Tech, and Chardon High School had been armed. That is the logic of the concealed-carry movement; that is how armed citizens have come to be patrolling the streets. That is not how civilians live. When carrying a concealed weapon for self-defense is understood not as a failure of civil society, to be mourned, but as an act of citizenship, to be vaunted, there is little civilian life left.

In 2002, Keene's son David Michael Keene was driving on the George Washington Memorial Parkway when, in a road rage incident, he fired a handgun at another motorist. He was sentenced to ten years in prison for "using, brandishing, and discharging a firearm in a crime of violence." I asked Keene if this private tragedy had left him uncertain about what the NRA had wrought. He said no: "You break the law, you pay the price."

I asked Keene if any public atrocity had given him pause. He explained that it is the NRA's policy never to comment on a shooting.

I asked him how he would answer critics who charge that no single organization has done more to weaken Americans' faith in government, or in one another, than the NRA.

"We live in a society now that's balkanized," Keene said. "But that has nothing to do with guns."

ON MONDAY, MARCH 26, 2012, thousands of students rallied in Atlanta, carrying signs that read I AM TRAYVON MARTIN, and DON'T SHOOT! One week later, in Oakland, a forty-three-year-old man named One Goh walked into Oikos University, a small Christian college. He was carrying a .45-caliber semiautomatic pistol and four magazines of ammunition. He grabbed Katleen Ping, a receptionist, and dragged her into a classroom. Nearby, Lucas Garcia, a thirty-three-year-old ESL teacher, heard a voice call out, "Somebody's got a gun!" He helped his students escape through a back door. Dechen Yangdon, twenty-seven, turned off the lights in her classroom and locked the door. She could hear Ping screaming, "Help, help, help!" "We were locked inside," Yangdon said later. "We couldn't help her."

Goh ordered the students to line up against the wall. He said, "I'm going to kill you all."

They had come from all over the world. Ping, twenty-four, was born in the Philippines. She was working at the school to support her parents, her brother, two younger sisters, and her four-year-old son, Kayzzer. Her husband was hoping to move to the United States. Tshering Rinzing Bhutia, thirty-eight, was born in Gyalshing, India, in the foothills of the Himalayas. He took classes during the day; at night, he worked as a janitor at San Francisco International Airport. Lydia Sim, twenty-one, was born in San Francisco, to Korean parents; she wanted to become a pediatrician. Sonam Choedon, thirty-three, belonged to a family living in exile from Tibet. A Buddhist, she came to the United States from Dharamsala, India. She was studying to become a nurse. Grace Eunhea Kim, twenty-three, was putting herself through school by working as a waitress. Judith Seymour was fifty-three. Her parents had moved back to their native Guyana; her two children were grown. She was about to graduate. Doris Chibuko, forty, was born in Enugu, in eastern Nigeria, where she practiced law. She immigrated in 2002. Her husband, Efanye, works as a technician for AT&T. They had three children, ages eight, five, and three. She was two months short of completing a degree in nursing.

Ping, Bhutia, Sim, Choedon, Kim, Seymour, and Chibuko: Goh shot and killed them all. Then he went from one classroom to another, shooting, before stealing a car and driving away. He threw his gun into a tributary of San Leandro Bay. Shortly afterward, he walked into a grocery store and said, "I just shot some people."

A multilingual memorial service was held at the Allen Temple Baptist Church. Oakland's mayor, Jean Quan, said, "Oakland is a city of dreams." A friend of Choedon's said, "Mainly, we're praying for her next life, that she can have a better one." In Gyalshing, Bhutia's niece, Enchuk Namgyal, asked that her uncle's body be sent home to be cremated in the mountains above the village, across the world from the country where he came for an education, religious freedom, and economic opportunity, and was shot to death.

Kids in Chardon High are back in school. Nickolas Walczak is in a wheelchair. There are Trayvon Martin T-shirts. Oikos University is closed. The NRA has no comment.

In an average year, roughly a hundred thousand Americans are killed or wounded with guns. On April 6, the police found One Goh's .45. Five days later, George Zimmerman was charged with second-degree murder. In May, T. J. Lane will appear at a hearing. Trials are to come. In each, introduced as evidence, will be an unloaded gun.

—2012

Postscript: No meaningful gun safety legislation has been passed in the ten years that have passed since I wrote this piece. The mass shootings continued. And in 2022, the Supreme Court sanctioned the reading of the Second Amendment the NRA had for so long been fighting for.

LONG DIVISION

T HE STUDY OF GOVERNMENT, LIKE THE GOVERN-
ment itself, is in a tight spot. In 2009, during a vote on a
House appropriations bill, Tom Coburn, a Republican senator from
Oklahoma, tried to abolish the National Science Foundation's Political Science Program, which supports academic research in "citizenship, government, and politics." The motion was tabled after the
American Political Science Association staged a same-day e-mail
campaign to oppose it. Last year, the measure met with success in
the House; House members who have few qualms about closing the
Centers for Disease Control are not, generally speaking, daunted by
the prospect of stifling the pursuit of social science. And, earlier this
year, when Coburn re-introduced his amendment in the Senate, it
passed with no more quibbling than the addition of a proviso that
some political science could be funded: research whose purpose is
"promoting national security or the economic interests of the United
States." The President signed the bill into law in March.

The movement to defund political science stems from the belief
that the National Science Foundation has no business funding
political science, because political science is all politics and no
science—except when it advances national security or boosts the
American economy, in which case it is, naturally, apolitical and
scientific. The political and unscientific stuff is the study of, for
instance, gridlock. According to Coburn, one reason the federal
government should not pay for political-science research is that
"studies of presidential executive power and Americans' attitudes
about the Senate filibuster hold little promise to save an American's
life from a threatening condition or to advance America's competi-
tiveness in the world"—a statement that is difficult to square with

the damage done to the U.S. economy by the ongoing budgetary brinkmanship.

Shutting down the federal government is expensive; irony is cheap. The N.S.F.'s Political Science Program was inaugurated in 1966. In 1970, it began supporting the work of a political scientist from the University of Michigan named Warren E. Miller, who, for two decades, had been collecting election returns and conducting interviews with voters as part of what came to be called the American National Election Studies project. Since 1977, the largest grants awarded by the Political Science Program have gone to this project, which conducts surveys every two years and is widely regarded as the most important collection of information about voting ever assembled. Another vast study concerns congressional voting. Beginning in the nineteen-eighties, the political scientists Keith T. Poole and Howard Rosenthal, then at Carnegie Mellon, received a series of N.S.F. grants to compile a record of all roll-call votes held in Congress. Their data now include the records of every roll-call decision made between 1789 and 2004: 2,844,164 roll calls in the Senate and 11,493,013 in the House. Political scientists analyzing these three compilations of longitudinal data—election results, interviews with voters, and congressional roll-call records—claim that voters and legislators alike are more polarized today than they have been at any time since the Confederacy seceded.

What's really going on could be anything from party realignment to the unravelling of the Republic. It's hard to know, though, what with a polarized Congress keen to defund the very scholarship that might cast light on the matter. Coburn is untroubled. "The University of Michigan may have some interesting theories about recent elections," he allowed, "but Americans who have an interest in electoral politics can turn to CNN, Fox News, MSNBC, the print media, and a seemingly endless number of political commentators on the Internet." This is a little like saying, when your kitchen is on fire, that it's O.K. because, in a cupboard above the stove, you keep fifty boxes of matches.

MODERN POLITICAL SCIENCE STARTED in the late nineteenth century as a branch of history. (The department in which I teach used to be the Department of History and Government; it split in two in 1910.) Political scientists have been arguing for more than a century over whether the study of government is a science. On the whole, Woodrow Wilson and Charles Beard thought not. By the end of the Second World War, science-y political scientists had allied themselves with the behavioral sciences, and, not long afterward, with rational-choice theory. They used quantitative methods to test theories about the political behavior of individuals. At the University of Michigan, Miller and his colleagues Philip Converse, Angus Campbell, and Donald Stokes used their survey data to produce a study called "The American Voter," in 1960. Four years later, elaborating on its findings, Converse published a landmark essay, "The Nature of Belief Systems in Mass Publics." Converse argued that the American electorate can be usefully divided into two groups: political élites, who are exceptionally well informed, follow politics closely, and adhere to a set of political beliefs so coherent as to constitute an ideology; and the mass public, whose specific knowledge of politics tends to be scant, resulting in a very loose and scattershot set of political beliefs. Political élites know "what-goes-with-what" (laissez-faire with free enterprise) and "what parties stand for" (Democrats favor labor, Republicans business), but much of the mass public does not.

In 1956 and 1960, the Michigan interviewers asked voters questions such as "Would you say that either one of the parties is *more conservative* or *more liberal* than the other?" Many voters could not answer that question. Others answered badly. There was a follow-up: "What do people have in mind when they say that the Republicans (Democrats) are more conservative than the Democrats (Republicans)?" This proved difficult to answer, too. Converse reported that the bottom thirty-seven per cent of respondents "could supply no meaning for the liberal-conservative distinction"; the top seventeen per cent gave what the interviewers deemed "best answers." Everyone else fell somewhere in between, but Converse and his colleagues were pretty sure that a lot of them were just guessing.

Converse reported as well on the relationship between what voters know and how they vote. Political élites vote in a more partisan fashion than the mass public; this tendency, too, follows a curve. The more you know, the more likely you are to vote in an ideologically consistent way, not just following your party but following a set of constraints dictated by a political ideology. (The parties, at the time, were not as ideologically uniform as they have since become.) What makes a voter a moderate, Converse concluded, is not knowing very much about politics. In the nineteen-fifties, there were a lot of moderates. Converse thought that this might be because only about ten per cent of the American electorate had graduated from college.

A great deal has changed since 1964. Voters have got better sorted by party; parties have got better sorted by ideology; and parties have got more ideological. The Republican Party has moved to the right and, to a much lesser degree, the Democratic Party has moved to the left. In 1964, the ideological position advocated by Barry Goldwater was nearly beyond the realm of the G.O.P. imagination; by 1980, Goldwater Republicanism was Reagan Republicanism; Newt Gingrich's 1994 Contract with America was well to the right of Reagan; and, in 2012, Mitt Romney ran to the right of the breakdown lane.

The changes within the Democratic Party are of a different nature. Ideologically, Democrats have not moved to the left; to the contrary, today's Democrats are significantly to the economic and social-welfare right of the antitrust Democrats of the eighteen-nineties, the New Deal Democrats of the nineteen-thirties, and the Great Society Democrats of the nineteen-sixties. Instead, the composition of the Party has shifted. In the civil-rights era, white Southern Democrats, who were conservatives, abandoned the Party; the Democrats left behind tended to be liberals. Then the complexion of the Democratic Party changed. In 1960, more than a quarter of African-Americans voted for Nixon over Kennedy; in 1972—after the 1964 Civil Rights Act and the 1965 Voting Rights Act—only one in ten African-Americans voted for Nixon over McGovern. Between 1992 and 2008, the nonwhite percentage of the U.S. electorate doubled, and, as Alan Abramowitz pointed out in "The

Disappearing Center" (2010), a growing racial divide within the electorate tends to widen the ideological divide, because nonwhite voters favor government-supported social programs more than white voters do. The labels "conservative" and "liberal" did not formerly correspond especially well to the terms "Republican" and "Democratic." They do now.

One of the most interesting explanations for the polarization of the electorate has to do with television. In "Post-Broadcast Democracy" (2007), Markus Prior observed that the period from the late nineteen-forties to the late nineteen-seventies—an era of remarkably low political polarization—was also the heyday of broadcast television. Prior thinks that during these decades a sizable number of Americans who had never cared much about politics got drawn into it because of television. At the time, television had essentially three channels, and, at six o'clock every night, the national news was broadcast on all of them. Nearly everyone watched it, even though a lot of people (Prior calls them "entertainment fans") would have rather watched just about anything else. When Election Day came around, these entertainment fans decided to vote. Relative to voters who actually like watching the news ("news viewers"), the entertainment fans were poorly informed, so they were moderates. Once cable television became available, starting in the late nineteen-seventies, entertainment fans gradually stopped watching the news, turned to dozens and then hundreds of other channels instead, and stopped voting. In the cable-and-Internet era of the past decade and a half, news viewers have more and different news choices. News viewers have always been voters; lately, they're more partisan, partly because the news is more partisan. The growth in polarization seen since 1980 is a result, according to Prior, of the failure of moderates to turn up at the polls and of the more partisan feeling of those people who do turn up.

This development may have reduced the quality of our political opinions. "Opinion quality" purports to measure the match between what we know and how we vote. If you know a lot about something and apply that information to a vote that matches your policy preferences, your opinion quality is high. In 2011, a team of political scientists led by James N. Druckman, of Northwestern University, conducted a survey of more than six hundred party-affiliated voters about drilling for oil and gas, framing the issue, for some respondents, with polarized terms and, for others, without. They found that in a polarized environment voters make worse choices and have more confidence in them. Their conclusion: "intense party competition degenerates opinion quality."

One element of voter behavior measured by the American National Election Studies project is the percentage of voters who do things like post yard signs in front of their houses or paste bumper stickers onto their cars. In 2004 and 2008, that percentage was higher than it had been at any time since the project began, in 1952. Nevertheless, there's dispute about whether ordinary voters are more polarized than before. "Most Americans are somewhat like the unfortunate citizens of some third-world countries who try to stay out of the crossfire while left-wing guerrillas and right-wing death squads shoot at each other," Morris Fiorina and his collaborators wrote in 2005, in "Culture War? The Myth of a Polarized America." Fiorina thinks that it's just party activists and party leaders who are polarized and that ordinary voters only *appear* polarized, because the candidates and party platforms we're stuck choosing between are so polarized. It's a subtle and illuminating argument. It doesn't quite explain the yard signs, though.

NO ONE SERIOUSLY QUESTIONS that members of Congress are more polarized than they used to be. This is borne out anecdotally, as social scientists like to say, by watching them on cable television, where you can see the spittle in HD. "We now live in an era where political elites literally hate each other," Nolan McCarty, Keith Poole, and Howard Rosenthal wrote in "Polarized America," in 2006. Poole and Rosenthal extended their earlier work on congressional roll-call votes by conducting another investigation funded by the National Science Foundation. They assembled a record of the ratings assigned to members of the U.S. Senate by thirty interest groups between 1959 and 1980. Interest groups rate members of Congress on a scale of zero to a hundred. The interest groups that Poole and Rosenthal studied included Americans for Democratic Action and the U.S. Chamber of Commerce. In 1984, Poole and Rosenthal reported the beginning of a significant increase in congressional polarization, fuelled by a development then already discernible: "Moderate Republicans are vanishing nationally." (This development tracks a trend charted by Warren Miller and M. Kent Jennings, who found that delegates to the Republican National Convention became increasingly conservative between 1972 and 1980.) The numbers have grown more dramatic since. In 1980, Americans for Democratic Action gave the North Carolina Republican Jesse Helms an 11 and the Pennsylvania Republican John Heinz a 50. In 1998, the A.D.A. gave a perfect conservative score of zero to Helms and to the Republican who eventually won Heinz's seat, Rick Santorum, while the Minnesota Democrat Paul Wellstone received a perfect liberal score of 100, and Ted Kennedy a 95.

This change is more notable when viewed across a longer stretch of time. Congressional polarization began to decline in the early twentieth century—chiefly because Republicans became more moderate—until the nineteen-seventies, when a surge began, chiefly because Republicans became more conservative. The migration of Southern Democrats to the G.O.P. explains only about a third of this shift.

Among the cable and Internet commentators upon whom Tom Coburn would like Americans to rely for the study of government, it is a commonplace that congressional polarization is being driven by gerrymandering, the redrawing of congressional districts along party lines. This explanation is wrong. First, polarization has taken place in both chambers at about the same time and rate and, since redistricting does not affect the Senate, it cannot wholly explain what's happened in the House. Second, much polarization in the House has taken place in districts that have not been redrawn by legislators. Third, much of the polarizing in gerrymandered districts preceded their redrawing. The best calculation is that redistricting accounts for no more than ten or twenty per cent of the polarization in the House.

Gerrymandering is bad for all kinds of reasons, but polarization isn't one of them.

There's lots more to count, if you like counting. In a paper published last year, a team of economists and a computer scientist tracked polarization by identifying "partisan phrases" in the *Congressional Record* and then searching, in Google Books, for those same phrases in more than two million books published in the United States in English since 1873. They identified partisan speech this way: "we impute both the partisanship (association with left- or right-wing ideology) and the polarization (distance from the ideological center) of phrases by correlating their frequency of use with the political party of the speaker." Using this metric, "protect American industry" was the most frequently used Republican phrase between 1893 and 1895; "men, women, and children" was the most frequently used Democratic phrase between 1929 and 1933. (Here's a finding you can test against your own impressions: between 2007 and 2009, during the 110th Congress, the most Republican phrases were "domestic energy product" and "*Wall Street Journal*" and the most Democratic were "education, health care" and "mental health service.") Next, the researchers compared their partisan-phrase data set with the roll-call vote records compiled by McCarty, Poole, and Rosenthal. Graphs on which partisan speech is plotted lined up very well with graphs on which polarization was plotted.

In this analysis, partisan speech in Google Books is better correlated with periods of legislative gridlock than partisan speech in the *Congressional Record*. It's not clear what, if anything, this explains. Both groups studied—members of Congress and authors of books about politics—are people whom Converse called "political élites," and what many political scientists would like to know is whether polarization is being driven by ordinary voters (few of whom write books) or by Congress. It's an important question. If polarization happens first among the electorate, and only later in Congress, then voters are driving it, in which case it might merit another, better name: "representation." If it happens first in Congress, and only later among voters, and especially if it's a consequence of legislators answering to special interests and campaign contributors rather than to voters, polarization in some instances might be more aptly called "corruption."

Studies that rely on Google Books can be fishy. People who write books about politics include everyone from John Rawls to Ted Cruz, who, in 2009, supplied a very interesting foreword to "U.S. Constitution for Dummies." Also on Google Books: James Carville and Paul Begala's "Buck Up, Suck Up . . . and Come Back When You Foul Up" and Karl Rove's "Courage and Consequence." Maybe a graph charting a surge in partisan speech in Google Books as indexed by the phrases most used by partisans in Congress is measuring nothing so much as the triumph of political consulting over political science.

IN 1950, when the distance between the parties was smaller than it had been before or has been since—and voters had a hard time figuring out which party was conservative and which liberal—the American Political Science Association's Committee on Political Parties issued a report called "Toward a More Responsible Two-Party System." The problem with American democracy, the committee argued, is that the parties are too alike, and too weak. It recommended strengthening every element of the party system, from national leadership committees to congressional caucuses, as well as establishing a starker difference between party platforms. "If the two parties do not develop alternative programs that can be executed," the committee warned, "the voter's frustration and the mounting ambiguities of national policy might set in motion more extreme tendencies to the political left and the political right."

In the decades since, the parties have become both more coherent and more organized. In the House, the majority party controls both the schedule and the rules: as Barbara Sinclair chronicled in "Party Wars" (2006), many of these changes, including new forms of control over the budgetary process, were instituted by House Democrats during their long years of majority. Party leadership controls the story that the party tells the press, Democrats through a Policy Committee and Republicans using a Theme Team. Congressional party leaders do their own counting: they assign a party-loyalty score to members, and hand out committee chairs to those with the highest scores.

Is polarization responsible for policy gridlock? You might think that a divided government, where one party controls the White House and the other Congress, is more likely to suffer from gridlock than a unified government. You might think, too, that a more polarized Congress will be more subject to gridlock. Both of these hypotheses have been tested. Working from sources like the end-of-session summaries printed in the *New York Times* and the *Washington Post*, David R. Mayhew generated a list of landmark laws passed in every Congress since the Second World War. (Mayhew once pointed out that political science began as a branch of history, became a species of sociology, and then turned into a kind of mathematics.) In "Divided We Govern" (1991), he reported that in the second half of the twentieth century a divided government did not produce fewer laws than a unified government.

In "Stalemate," published in 2003, Sarah Binder questioned Mayhew's findings. Mayhew had conceded that he used a numerator without a denominator: he counted how many laws were passed but not how many were urged. Binder devised a denominator. Using the unsigned editorials that appear every day in the *Times*, she reconstructed each party's national legislative agenda. Together, those issues added up to the number Binder placed in her denominator, allowing her to calculate a "gridlock score" for every Congress: the number of failed agenda items divided by the number of items on the agenda. The size of the agenda for unified and divided governments is roughly equal (an average of a hundred and seven for unified and a hundred and twenty-three for divided). Between 1947 and 2000, the most productive Congress was the Eighty-ninth, the unified government under the Johnson Administration; its gridlock score is 35. The least productive, with a gridlock score of 65, was the 105th, in a divided government headed by Bill Clinton. Where Mayhew had argued that there was no difference in performance by unified and divided governments, Binder found that split-party governments are less productive.

She also calculated a "polarization score": she divided the number of moderates in the House and the Senate by the distance between the ideological medians of each party, as measured by placing them on a numerical spectrum not unlike the interest-group ratings scale. The more polarized its members, and the fewer the moderates, the less productive the Congress. Binder also examined, as another measure of legislative efficacy, the number of days late that Congress reached a budget resolution, for every year from 1976 (the first session subject to the Congressional Budget Act of 1974). Budget resolutions were an average of eleven days late when government was unified and nearly two months late when government was divided. Polarization slows down the budgetary process, too. In Congress, moderates aren't people who don't know much about politics. Moderates are people who get laws passed.

NOT EVERYTHING CAN BE LASHED TO A RULER. In an opinion essay in the *Times* this past summer, the political theorist Jacqueline Stevens argued that the discipline has failed to anticipate just about every important political development of recent history, from the end of the Cold War to the polarization of American politics. Stevens was dismayed by the American Political Science Association's reaction to the movement to defund the N.S.F.'s Political Science Program: "Why are my colleagues kowtowing to Congress for research money that comes with ideological strings attached?"

To say that there are limits to what this research can explain is not to say that it lacks value. The collection of the data alone is invaluable, and the best work is formidable. The strength of any analysis, though, lies in its independence from the policy agendas of politicians. Accepting money from the federal government to conduct research places academic inquiry in the service of national interests. In 1966, when the Political Science Program was founded, a year after the passage of the Voting Rights Act, equality of political participation was chief among what were then understood to be the nation's interests. That's the spirit in which the N.S.F. began funding the American National Election Studies project and, soon afterward, the study of congressional roll-call decisions. The 2013 proviso to the Coburn amendment, stipulating that the purpose of any political-science research funded by the N.S.F. must be to stimulate the American economy or improve national security, places an academic discipline in the service of a set of national interests different from those current in 1966, which had to do with democracy and equality. Easy money it is not.

Is the study of government a science? In more analytically luxuriant times, political scientists debated some of the very questions raised by Coburn in much the same way that, before the denial of climate change, certain philosophers of science argued that all science is interpretation. Other moves have been made since. But intellectuals, as Bruno Latour once pointed out, are nearly always one critique too late: "entire Ph.D. programs are still running to make sure that good American kids are learning the hard way that facts are made up, that there is no such thing as natural, unmediated, unbiased access to truth, that we are always prisoners of language, that we always speak from a particular standpoint, and so on, while dangerous extremists are using the very same argument of social construction to destroy hard-won evidence that could save our lives."

Irony is cheap, not painless. One well-established fact is that polarization in Congress maps onto one measure better than any other: economic inequality. The smaller the gap between rich and poor, the more moderate our politicians; the greater the gap, the greater the disagreement between liberals and conservatives. The greater the disagreement between liberals and conservatives, the less Congress is able to get done; the less Congress gets done, the greater the gap between rich and poor. That's not bad math. That's what happens when the kitchen's on fire and all you've got is matches.

—2013

RICHER AND POORER

FOR ABOUT A CENTURY, ECONOMIC INEQUALITY HAS been measured on a scale, from zero to one, known as the Gini index and named after an Italian statistician, Corrado Gini, who devised it in 1912, when he was twenty-eight and the chair of statistics at the University of Cagliari. If all the income in the world were earned by one person and everyone else earned nothing, the world would have a Gini index of one. If everyone in the world earned exactly the same income, the world would have a Gini index of zero. The United States Census Bureau has been using Gini's measurement to calculate income inequality in America since 1947. Between 1947 and 1968, the U.S. Gini index dropped to .386, the lowest ever recorded. Then it began to climb.

Income inequality is greater in the United States than in any other democracy in the developed world. Between 1975 and 1985, when the Gini index for U.S. households rose from .397 to .419, as calculated by the U.S. Census Bureau, the Gini indices of the United Kingdom, the Netherlands, France, Germany, Sweden, and Finland ranged roughly between .200 and .300, according to national data analyzed by Andrea Brandolini and Timothy Smeeding. But historical cross-country comparisons are difficult to make; the data are patchy, and different countries measure differently. The Luxembourg Income Study, begun in 1983, harmonizes data collected from more than forty countries on six continents. According to the L.I.S.'s adjusted data, the United States has regularly had the highest Gini index of any affluent democracy. In 2013, the U.S. Census Bureau reported a Gini index of .476.

The evidence that income inequality in the United States has been growing for decades and is greater than in any other developed democracy is not much disputed. It is widely known and widely studied.

Economic inequality has been an academic specialty at least since Gini first put chalk to chalkboard. In the nineteen-fifties, Simon Kuznets, who went on to win a Nobel Prize, used tax data to study the shares of income among groups, an approach that was further developed by the British economist Anthony Atkinson, beginning with his 1969 paper "On the Measurement of Inequality," in the *Journal of Economic Theory*. Last year's unexpected popular success of the English translation of Thomas Piketty's "Capital in the Twenty-first Century" drew the public's attention to measurements of inequality, but Piketty's work had long since reached American social scientists, especially through a 2003 paper that he published with the Berkeley economist Emmanuel Saez, in *The Quarterly Journal of Economics*. Believing that the Gini index underestimates inequality, Piketty and Saez favor Kuznets's approach. (Atkinson, Piketty, Saez, and Facundo Alvaredo are also the creators of the World Top Incomes Database, which collects income-share data from more than twenty countries.) In "Income Inequality in the United States, 1913-1998," Piketty and Saez used tax data to calculate what percentage of income goes to the top one per cent and to the top ten per cent. In 1928, the top one per cent earned twenty-four per cent of all income; in 1944, they earned eleven per cent, a rate that began to rise in the nineteen-eighties. By 2012, according to Saez's updated data, the top one per cent were earning twenty-three per cent of the nation's income, almost the same ratio as in 1928, although it has since dropped slightly.

Political scientists are nearly as likely to study economic inequality as economists are, though they're less interested in how much inequality a market can bear than in how much a democracy can bear, and here the general thinking is that the United States is nearing its breaking point. In 2001, the American Political Science Association formed a Task Force on Inequality and American Democracy; a few years later, it concluded that growing economic inequality was threatening fundamental American political institutions. In 2009, Oxford University Press published both a seven-hundred-page "Handbook of Economic Inequality" and a collection of essays about the political consequences of economic inequality whose argument is its title: "The Unsustainable American State." There's a global version of this argument, too. "Inequality Matters," a 2013 report by the United Nations, took the view—advanced by the economist Joseph Stiglitz in his book "The Price of Inequality"—that growing income inequality is responsible for all manner of political instability, as well as for the slowing of economic growth worldwide. Last year, when the Pew Research Center conducted a survey about which of five dangers people in forty-four countries consider to be the "greatest threat to the world," many of the countries polled put religious and ethnic hatred at the top of their lists, but Americans and many Europeans chose inequality.

What's new about the chasm between the rich and the poor in the United States, then, isn't that it's growing or that scholars are studying it or that people are worried about it. What's new is that American politicians of all spots and stripes are talking about it, if feebly: inequality this, inequality that. In January, at a forum sponsored by Freedom Partners (a free-market advocacy group with ties to the Koch brothers), the G.O.P. Presidential swains Ted Cruz, Rand Paul, and Marco Rubio battled over which of them disliked inequality more, agreeing only that its existence wasn't their fault. "The top one per cent earn a higher share of our income, nationally, than any year since 1928," Cruz said, drawing on the work of Saez and Piketty. Cruz went on, "I chuckle every time I hear Barack Obama or Hillary Clinton talk about income inequality, because it's increased dramatically under their policies." No doubt there has been a lot of talk. "Let's close the loopholes that lead to inequality by allowing the top one per cent to avoid paying taxes on their accumulated wealth," Obama said during his State of the Union address. Speaker of the House John Boehner countered that "the President's policies have made income inequality worse."

The reason Democrats and Republicans are fighting over who's to blame for growing economic inequality is that, aside from a certain amount of squabbling, it's no longer possible to deny that it exists—a development that's not to be sneezed at, given the state of the debate on climate change. That's not to say the agreement runs deep; in fact, it couldn't be shallower. The causes of income inequality are much disputed; so are its costs. And knowing the numbers doesn't appear to be changing anyone's mind about what, if anything, should be done about it.

ROBERT PUTNAM'S 2015 BOOK, "Our Kids: The American Dream in Crisis," is an attempt to set the statistics aside and, instead, tell a story. "Our Kids" begins with the story of the town where Putnam grew up, Port Clinton, Ohio. Putnam is a political scientist, but his argument is historical—it's about change over time—and fuelled, in part, by nostalgia. "My hometown was, in the 1950s, a passable embodiment of the American Dream," he writes, "a place that offered decent opportunity for all the kids in town, whatever their background." Sixty years later, Putnam says, Port Clinton "is a split-screen American nightmare, a community in which kids from the wrong side of the tracks that bisect the town can barely imagine the future that awaits the kids from the right side of the tracks."

Inequality-wise, Port Clinton makes a reasonable Middletown. According to the American Community Survey conducted by the U.S. Census Bureau, Port Clinton's congressional district, Ohio's ninth, has a Gini index of .467, which is somewhat lower than the A.C.S.'s estimate of the national average. But "Our Kids" isn't a book about the Gini index. "Some of us learn from numbers, but more of us learn from stories," according to an appendix that Putnam co-wrote with Jennifer M. Silva. Putnam, the author of "Bowling Alone," is the director of the Saguaro Seminar for civic engagement at Harvard's Kennedy School of Government; Silva, a sociologist, has been a postdoctoral fellow there. In her 2013 book "Coming Up Short: Working-Class Adulthood in an Age of Uncertainty" (Oxford), Silva reported the results of interviews she conducted with a hundred working-class adults in Lowell, Massachusetts and Richmond, Virginia, described her account of the structural inequalities that shape their lives as "a story of institutions—not individuals or their families," and argued that those inequalities are the consequence of the past half century's "massive effort to roll back social protections from the market." For "Our Kids," Silva visited Robert Putnam's home town and interviewed young people and their parents. Putnam graduated from Port Clinton High School in 1959. The surviving members of his class are now in their mid-seventies. Putnam and Silva sent them questionnaires; seventy-five people returned them. Silva also spent two years interviewing more than a hundred young adults in nine other cities and counties across the nation. As Putnam and Silva note, Silva conducted nearly all of the interviews Putnam uses in his book.

"Our Kids" is a heartfelt portrait of four generations: Putnam's fellow 1959 graduates and their children, and the kids in Port Clinton and those nine other communities today and their parents. The book tells more or less the same story that the numbers tell; it's just got people in it. Specifically, it's got kids: the kids Putnam used to know, and, above all, the kids Silva interviewed. The book proceeds from the depressing assumption that presenting the harrowing lives of poor young people is the best way to get Americans to care about poverty.

Putnam has changed the names of all his subjects and removed certain identifying details. He writes about them as characters. First, there's Don. He went to Port Clinton High School with Putnam. His father worked two jobs: an eight-hour shift at Port Clinton Manufacturing, followed by seven and a half hours at a local canning plant. A minister in town helped Don apply to university. "I didn't know I was poor until I went to college," Don says. He graduated from college, became a minister, and married a high-school teacher; they had one child, who became a high-school librarian. Libby, another member of Putnam's graduating class, was the sixth of ten children. Like Don's parents, neither of Libby's parents finished high school. Her father worked at Standard Products, a factory on Maple Street that made many different things out of rubber, from weather stripping to tank treads. Libby won a scholarship to the University of Toledo, but dropped out to get married and have kids. Twenty years later, after a divorce, she got a job as a clerk in a lumberyard, worked her way up to becoming a writer for a local newspaper, and eventually ran for countywide office and won.

ALL BUT TWO OF THE MEMBERS of Putnam's graduating class were white. Putnam's wistfulness toward his childhood home town is at times painful to read. The whiteness of Port Clinton in the nineteen-fifties was not mere happenstance but the consequence of discriminatory housing and employment practices. I glanced through the records of the Ohio chapter of the N.A.A.C.P., which included a branch in Port Clinton. The Ohio chapter's report for 1957 chronicles, among other things, its failed attempt to gain passage of statewide Fair Housing legislation; describes how "cross burnings occurred in many cities in Ohio"; recounts instances of police brutality, including in Columbus, where a patrolman beat a woman "with the butt of his pistol all over her face and body"; and states that in Toledo, Columbus, "and in a number of other communities, the Association intervened in situations where violence flared up or was threatened when Negro families moved into formerly 'all-white neighborhoods.' " Thurgood Marshall, the director of the N.A.A.C.P.'s Legal Defense and Educational Fund, spoke in Ohio in 1958, after which a sympathetic Cleveland newspaper wrote that Marshall "will never be named to the Supreme Court." In 1960, the Ohio N.A.A.C.P. launched a statewide voter-registration drive. One pamphlet asked, "Are you permitted to live wherever you please in any Ohio City?" Putnam acknowledges that there was a lot of racism in Port Clinton, but he suggests that, whatever hardships the two black kids in his class faced because they were black, the American dream was nevertheless theirs. This fails to convince. As one of those two kids, now grown, tells Putnam, "Your then was not my then, and your now isn't even my now."

In any case, the world changed, and Port Clinton changed with it. "Most of the downtown shops of my youth stand empty and derelict," Putnam writes. In the late nineteen-sixties, the heyday of the Great Society, when income inequality in the United States was as low as it has ever been, the same was probably true of Port Clinton. But in the nineteen-seventies the town's manufacturing base collapsed. Standard Products laid off more than half of its workers. In 1993, the plant closed. Since then, unemployment has continued to rise and wages to fall. Between 1999 and 2013, the percentage of children in Port Clinton living in poverty rose from ten to forty.

Silva found David hanging out in a park. His father, currently in prison, never had a steady job. David's parents separated when he was a little boy. He bounced around, attending seven elementary schools. When he was thirteen, he was arrested for robbery. He graduated from high school only because he was given course credit for hours he'd worked at Big Boppers Diner (from which he was fired after graduation). In 2012, when David was eighteen, he got his girlfriend pregnant. "I'll never get ahead," he posted on his Facebook page last year, after his girlfriend left him. "I'm *FUCKING DONE.*"

Wealthy newcomers began arriving in the nineteen-nineties. On the shores of Lake Erie, just a few miles past Port Clinton's trailer parks, they built mansions and golf courses and gated communities. "Chelsea and her family live in a large white home with a wide porch overlooking the lake," Putnam writes, introducing another of his younger characters. Chelsea was the president of her high school's student body and editor of the yearbook. Her mother, Wendy, works part time; her father, Dick, is a businessman. In the basement of their house, Wendy and Dick had a "1950s-style diner" built so that Chelsea and her brother would have a place to hang out with their friends. When Chelsea's brother got a bad grade in school, Wendy went all the way to the school board to get it changed. Chelsea and her brother are now in college. Wendy does not appear to believe in welfare. "You have to work if you want to get rich," she says. "If my kids are going to be successful, I don't think they should have to pay other people who are sitting around doing nothing for their success."

Aside from the anecdotes, the bulk of "Our Kids" is an omnibus of social-science scholarship. The book's chief and authoritative contribution is its careful presentation for a popular audience of important work on the erosion, in the past half century, of so many forms of social, economic, and political support for families, schools, and communities—with consequences that amount to what Silva and others have called the "privatization of risk." The social-science literature includes a complicated debate about the relationship between inequality of outcome (differences of income and of wealth) and inequality of opportunity (differences in education and employment). To most readers, these issues are more familiar as a political disagreement. In American politics, Democrats are more likely to talk about both kinds of inequality, while Republicans tend to confine their concern to inequality of opportunity. According to Putnam, "All sides in this debate agree on one thing, however: as income inequality expands, kids from more privileged backgrounds start and probably finish further and further ahead of their less privileged peers, even if the rate of socioeconomic mobility is unchanged." He also takes the position, again relying on a considerable body of scholarship, that, "quite apart from the danger that the opportunity gap poses to American prosperity, it also undermines our democracy." Chelsea is interested in politics. David has never voted.

The American dream is in crisis, Putnam argues, because Americans used to care about other people's kids and now they only care about their own kids. But, he writes, "America's poor kids do belong to us and we to them. They are our kids." This is a lot like his argument in "Bowling Alone." In high school in Port Clinton, Putnam was in a bowling league; he regards bowling leagues as a marker of community and civic engagement; bowling leagues are in decline; hence, Americans don't take care of one another anymore. "Bowling Alone" and "Our Kids" also have the same homey just-folksiness. And they have the same shortcomings. If you don't miss bowling leagues or all-white suburbs where women wear aprons—if Putnam's then was not your then and his now isn't your now—his well-intentioned "we" can be remarkably grating.

In story form, the argument of "Our Kids" is that while Wendy and Dick were building a fifties-style diner for their kids in the basement of their lakefront mansion, grade-grubbing with their son's teachers, and glue-gunning the decorations for their daughter's prom, every decent place to hang out in Port Clinton closed its doors, David was fired from his job at Big Boppers, and he got his girlfriend pregnant because, by the time David and Chelsea were born, in the nineteen-nineties, not only was Standard Products out of business but gone, too, was the sense of civic obligation and commonweal—everyone caring about everyone else's kids—that had made it possible for Don and Libby to climb out of poverty in the nineteen-fifties and the nineteen-sixties. "Nobody gave a shit," David says. And he's not wrong.

"Our Kids" is a passionate, urgent book. It also has a sad helplessness. Putnam tells a story teeming with characters and full of misery but without a single villain. This is deliberate. "This is a book without upper-class villains," he insists in the book's final chapter. In January, Putnam tweeted, "My new book 'Our Kids' shows a growing gap between rich kids and poor kids. We'll work with all sides on solutions." It's easier to work with all sides if no side is to blame. But Putnam's eagerness to influence Congress has narrative consequences. If you're going to tell a story about bad things happening to good people, you've got to offer an explanation, and, when you make your arguments through characters, your reader will expect that explanation in the form of characters. I feel bad for Chelsea. But I feel worse for David. Am I supposed to hate Wendy?

Some people make arguments by telling stories; other people make arguments by counting things. Charles Dickens was a story man. In "Hard Times" (1854), a novel written when statistics was on the rise, Dickens's villain, Thomas Gradgrind, was a numbers man, "a man of facts and calculations," who named one of his sons Adam Smith and another Malthus. "With a rule and a pair of scales, and the multiplication table always in his pocket, Sir, ready to weigh and measure any parcel of human nature, and tell you exactly what it comes to."

Numbers men are remote and cold of heart, Dickens thought. But, of course, the appeal of numbers lies in their remoteness and coldness. Numbers depersonalize; that remains one of their chief claims to authority, and to a different explanatory force than can be found in, say, a poem. "Quantification is a technology of distance," as the historian of science Theodore Porter has pointed out. "Reliance on numbers and quantitative manipulation minimizes the need for intimate knowledge and personal trust." It's difficult to understand something like income inequality across large populations and to communicate your understanding of it across vast distances without counting. But quantification's lack of intimacy is also its weakness; it represents not only a gain but also a loss of knowledge.

Corrado Gini, he of the Gini index, was a numbers man, at a time when statistics had become a modern science. In 1925, four years after Gini wrote "Measurement of Inequality of Incomes," he signed the "Manifesto of Fascist Intellectuals" (he was the only statistician to do so) and was soon running the Presidential Commission for the Study of Constitutional Reforms. As Jean-Guy Prévost reported in "A Total Science: Statistics in Liberal and Fascist Italy" (2009), Gini's work was so closely tied to the Fascist state that, in 1944, after the regime fell, he was tried for being an apologist for Fascism. In the shadow of his trial, he joined the Movimento Unionista Italiano, a political party whose objective was to annex Italy to the United States. "This would solve all of Italy's problems," the movement's founder, Santi Paladino, told a reporter for *Time*. ("Paladino has never visited the U.S., though his wife Francesca lived 24 years in The Bronx," the magazine noted.) But, for Gini, the movement's purpose was to provide him with some anti-Fascist credentials.

The story of Gini is a good illustration of the problem with stories, which is that they personalize (which is also their power). His support for Fascism doesn't mean that the Gini index isn't valuable. It is valuable. The life of Corrado Gini can't be used to undermine all of statistical science. Still, if you wanted to write an indictment of statistics as an instrument of authoritarian states, and if you had a great deal of other evidence to support that indictment—including other stories and, ideally, numbers—why yes, Gini would be an excellent character to introduce in Chapter 1.

Because stories contain one kind of truth and numbers another, many writers mix and match, telling representative stories and backing them up with aggregate data. Putnam, though, doesn't so much mix and match as split the difference. He tells stories about kids but presents data about the economy. That's why "Our Kids" has heaps of victims but not a single villain. "We encounter Elijah in a dingy shopping mall on the north side of Atlanta, during his lunch break from a job packing groceries," Putnam writes. "Elijah is thin and small in stature, perhaps five foot seven, and wears baggy clothes that bulk his frame: jeans belted low around his upper thighs, a pair of Jordans on his feet." As for why Elijah is packing groceries, the book offers not characters—there are no interviews, for instance, with members of the Georgia legislature or the heads of national corporations whose businesses have left Atlanta—but numbers, citing statistics about the city ("Large swaths of southern and western Atlanta itself are over 95 percent black, with child poverty rates ranging from 50 percent to 80 percent") and providing a series of charts reporting the results of studies about things like class differences in parenting styles and in the frequency of the family dinner.

IN "THE AGE OF ACQUIESCENCE: The Life and Death of American Resistance to Organized Wealth and Power," Steve Fraser fumes that what's gone wrong with political discourse in America is that the left isn't willing to blame anyone for anything anymore. There used to be battle cries. No more kings! Down with fat cats! Damn the moneycrats! Like Putnam's argument, Fraser's is both historical and nostalgic. Fraser longs for the passion and force with which Americans of earlier generations attacked aggregated power. Think of the way Frederick Douglass wrote about slavery, Ida B. Wells wrote about lynching, Ida Tarbell wrote about Standard Oil, Upton Sinclair wrote about the meatpacking industry, and Louis Brandeis wrote about the money trust. These people weren't squeamish about villains.

To chronicle the rise of acquiescence, Fraser examines two differences between the long nineteenth century and today. "The first Gilded Age, despite its glaring inequities, was accompanied by a gradual rise in the standard of living; the second by a gradual erosion," he writes. In the first Gilded Age, everyone from reporters to politicians apparently felt comfortable painting plutocrats as villains; in the second, this is, somehow, forbidden. "If the first Gilded Age was full of sound and fury," he writes, "the second seemed to take place in a padded cell." Fraser argues that while Progressive Era muckrakers ended the first Gilded Age by drawing on an age-old tradition of dissent to criticize prevailing economic, social, and political arrangements, today's left doesn't engage in dissent; it engages in consent, urging solutions that align with neoliberalism, technological determinism, and global capitalism: "Environmental despoiling arouses righteous eating; cultural decay inspires charter schools; rebellion against work becomes work as a form of rebellion; old-form anticlericalism morphs into the piety of the secular; the break with convention ends up as the politics of style; the cri de coeur against alienation surrenders to the triumph of the solitary; the marriage of political and cultural radicalism ends in divorce." Why not blame the financial industry? Why not blame the Congress that deregulated it? Why not blame the system itself? Because, Fraser argues, the left has been cowed into silence on the main subject at hand: "What we could not do, what was not even speakable, was to tamper with the basic institutions of financial capitalism."

Putnam closes "Our Kids" with a chapter called "What Is to Be Done?" Tampering with the basic institutions of financial capitalism is not on his to-do list. The chapter includes one table, one chart, many stories, and this statement: "The absence of personal villains in our stories does not mean that no one is at fault." At fault are "social policies that reflect collective decisions," and, "insofar as we have some responsibility for those collective decisions, we are implicated by our failure to address removable barriers to others' success." What can Putnam's "we" do? He proposes changes in four realms: family structure, parenting, school, and community. His policy recommendations include expanding the earned-income tax credit and protecting existing anti-poverty programs; implementing more generous parental leaves, better child-care programs, and state-funded preschool; equalizing the funding of public schools, providing more community-based neighborhood schools, and increasing support for vocational high-school programs and for community colleges; ending pay-to-play extracurricular activities in public schools and developing mentorship programs that tie schools to communities and community organizations.

All of these ideas are admirable, many are excellent, none are new, and, at least at the federal level, few are achievable. The American political imagination has become as narrow as the gap between rich and poor is wide.

"INEQUALITY: WHAT CAN BE DONE?," by Anthony Atkinson, was published in 2015. Atkinson is a renowned expert on the measurement of economic inequality, but in "Inequality" he hides his math. "There are a number of graphs, and a small number of tables," he writes, by way of apology, and he paraphrases Stephen Hawking: "Every equation halves the number of readers."

Much of the book is a discussion of specific proposals. Atkinson believes that solutions like Putnam's, which focus on inequality of opportunity, mainly through reforms having to do with public education, are inadequate. Atkinson thinks that the division between inequality of outcome and inequality of opportunity is largely false. He believes that tackling inequality of outcome is a very good way to tackle inequality of opportunity. (If you help a grownup get a job, her kids will have a better chance of climbing out of poverty, too.) Above all, he disagrees with the widespread assumption that technological progress and globalization are responsible for growing inequality. That assumption, he argues, is wrong and also dangerous, because it encourages the belief that growing inequality is inevitable.

Atkinson points out that neither globalization nor rapid technological advance is new and there are, therefore, lessons to be learned from history. Those lessons do not involve nostalgia. (Atkinson is actually an optimistic sort, and he spends time appreciating rising standards of living, worldwide.) One of those lessons is that globalizing economies aren't like hurricanes or other acts of God or nature. Instead, they're governed by laws regulating things like unions and trusts and banks and wages and taxes; laws are passed by legislators; in democracies, legislators are elected. So, too, new technologies don't simply fall out of the sky, like meteors or little miracles. "The direction of technological change is the product of decisions by firms, researchers, and governments," Atkinson writes. The iPhone exists, as Mariana Mazzucato demonstrated in her 2013 book "The Entrepreneurial State," because various branches of the U.S. government provided research assistance that resulted in several key technological developments, including G.P.S., multi-touch screens, L.C.D. displays, lithium-ion batteries, and cellular networks.

Atkinson isn't interested in stories the way Putnam is interested in stories. And he isn't interested in villains the way Fraser is interested in villains. But he is interested in responsible parties, and in demanding government action. "It is not enough to say that rising inequality is due to technological forces outside our control," Atkinson writes. "The government can influence the path taken." In "Inequality: What Can Be Done?," he offers fifteen proposals, from the familiar (unemployment programs, national savings bonds, and a more progressive tax structure) to the novel (a governmental role in the direction of technological development, a capital endowment or "minimum inheritance" paid to everyone on reaching adulthood), along with five "ideas to pursue," which is where things get Piketty (a global tax on wealth, a minimum tax on corporations).

In Port Clinton, Ohio, a barbed-wire fence surrounds the abandoned Standard Products factory; the E.P.A. has posted signs warning that the site is hazardous. There's no work there anymore, only poison. Robert Putnam finds that heartbreaking. Steve Fraser wishes people were angrier about it. Anthony Atkinson thinks something can be done. Atkinson's specific policy recommendations are for the United Kingdom. In the United States, most of his proposals are nonstarters, no matter how many times you hear the word "inequality" on "Meet the Press" this year.

It might be that people have been studying inequality in all the wrong places. A few years ago, two scholars of comparative politics, Alfred Stepan, at Columbia, and the late Juan J. Linz—numbers men—tried to figure out why the United States has for so long had much greater income inequality than any other developed democracy. Because this disparity has been more or less constant, the question doesn't lend itself very well to historical analysis. Nor is it easily subject to the distortions of nostalgia. But it does lend itself very well to comparative analysis.

Stepan and Linz identified twenty-three long-standing democracies with advanced economies. Then they counted the number of veto players in each of those twenty-three governments. (A veto player is a person or body that can block a policy decision. Stepan and Linz explain, "For example, in the United States, the Senate and the House of Representatives are veto players because without their consent, no bill can become a law.") More than half of the twenty-three countries Stepan and Linz studied have only one veto player; most of these countries have unicameral parliaments. A few countries have two veto players; Switzerland and Australia have three. Only the United States has four. Then they made a chart, comparing Gini indices with veto-player numbers: the more veto players in a government, the greater the nation's economic inequality. This is only a correlation, of course, and cross-country economic comparisons are fraught, but it's interesting.

Then they observed something more. Their twenty-three democracies included eight federal governments with both upper and lower legislative bodies. Using the number of seats and the size of the population to calculate malapportionment, they assigned a "Gini Index of Inequality of Representation" to those eight upper houses, and found that the United States had the highest score: it has the most malapportioned and the least representative upper house. These scores, too, correlated with the countries' Gini scores for income inequality: the less representative the upper body of a national legislature, the greater the gap between the rich and the poor.

The growth of inequality isn't inevitable. But, insofar as Americans have been unable to adopt measures to reduce it, the numbers might seem to suggest that the problem doesn't lie with how Americans treat one another's kids, as lousy as that is. It lies with Congress.

—2015

POLITICS AND THE
NEW MACHINE

"I AM WHO I AM," DONALD J. TRUMP SAID IN AUGUST, on the eve of 2015's first GOP presidential debate, and what he meant by that was this: "I don't have a pollster." The word "poll-ster," when it was coined, was meant as a slur, like "huckster." That's the way Trump uses it. Other candidates have pollsters: "They pay these guys two hundred thousand dollars a month to tell them, 'Don't say this, don't say that.'" Trump has none: "No one tells me what to say."

Every election is a morality play. The Candidate tries to speak to the People but is thwarted by Negative Campaigning, vilified by a Biased Media, and haunted by a War Record. I am who I am, the Candidate says, and my Opponents are flunkies. Trump makes this claim with unrivaled swagger, but citing his campaign's lack of a pollster as proof of his character, while fascinating, is utterly disin-genuous. The Path to Office is long. To reach the Land of Caucuses and Primaries, the Candidate must first cross the Sea of Polls. Trump is a creature of that sea.

Lately, the Sea of Polls is deeper than ever before, and darker. From the late 1990s to 2012, twelve hundred polling organizations conducted nearly thirty-seven thousand polls by making more than three billion phone calls. Most Americans refused to speak to them. This skewed results. Mitt Romney's pollsters believed, even on the morning of the election, that Romney would win. A 2013 study—a poll—found that three out of four Americans suspect polls of bias. Presumably, there was far greater distrust among the people who refused to take the survey.

The modern public opinion poll has been around since the Great Depression, when the response rate—the number of people who take a survey as a percentage of those who were asked—was more than ninety. The participation rate—the number of people who take a survey as a percentage of the population—is far lower. Election pollsters sample only a minuscule portion of the electorate, not uncommonly something on the order of a couple of thousand people out of the more than two hundred million Americans who are eligible to vote. The promise of this work is that the sample is exquisitely representative. But the lower the response rate the harder and more expensive it becomes to realize that promise, which requires both calling many more people and trying to correct for "non-response bias" by giving greater weight to the answers of people from demographic groups that are less likely to respond. Pollster.com's Mark Blumenthal has recalled how, in the 1980s, when the response rate at the firm where he was working had fallen to about 60 percent, people in his office said, "What will happen when it's only twenty? We won't be able to be in business!" A typical response rate is now in the single digits.

Meanwhile, polls are wielding greater influence over American elections than ever. In May 2015, Fox News announced that, in order to participate in its first prime-time debate, hosted jointly with Facebook, Republican candidates had to "place in the top ten of an average of the five most recent national polls." Where the candidates stood on the debate stage would also be determined by their polling numbers. (Ranking in the polls had earlier been used to exclude third-party candidates.) Scott Keeter, Pew's director of survey research, is among the many public opinion experts who found Fox News's decision insupportable. "I just don't think polling is really up to the task of deciding the field for the headliner debate," Keeter told me. Bill McInturff doesn't think so, either. McInturff is a cofounder of Public Opinion Strategies, the leading Republican polling organization; with its Democratic counterpart, Hart Research Associates, he conducts the NBC News/*Wall Street Journal* poll. "I didn't think my job was to design polling so that Fox could pick people for a debate," McInturff told me. Really, it's not possible to design a poll to do that.

Even if more people could be persuaded to answer the phone, polling would still be teetering on the edge of disaster. Few American adults any longer had landlines, and the 1991 Telephone Consumer Protection Act bans autodialing to cell phones. (The law applies both to public opinion polling, a billion-dollar-a-year industry, and to market research, a twenty-billion-dollar-a-year industry.) In 2015 Gallup Inc. agreed to pay twelve million dollars to settle a class action lawsuit filed on behalf of everyone in the United States who, between 2009 and 2013, received an unbidden cell phone call from the company seeking an opinion about politics. (Gallup denies any wrongdoing.) The FCC issued a ruling reaffirming and strengthening the prohibition on random autodialing to cell phones. During congressional hearings, Greg Walden, a Republican from Oregon, who is the chair of the House Subcommittee on Communications and Technology, asked FCC chairman Tom Wheeler if the ruling meant that pollsters would go "the way of blacksmiths." "Well," he said, "they have been, right?"

Internet pollsters have not replaced them. Using methods designed for knocking on doors to measure public opinion on the internet is like trying to shoe a horse with your operating system. Internet pollsters can't call you; they have to wait for you to come to them. Not everyone uses the internet, and, at the moment, the people who do, and who complete online surveys, are younger and leftier than people who don't, while people who have landlines, and who answer the phone, are older and more conservative than people who don't. Some pollsters, both here and around the world, rely on a combination of telephone and internet polling; the trick is to figure out just the right mix. So far, it isn't working. In Israel in March 2015, polls failed to predict Benjamin Netanyahu's victory. That May in the UK, every major national poll failed to forecast the Conservative Party's win.

"It's a little crazy to me that people are still using the same tools that were used in the 1930s," Dan Wagner told me when I asked him about the future of polling. Wagner was the chief analytics officer on the 2012 Obama campaign and is the CEO of Civis Analytics, a data-science technology and advisory firm. Companies like Civis have been collecting information about you and people like you in order to measure public opinion and, among other things, forecast elections by building predictive models and running simulations to determine what issues you and people like you care about, what kind of candidate you'd give money to, and, if you're likely to turn out on Election Day, how you'll vote. They might call you, but they don't need to.

Still, data science can't solve the biggest problem with polling, because that problem is neither methodological nor technological. It's political. Pollsters rose to prominence by claiming that measuring public opinion is good for democracy. But what if it's bad?

A "poll" used to mean the top of your head. Ophelia says of Polonius, "His beard as white as snow: All flaxen was his poll." When voting involved assembling (all in favor of Smith stand here, all in favor of Jones over there), counting votes required counting heads; that is, counting polls. Eventually, a "poll" came to mean the count itself. By the nineteenth century, to vote was to go "to the polls," where, more and more, voting was done on paper. Ballots were often printed in newspapers: you'd cut one out and bring it with you. With the turn to the secret ballot, beginning in the 1880s, the government began supplying the ballots, but newspapers kept printing them; they'd use them to conduct their own polls, called "straw polls." Before the election, you'd cut out your ballot and mail it to the newspaper, which would make a prediction. Political parties conducted straw polls, too. That's one of the ways the political machine worked.

Straw polls were usually conducted a few days or weeks before an election. In August 2015, to cull the field for the first GOP debate, Fox News used polls conducted more than four hundred and sixty days before the general election. (These early polls have become so unreliable that neither Gallup nor Pew conducts them.) The question asked ordinarily takes the form of "If the election were held tomorrow . . ." The circumstances under which the next U.S. presidential election would actually be held tomorrow involve, essentially, Armageddon. Trump won. All flaxen was his poll.

A century ago, newspapers that wanted to predict the outcome of a presidential election had to join forces. In 1908, the *New York Herald*, the *Cincinnati Enquirer*, the *Chicago Record-Herald*, and the *St. Louis Republic* tallied their straws together. William Randolph Hearst's newspapers did the same thing. But the best predictions were made by a national magazine, the *Literary Digest*, beginning in 1916. It regularly miscalculated the popular vote, but for a long time it got the Electoral College winner right. In 1920, the *Digest* mailed out eleven million ballots. By 1932, its mailing list had swelled to twenty million. Most of those names were taken from telephone directories and automobile-registration files. George Gallup was one of the few people who understood that the *Digest* risked underestimating Democratic votes, especially as the Depression deepened, because its sample, while very big, was not very representative: people who supported FDR were much less likely than the rest of the population to own a telephone or a car.

Gallup was borrowing from the insights of social science. Social surveys, first conducted in the 1890s, had been a hallmark of Progressive Era social reform. In 1896, W. E. B. Du Bois went door to door in Philadelphia's Seventh Ward and interviewed some five thousand people in order to prepare his study *The Philadelphia Negro*. In the 1930s, social scientists argued for the merits of a shortcut that relied on statistical science: surveying a tiny but representative sample of a population.

Gallup had always wanted to be a newspaper editor, but after graduating from the University of Iowa, in 1923, he entered a PhD program in applied psychology. In 1928, in a dissertation called "An Objective Method for Determining Reader Interest in the Content of a Newspaper," Gallup argued that "at one time the press was depended upon as the chief agency for instructing and informing the mass of people" but that newspapers no longer filled that role and instead ought to meet "a greater need for entertainment." He therefore devised a method: he'd watch readers go through a newspaper column by column and mark up the parts they liked, so that he could advise an editor which parts of the paper to keep printing and which parts to scrap.

In 1932, when Gallup was a professor of journalism at North-western, his mother-in-law, Ola Babcock Miller, ran for secretary of state in Iowa. Her late husband had run for governor; her nomination was largely honorary and she was not expected to win. Gallup had read the work of Walter Lippmann. Lippmann believed that "public opinion" is a fiction created by political elites to suit and advance their interests. Gallup disagreed, and suspected that public opinion, like reader interest, could be quantified. To get a sense of his mother-in-law's chances, Gallup began applying psychology to politics. The year of the race (she won), Gallup moved to New York, and began working for an advertising agency while also teaching at Columbia and running an outfit he called the Editors' Research Bureau, selling his services to newspapers. Gallup thought of this work as "a new form of journalism." But he decided that it ought to sound academic, too. In 1935, in Princeton, he founded the American Institute of Public Opinion, with funding provided by more than a hundred newspapers.

In 1936, in his syndicated column Gallup predicted that the *Literary Digest* would calculate that Alf Landon would defeat FDR in a landslide and that the *Digest* would be wrong. He was right on both counts. This was only the beginning. "I had the idea of polling on every major issue," Gallup explained. He began insisting that this work was essential to democracy. Elections come only every two years, but "we need to know the will of the people at all times." Gallup claimed that his polls had rescued American politics from the political machine and restored it to the American pastoral, the New England town meeting. Elmo Roper, another early pollster, called the public opinion survey "the greatest contribution to democracy since the introduction of the secret ballot."

Gallup's early method is known as "quota sampling." He determined what proportion of the people are men, women, Black, white, young, and old. The interviewers who conducted his surveys had to fill a quota so that the population sampled would constitute an exactly proportionate mini-electorate. But what Gallup presented as "public opinion" was the opinion of Americans who were disproportionately educated, white, and male. Nationwide, in the 1930s and '40s, Blacks constituted about 10 percent of the population but made up less than 2 percent of Gallup's survey respondents. Because Blacks in the South were generally prevented from voting, Gallup assigned no "Negro quota" in those states. As the historian Sarah Igo has pointed out, "Instead of functioning as a tool for democracy, opinion polls were deliberately modeled upon, and compounded, democracy's flaws."

Ever since Gallup, two things have been called polls: surveys of opinions and forecasts of election results. (Plenty of other surveys, of course, don't measure opinions but instead concern status and behavior: Do you own a house? Have you seen a doctor in the past month?) It's not a bad idea to reserve the term "polls" for the kind meant to produce election forecasts. When Gallup started out, he was skeptical about using a survey to forecast an election: "Such a test is by no means perfect, because a preelection survey must not only measure public opinion in respect to candidates but must also predict just what groups of people will actually take the trouble to cast their ballots." Also, he didn't think that predicting elections constituted a public good: "While such forecasts provide an interesting and legitimate activity, they probably serve no great social purpose." Then why do it? Gallup conducted polls only to prove the accuracy of his surveys, there being no other way to demonstrate it. The polls themselves, he thought, were pointless.

DONALD TRUMP DIDN'T HAVE a campaign pollster, but in 2015, while he was leading them, his campaign loved polls. Polls admitted Trump into the first GOP debate and polls handed him a victory. "Donald J. Trump Dominates *Time* Poll," the Trump campaign posted on its website following the August debate, linking to a story in which *Time* reported that 47 percent of respondents said that Trump had won. *Time*'s "poll" was conducted by PlayBuzz, a viral-content provider that embeds quizzes, polls, lists, and other "playful content" items onto websites to attract traffic. PlayBuzz collected more than seventy-seven thousand "votes" from visitors to *Time*'s website in its instant opt-in internet poll. *Time* posted a warning: "The results of this poll are not scientific."

Because most polls do not come with warnings, many reporters and news organizations have been trying to educate readers about polling methods. The day after the first GOP debate, *Slate* published a column called "Did Trump Actually Win the Debate? How to Understand All Those Instant Polls That Say Yes." This, though, didn't stop *Slate* from conducting its own instant poll. "TV talking heads won't decide this election," *Slate*'s pollster promised. "The American people will."

The statistician Nate Silver began explaining polls to readers in 2008; the *Times* ran his blog, FiveThirtyEight, for four years. Silver makes his own predictions by aggregating polls, giving greater weight to those which are more reliable. This is helpful, but it's a patch, not a fix. The distinction between one kind of poll and another is important, but it is also often exaggerated. Polls drive polls. Good polls drive polls and bad polls drive polls, and when bad polls drive good polls they're not so good anymore.

Laws govern who can run for office and how. There are laws about who can vote, and where, and when. Seven constitutional amendments and countless Supreme Court cases concern voting. But polls are largely free from government regulation, or even scrutiny. (This is not true in other countries; Canadian election law, for instance, regulates the disclosure of election polls.)

This wasn't always the case. In the 1930s and '40s, motions were regularly introduced in Congress calling for an investigation into the influence of public opinion polling on the political process. "These polls are a racket, and their methods should be exposed to the public," Walter Pierce, a Democratic member of the House, wrote in 1939, the year *Time* first called George Gallup a "pollster." One concern was that polls were jury-rigged. In the presidential election of 1944, George Gallup underestimated Democratic support in two out of three states. When Congress called him in for questioning to answer the charge that "the Gallup poll was engineered in favor of the Republicans," Gallup explained that, anticipating a low turnout, he had taken two points off the projected vote for FDR. In another instance, a congressman voiced concern that polls "are in contradiction to representative government": pollsters appeared to believe that the United States is or ought to be a direct democracy.

Social scientists began criticizing pollsters, too. In 1947, in an address to the American Sociological Association, Herbert Blumer argued that public opinion does not exist, absent its measurement. Pollsters proceed from the assumption that "public opinion" is an aggregation of individual opinions, each given equal weight—an assumption Blumer demonstrated to be preposterous, since people form opinions "as a function of a society in operation." We come to hold and express our opinions in conversation, and especially in debate, over time, and different people and groups influence us, and we them, to different degrees.

Gallup got his back up. In 1948, the week before Election Day, he said, "We have never claimed infallibility, but next Tuesday the whole world will be able to see down to the last percentage point how good we are." He predicted that Dewey would beat Truman. He was quite entirely wrong.

Gallup liked to say that pollsters take the "pulse of democracy." "Although you can take a nation's pulse," E. B. White wrote after the election, "you can't be sure that the nation hasn't just run up a flight of stairs."

In the wake of polling's most notorious failure, the political scientist Lindsay Rogers published a book called *The Pollsters: Public Opinion, Politics, and Democratic Leadership*. Rogers, the Burgess Professor of Public Law at Columbia, had started out as a journalist, and, as a scholar, he was a humanist at a time when most students of government had turned away from the humanities and toward social science. (Amy Fried, in an essay about what was lost in that abandonment, has called him "the Forgotten Lindsay Rogers.") He had drafted *The Pollsters* before the election debacle; his concern had very little to do with miscalculation. Where Blumer argued that polling rests on a misapplication of social science, Rogers argued that it rests on a misunderstanding of American democracy. Even if public opinion could be measured (which Rogers doubted), he believed that legislators' use of polls to inform their votes would be inconsistent with their constitutional duty. The United States has a representative government for many reasons, among them that it protects the rights of minorities against the tyranny of a majority. "The pollsters have dismissed as irrelevant the kind of political society in which we live and which we, as citizens, should endeavor to strengthen," Rogers wrote. Polls, Rogers believed, are a majoritarian monstrosity.

The alarms raised by Blumer and Rogers went unheeded. Instead, many social scientists came to believe that, if the pollsters failed, social science would fail with them (not least by losing foundation and federal research money). Eight days after Truman beat Dewey, the Social Science Research Council appointed an investigative committee, explaining that "extended controversy regarding the preelection polls among lay and professional groups might have extensive and unjustified repercussions upon all types of opinion and attitude studies and perhaps upon social science research generally." The committee concluded that the problem was, in part, quota sampling, but, in any case, the main work of the report was to defend the sample-survey method, including a landmark project founded at the University of Michigan in 1948, which became the most ambitious and most significant survey of American voters: the American National Election Survey.

In 1952, Eisenhower unexpectedly defeated Stevenson. "Yesterday the people surprised the pollsters, the prophets, and many politicians," Edward R. Murrow said on CBS Radio. "They are mysterious and their motives are not to be measured by mechanical means." But politicians don't want the people to be mysterious. Soon, not only political candidates but officeholders—including presidents—began hiring pollsters. Meanwhile, pollsters claim to measure opinions as elusive as Americans' belief in God, as the sociologist Robert Wuthnow points out in a compelling and disturbing book, *Inventing American Religion: Polls, Surveys, and the Tenuous Quest for a Nation's Faith*. In 1972, when Congress debated a Truth in Polling Act, longtime pollsters like Gallup attempted to distance themselves from campaign and media pollsters. Called to testify, Gallup supported the bill, objecting only to the requirement that pollsters report their response rates. That same year, in *Public Opinion Does Not Exist*, the French sociologist Pierre Bourdieu revisited arguments made by Herbert Blumer. As these and other critics have demonstrated again and again, a sizable number of people polled either know nothing about the matters those polls purport to measure or hold no opinion about them. "The first question a pollster should ask," the sociologist Leo Bogart advised in 1972, is " 'Have you thought about this at all? Do you *have* an opinion?' "

Despite growing evidence of problems known as non-opinion, forced opinion, and exclusion bias, journalists only relied on Gallup-style polling more, not less, and they began, too, to do it themselves. In 1973, in *Precision Journalism*, Philip Meyer urged reporters to conduct their own surveys: "If your newspaper has a data-processing department, then it has key-punch machines and people to operate them." Two years later, the *Times* and CBS released their first joint poll, and we've been off to the races ever since, notwithstanding the ongoing concerns raised by critics who point out, as has Gallup Poll's former managing editor David Moore, that "media polls give us distorted readings of the electoral climate, manufacture a false public consensus on policy issues, and in the process undermine American democracy." Polls don't take the pulse of democracy; they raise it.

BY THE END OF AUGUST 2015, Trump, faltering, revealed that he was of course obsessed with his standing in the polls. "I won in every single poll of the debate," he boasted. "I won in *Time* magazine." Trump's lead in the polls had taken so many political reporters by surprise that some people who cover polls—"data journalists" is, broadly, the term of art—began turning to data-science firms like Civis Analytics, wondering whether they, too, saw Trump in the lead.

If public opinion polling is the child of a strained marriage between the press and the academy, data science is the child of a rocky marriage between the academy and Silicon Valley. The term "data science" was coined in 1960, one year after the Democratic National Committee (DNC) hired Simulmatics Corporation, a company founded by Ithiel de Sola Pool, a political scientist from MIT, to provide strategic analysis in advance of the upcoming presidential election. Pool and his team collected punch cards from pollsters who had archived more than sixty polls from the elections of 1952, 1954, 1956, 1958, and 1960, representing more than a hundred thousand interviews, and fed them into a UNIVAC. They then sorted voters into four hundred and eighty possible types (for example, "Eastern, metropolitan, lower-income, white, Catholic, female Democrat") and sorted issues into fifty-two clusters (for example, foreign aid). Simulmatics' first task, completed just before the Democratic National Convention, was a study of "the Negro vote in the North." Its report, which is thought to have influenced the civil rights paragraphs added to the party's platform, concluded that between 1954 and 1956 "a small but significant shift to the Republicans occurred among Northern Negroes, which cost the Democrats about 1 percent of the total votes in 8 key states." After the nominating convention, the DNC commissioned Simulmatics to prepare three more reports, including one that involved running simulations about different ways in which Kennedy might discuss his Catholicism.

In 1964, a political scientist named Eugene Burdick wrote a novel called *The 480*, about the work done by Simulmatics. He was worried about its implications:

> There is a benign underworld in American politics. It is not the underworld of cigar-chewing pot-bellied officials who mysteriously run "the machine." Such men are still around, but their power is waning. They are becoming obsolete though they have not yet learned that fact. The new underworld is made up of innocent and well-intentioned people who work with slide rules and calculating machines and computers which can retain an almost infinite number of bits of information as well as sort, categorize, and reproduce this information at the press of a button. Most of these people are highly educated, many of them are Ph.D.s, and none that I have met have malignant political designs on the

American public. They may, however, radically reconstruct the American political system, build a new politics, and even modify revered and venerable American institutions—facts of which they are blissfully innocent. They are technicians and artists; all of them want, desperately, to be scientists.

Burdick's dystopianism is vintage Cold War: the Strangelovian fear of the machine. (Burdick also cowrote *Fail-Safe*, in which a computer error triggers a nuclear war.) But after 1960 the DNC essentially abandoned computer simulation. One reason may have been that LBJ wasn't as interested in the work of MIT scientists as Kennedy had been. For decades, Republicans were far more likely than Democrats to use computer-based polling. In 1977, the Republican National Committee (RNC) acquired a mainframe computer, while the DNC got its own mainframe in the eighties. The political scientist Kenneth Janda speculates that the technological advantage of the Republican Party during these years stemmed from its ties to big business. Democratic technological advances awaited the personal computer; the RNC is to IBM as the DNC is to Apple. In the internet era, beginning with the so-called MoveOn effect, technology at least briefly favored Democrats but, as Matthew Hindman argued in *The Myth of Digital Democracy*, it has not favored democracy.

DOUGLAS RIVERS IS A PROFESSOR of political science at Stanford and the chief scientist at YouGov. He started trying to conduct public opinion surveys via the internet in the nineties, and has done much of the best and most careful work in the field. When he cofounded Knowledge Networks and conducted polls through Web TV, he used probability sampling as an alternative to quota sampling. The initial response rate was something like 50 percent, but over time the rate fell into the single digits. After the dot-com crash, "we slimmed down," Rivers told me when I visited him in Palo Alto. "I went back to teaching."

Rivers then started a company called Polimetrix, which he sold to YouGov for an estimated thirty-five million dollars. There he developed a method called "matched sampling": he uses the U.S. Census Bureau's American Community Survey, which surveys a million people a year, to generate a random sample according to "fifteen variables of representativeness" and to determine who will participate in polls. "You get a million people to take the poll, but you only need a thousand, so you pick the thousand that match your target population," he explained to me.

Sometimes when political scientists are hired by corporations their research becomes proprietary. "When I say I don't know the secret sauce, I really don't know it," Arthur Lupia says of political scientists who sell their research to businesses rather than publish it in journals that would require them to reveal their methodologies. Lupia is a professor of political science at the University of Michigan, a former director of the American National Election Survey, and the lead author of "Improving Public Perceptions of Political Science's Value," a 2014 report prepared by a task force established by the American Political Science Association. Where once social scientists avidly defended the polling industry, many have grown alarmed that media-run horse-race polls may be undermining the public's perception of the usefulness of social science surveys. (Lupia jokes that horse-race polls ought to have a warning label that reads FOR ENTERTAINMENT PURPOSES ONLY.) Like Rivers, Lupia ardently believes in the importance of measuring public opinion. "It is critical for a nation that cherishes its democratic legitimacy to seek credible measures of how citizens think, feel, and act in electoral contexts," Lupia and the political scientist Jon Krosnick have written. Otherwise, "there will be no strong evidentiary basis for differentiating propagandistic tall tales from empirically defensible and logically coherent readings of electoral history."

It's an important point. But it may be that media-run polls have endangered the academic study of public opinion and of political behavior. Public disaffection with the polling industry has contributed to a plummeting response rate for academic and government surveys.

Those surveys are invaluable, the political scientist Sidney Verba has argued. "Surveys produce just what democracy is supposed to produce—equal representation of all citizens," Verba said in a presidential address before the American Political Science Association in 1995. "The sample survey is rigorously egalitarian; it is designed so that each citizen has an equal chance to participate and an equal voice when participating." Verba sees surveying public opinion not only as entirely consistent with democratic theory but as a corrective to democracy's flaws. Surveys, Verba argues, achieve representativeness through science.

The best and most responsible pollsters, whether Democratic, Republican, or nonpartisan, want nothing so much as reliable results. Today, with a response rate in the single digits, they defend their work by pointing out that the people who do answer the phone are the people who are most likely to vote. Bill McInturff, of Public Opinion Strategies, told me, "The people we have trouble getting are less likely to vote." But the difficulty remains. Surveying only likely voters might make for a better election prediction, but it means that the reason for measuring public opinion, the entire justification for the endeavor, has been abandoned. Public opinion polling isn't enhancing political participation. Instead, it's a form of disenfranchisement.

"There are all kinds of problems with public opinion research, as done by surveys," Lupia admits. "But a lot of the alternatives are worse. A lot of what we'd have would be self-serving stories about what's good for people. 'When given a clear choice between eggs and bananas, ninety-eight percent of the people prefer one or the other.' Prior to the polls, I can say that, and you have no check on me. But if there's a poll you have a check."

That's a good point, too, except that there isn't much of a check on political scientists who don't reveal their methods because they've sold their algorithms to startups for millions of dollars. Whether or not they're making money, people who predict elections want to be right, and they believe, as fiercely as Lupia does, that they are engaged in a public good. I asked Doug Rivers what role the measurement of public opinion plays in a democracy. He said, "The cynical answer is 'Once the rockets are up, who cares where they come down.'" (He was quoting a Tom Lehrer song.) But Rivers isn't cynical. He believes that polling "improves the quality of representation." I asked him to give me an example. He said, "You couldn't have had the change in gay marriage without the polling data." Everyone cares where the rockets come down.

THE DAY I VISITED CROWDPAC, at the back of a one-story office building in Menlo Park, the staff was having a debate about what kind of takeout to order during the GOP debate. "What is GOP food? BBQ?" A piece of computer hardware labeled "Hillary's Hard Drive: HEAVY USE: Now Perfectly Clean" rested on a coffee table. There were Bernie Sanders posters on the walls and cutouts of Rand Paul's head popping out of a jar of pencils. Crowdpac is the brainchild of Steve Hilton, a former senior adviser to David Cameron, and Adam Bonica, a young Stanford political scientist. Their idea is to use data science to turn public opinion polling upside down. "There had been an explosion in the use of data, all structured to advance campaigns," Bonica says. "They'd take information from voters and manipulate it to the politicians' advantage. But what if it could go the other way?" The company's unofficial motto on its website used to be "Now you can get the data on them!"

Crowdpac is just getting off the ground, but it has provided an interactive Voter's Guide for several federal, state, and citywide elections from Philadelphia to San Francisco and encouraged people to run for office. Liz Jaff, Crowdpac's Democratic political director (she has a Republican counterpart), showed me a beta site she'd set up, whereby visitors who supported Planned Parenthood could look up all the unopposed GOP candidates who have promised to defund Planned Parenthood and then pledge money to anyone who would run against them. The pledges would be converted to donations automatically, as soon as someone decided to run. Candidates could see how much money they would have, right out of the gate, and their opponents could see, too. "If you get a tweet saying you just got five hundred thousand dollars pledged against you, that sends a message," Jaff said.

"We are trying to figure out what drives people to be interested in politics," Hilton told me. "We are working on tools that help people get engaged with particular issues. If you care about fracking—for or against—what should you do? What candidate should you give money to? What people should you urge to run for office? We are uncovering the hidden political wiring of politics."

I asked him if that wasn't the role of the press.

"Maybe once," he said.

Data science may well turn out to be as flawed as public opinion polling. But a stage in the development of any new tool is to imagine that you've perfected it, in order to ponder its consequences. I asked Hilton to suppose that there existed a flawless tool for measuring public opinion, accurately and instantly, a tool available to voters and politicians alike. Imagine that you're a member of Congress, I said, and you're about to head into the House to vote on an act—let's call it the Smeadwell-Nutley Act. As you do, you use an app called iThePublic to learn the opinions of your constituents. You oppose Smeadwell-Nutley; your constituents are 79 percent in favor of it. Your constituents will instantly know how you've voted, and many have set up an account with Crowdpac to make automatic campaign donations. If you vote against the proposed legislation, your constituents will stop giving money to your reelection campaign. If, contrary to your convictions but in line with your iThePublic, you vote for Smeadwell-Nutley, would that be democracy?

A worried look crossed Hilton's face. Lindsay Rogers has long since been forgotten. But the role of public opinion measurement in a representative government is more troubling than ever.

Hilton shook his head. "You can't solve every problem with more democracy," he said.

TO WINNOW THE FIELD OF CANDIDATES who would hold the main stage in the second GOP debate, in September 2015, CNN had intended to use the average of national polls conducted over the summer. But after Carly Fiorina's campaign complained that the method was unfair, CNN changed its formula. The decision had very little to do with American democracy or social science. It had to do with the practice of American journalism. It would make better television if

Fiorina was on the same stage as Trump, since he'd made comments about her appearance. ("Look at that face!" he said.)

"No one tells me what to say," Trump had said in August. By September, on the defensive about Fiorina, he insisted—he knew—that he had the will of the people behind him. "If you look at the polls," he said, "a lot of people like the way I talk."

Donald Trump is a creature of the polls. He is his numbers. But he is only a sign of the times. Turning the press into pollsters has made American political culture Trumpian: frantic, volatile, shortsighted, sales-driven, and antidemocratic.

He kept his lead nearly till the end of October. "Do we love these polls?" he called out to a crowd in Iowa. "Somebody said, 'You love polls.' I said that's only because I've been winning every single one of them. Right? Right? Every single poll." Two days later, when he lost his lead in Iowa to Ben Carson, he'd grown doubtful: "I honestly think those polls are wrong." By the week of the third GOP debate, he'd fallen behind in a national CBS/NYT poll. "The thing with these polls, they're all so different," Trump said, mournfully. "It's not very scientific."

—2015

Postscript: In 2016, all major polling organizations predicted Hillary Clinton would defeat Donald Trump.

PARTY CRASHERS

THE CLOCK ON THE WALL IN THE CAFETERIA AT Winnacunnet High School, in Hampton, New Hampshire, is mounted behind a wire cage that protects its face from the likeliest weapons (French fries, foam balls) deployed in the uprisings of adolescents (food fights, dodgeball). Or maybe that was to prepare it for politics. Two weeks ago, the day after the Iowa caucuses and one week before the New Hampshire primary, a makeshift stage had been built at the far end of the cafeteria, catercornered from the caged clock. Its backdrop was an American flag; a campaign poster, an "H" with an arrow running through it; and three rows of Granite State citizens, a political Greek chorus positioned behind the lectern, awaiting the candidate. Minutes passed. The slender black hand of the clock ticked and twitched, like an old man tapping and jerking his cane. Hillary Rodham Clinton was running late.

"I feel great being back in New Hampshire after winning in Iowa!" she said when she finally arrived, walking onto the stage with Gabrielle Giffords, the former U.S. congresswoman from Arizona who was shot in the head while meeting with voters in 2011, and Giffords's husband, the astronaut Mark Kelly. In the 2016 Democratic primaries, Clinton had won in Iowa, but just barely. Her only remaining rival, Bernie Sanders, was expected to win New Hampshire, and by a wide margin. She didn't look like she was feeling great. And after the New Hampshire results came in—Sanders went on to win, in a rout—she'd have cause to feel worse.

During their months vying for the right to carry the Democratic Party standard, the former Secretary of State and the senator from Vermont have been on the same stage often, if not always at the same time. Sanders had spoken in this very school in December. "Winnacunnet High School Feels the Bern," ran the headline of a lead story in the Winnachronicle, the school newspaper. Two crackerjack student staff writers had reported, "The senator ended his speech by saying, 'Brothers and sisters, welcome to the political revolution.'"

For Clinton's visit, the cafeteria was packed with stalwart Clinton supporters, mostly women, mostly white, mostly within a decade of Clinton's age. Members of the press had been escorted through the kitchen, and then corralled into a pen at the rear of the cafeteria, separated from the rest of the room by steel police barriers. Those who stood shouldered cameras; those who sat cradled laptops. Instruction sheets had been taped to the chairs:

WIFI
Network: WHS Public
Password: warriors

Three television reporters sat in a row: ABC, CBS, CNN. "We're the slow-news team," one of them told me. A hipster photographer had perched his super-skinny tripod atop a blue plastic chair, setting its camera to peer over the crowd. He'd found a good spot, but his unobstructed view didn't last for long. The instant Clinton began speaking, dozens of arms reached high into the air, all across the room, wielding smartphones. It was like watching a flock of ostriches awaken, the arms their necks, the phones their heads, the red recording buttons their wide, blinking eyes.

Clinton and Sanders had been waging a remarkably polite battle. "I'm proud of the campaign we're running on the Democratic side," Clinton told the crowd. "It's in stark contrast to the insults you see on the other side."

Less than ten miles away, Marco Rubio had just finished speaking at the town hall in Exeter, a brick Federal-style building made famous by Abraham Lincoln, who spoke there in 1860. A statue of Justice stood on the cupola, high above an asphalt lot where satellite-dish-equipped television trucks were parked, one from Liberty Uplink, another from the Freedom Broadcast Group. On the front steps were stacks of yard signs: "Don't Believe the Liberal Media."

Rubio had made a strong third-place showing in the G.O.P. race in Iowa, not far behind Ted Cruz and Donald Trump. Before Chris Christie deflated him in a debate over the weekend, he seemed to be surging, the establishment's last best hope, not too weak, not too mean, not too wild, not too bland, the G.O.P.'s Goldilocks. The hall in Exeter had filled early with an enthusiastic crowd, more men than women: blue Red Sox caps, black knitted Bruins hats. Police officers stationed at the doors had turned away disappointed latecomers. Inside, where the walls are painted Colonial green, blue-and-white campaign banners had been draped across the balconies: "New Hampshire Is Marco Rubio Country."

Rubio has an appealing Mickey Mousiness. Also, he can be funny, especially if you haven't seen his shtick more than a few times. (A stump speech at a campaign stop is a lot like standup comedy. It would turn out that Rubio had learned his lines only too well.) While he was listing all the things he'd do on his first day in office—swear to uphold the Constitution, defend the Second Amendment, and repeal "every single one of Obama's illegal and unconstitutional executive orders"—the crowd began chanting, "Mar-co, Mar-co, Mar-co."

"As long as you don't say 'Polo,' " Rubio said. He smiled. "I hated that game." He made as if he were returning to his Oval Office to-do list. "When I'm President, we're banning that game!"

Rubio is funny mainly in order to call out his seriousness. He offered another of his one-liners: "Bernie Sanders is actually a nice guy, and he'd be a really good candidate for President—of Sweden." Then he gathered himself up, turning grave: "Hillary Clinton is no laughing matter." Rubio says that Clinton is not qualified to be President.

The scene in Exeter, uplinked by Liberty and broadcast by Freedom, was captured by a media army composed of artillery (five large video cameras mounted on a stage at the rear of the hall, and a dozen more perched on each of the hall's balconies) and infantry (reporters propping computers in their laps). But with every third person in the crowd tapping at a phone, sending words and pictures out to the world, it was hard to tell the civilians from the military. Who are the people, and who are the press? "I wasn't tweeting," a young long-haired woman in a blue wool coat told me. "I was Snapchatting." Even before Rubio finished delivering his stump speech, an A.P. photographer plunked down on the floor, opened his laptop, and began cropping a shot. "I can't talk now," he said, excusing himself. "I'm filing right now."

IN THE RIGHT NOW, when what happened in New Hampshire already feels as old as the Parthenon, it's hard to care about the long ago, but there haven't always been parties, and there haven't always been primaries, and this may be the first Presidential-primary season with free Wi-Fi pretty much everywhere. A lot of people, not least the candidates themselves, have been talking about political revolution and, more modestly, about party realignment. None of the candidates, not even the party favorites, are campaigning on behalf of their party; most are campaigning to crash it. Outsiders are in. Insiders are out. "We've always taken on the establishment," Rubio says. "Of course we're an underdog," Sanders says. On the day of the Iowa caucuses, Cruz's campaign called voters and sent out an e-mail blast suggesting that Carson was about to quit the race, and so Trump was saying that Cruz had stolen the election. Rush Limbaugh took Trump's protest as the latest, best evidence that "Trump is not your typical Republican-establishment candidate."

The people who turn up at Sanders and Trump rallies are wed, across the aisle, in bonds of populist unrest. They're revolting against party élites, and especially against the all-in-the-family candidates anointed by the Democratic and the Republican leadership: Clinton and Bush, the wife and brother of past party leaders. (More attention has been paid to the unravelling of the G.O.P.; the Democratic Party is no less frayed.) There is, undoubtedly, a great deal of discontent, particularly with the role of money in elections: both Sanders and Trump damn the campaign-finance system as rigged

and the establishment as corrupt. But to call the current state of
affairs, in either party, a political revolution isn't altogether accurate.
The party system, like just about every other old-line industry and
institution, is struggling to survive a communications revolution.
Accelerated political communication can have all manner of good
effects for democracy, spreading news about rallies, for instance, or
getting hundreds of thousands of signatures on a petition lickety-
split. Less often noticed are the ill effects, which include the atomizing
of the electorate. There's a point at which political communication
speeds past the last stop where democratic deliberation, the genu-
ine consent of the governed, is possible. An instant poll, of the sort
that pops up on your screen while you're attempting to read debate
coverage, encourages snap and solitary judgment, the very opposite
of what's necessary for the exercise of good citizenship. Democracy
takes time. It requires civic bonds, public institutions, and a free
press. And in the United States, so far, it has needed parties.

THE AMERICAN TWO-PARTY SYSTEM is a creation of the press.
"The idea of a party system," as Richard Hofstadter once pointed out,
is an American invention, one that not only tolerates but requires the
practice of loyal opposition, political criticism, and organized dissent.
It began in 1787, during the debate over the Constitution, a debate
waged in ratifying conventions but also, more thrillingly, in the
nation's hundreds of weekly newspapers. Some favored ratification;
these became Federalist newspapers. Others, the Anti-Federalist newspapers, opposed it. If it hadn't been for the all-or-nothing dualism of
this choice, the United States might well have a multiparty political
culture. But the model held, and the Federalist–Anti-Federalist cleav-
age, with some adjustments, became the basis of the first party system,
which took shape in 1796. It pitted Federalists, who supported the
election of John Adams, against the Democratic-Republicans, who
supported Thomas Jefferson. In the seventeen-nineties, the number
of newspapers, each of them partisan, grew four times as fast as the
population. At a time when there were very few national institutions,
parties exerted a tremendous, and vital, nationalizing force. Once

much maligned as destructive of public life, parties, driven by newspapers, became its machinery. "The engine," Jefferson said, "is the press."

The men who drafted the Constitution hadn't anticipated parties, and made no provision for them. Parties are an add-on. They make their own rules. At first, they chose their Presidential nominees by legislative caucus: each party's congressional caucus nominated its Presidential candidate. That practice lasted until Andrew Jackson campaigned against "King Caucus," calling the method anti-democratic, and said that the people needed to have a more direct role in the choice of the party nominee. Jackson came to power through a new form of political communication, the campaign biography: after the publication of "The Life of Jackson," in 1824 (when Jackson won the popular vote but lost the election), no campaign season was ever again without one. Jackson's rise also marked the end of the first party system and the beginning of the second: Jacksonian Democrats versus Whigs. Historians like to date the shift from one party system to another to a single year—in this case, 1828, the year Jackson won—but, in truth, such shifts are, by their very nature, gradual. And, while they're obviously driven by ideological movements, by the emergence of new economic issues and circumstances, and, especially, by changes in the composition of the electorate, they're also influenced by novel forms of political communication.

So are the methods by which Americans elect their Presidents. The first Presidential nominating convention was held in 1832; state delegates met to make the choice after hearing stump speeches from the contenders. Critics said this was a bad idea, too. "This convention system, if adopted by both parties, will make our government a prize to be sought after by political gamblers," the governor of Illinois warned.

The second party system lasted until 1854, by which time its inability to address the matter of slavery was proving to be the undoing of the Whigs, and the Know-Nothings, and the Free Soilers, and the Liberty Party. It wasn't only slavery, though. The system had entered a state of disequilibrium because political communication was undergoing a revolution. Revolutions in communication tend to pull the people away from the élites. (The printing press is the classic example; think of its role in the Reformation. But this happens, to varying degrees, every time the speed and scale of communication makes a leap.) In 1833, refinements in printing technology lowered the cost of a daily newspaper to a penny or two; in the eighteen-forties, newspapers got their news by telegraph; the post office set a special, cheaper rate for newspapers; and, in the eighteen-fifties, newspapers began printing illustrations based on photographs. Meanwhile, literacy rates were skyrocketing. Candidates began campaigning, speaking and writing to the people directly. For a while, party élites lost control, until the system reached equilibrium in the form of a relatively stable contest between Democrats and a new party, the Republicans. Walt Whitman complained about "the neverending audacity of elected persons," damning men in politics as members of the establishment, but voter turnout rose from 36.9 per cent in 1824 to 57.6 per cent in 1838 and 80.2 per cent in 1840. And so it churned, and so it churns.

The third party system lasted until 1896. (Dating party realignments is an uncertain affair; it depends on how and what you're measuring. By some accounts, the second party system ended in 1860, and we're still in the third.) Like the first party system, it came to an end with a populist revolt, which took place during another acceleration in the speed of communication, brought about by the telephone, the Linotype, and halftone printing, technologies that allowed daily newspapers and illustrated magazines, in particular, to carry political news faster, and to more readers, than ever before. The eighteen-nineties saw a war between the Pulitzer and the Hearst newspaper empires; the number of newspapers exceeded ten thousand, including more dailies than exist today, some with a circulation of more than a million. Meanwhile, campaign posters papered the walls of buildings on every city block. In 1896, Puck printed a two-page color spread called "The Poster Craze in Candidateville": a lanky Uncle Sam strolls down Presidential Avenue, inspecting posters for a slew of Presidential aspirants, among them William

McKinley and William B. Allison, the "Farmer's Friend." Everyone ran as an outsider.

The disequilibrium of that political moment led not only to the beginning of the fourth party system but also to the birth of the primary system. Once the fourth party system got started, populists and progressive reformers began making the same complaints about the nominating convention that Jacksonians had made about the legislative caucus: the choice of the parties' Presidential nominees shouldn't be in the hands of a select group of party leaders, whether legislators or convention delegates. By 1917, states had started holding direct primaries, mini-elections in which all party members get to vote for the Presidential nominee. But the fourth party system was short-lived, toppled by a new media era. William Jennings Bryan recorded campaign speeches on wax cylinders in 1908. By the end of the First World War, the speed and the spread of political communication had picked up again. In 1920, Warren Harding became the last Presidential candidate to send his speeches to voters, on a phonograph record. His successors turned to radio. *Time*, the first weekly news-magazine, débuted in 1923; its aim was to cut the time it takes to read a week's worth of news down to an hour. Radio started reaching everyday Americans in 1926, when NBC began broadcasting, followed by CBS in 1928. A Presidential campaign speech, by F.D.R., was recorded, and heard and seen, in movie theatres in 1932, the year that marked the end of the fourth party system, as both the Democratic and the Republican Parties rearranged themselves around the New Deal coalition.

The fifth party system began in 1932, the very year that George Gallup started conducting pre-election public-opinion polls and just months before the founding of the world's first political consulting firm, Campaigns, Inc. These forms of political communication—voters communicating with candidates through polls, and candidates communicating with voters through consultants—characterize the era of the fifth party system, as much as the ideological positions of the parties themselves. Despite the upheavals of the Depression, the Second World War, the Cold War, and Vietnam, the era of national newsmagazines, newsreels, and network broadcasting was a period of remarkable party stability. True, with campaign ads from every side being broadcast night after night, voters might have been muddled. In one television ad from 1956— produced by political consultants, relying on public-opinion polling—a cartoon voter despairs, "I've listened to everybody. On TV and radio. I've read the papers and magazines. I've tried! But I'm still confused. Who's right? What's right? What should I believe? What are the facts? How can I tell?" But the parties made their choices clear: "Words have been flying at you hot and heavy," a comforting narrator tells the cartoon voter, who considers the evidence and concludes, "Me? I like Ike!"

Historians and political scientists have been arguing for a long time about when the fifth party system yielded to a sixth. Some say it happened in 1964, with Barry Goldwater and the G.O.P.'s conservative turn. Some say 1968, given the mayhem at the nominating conventions. A great many, with good evidence, date the beginning of the sixth party system to 1972, by which time Southern whites had abandoned the Democratic Party and the G.O.P., having lost African-Americans to the opposition, began folding evangelicals into its ranks. This was when the current era of political polarization arose; it was about then that "Republican" began meaning conservative and "Democratic" began meaning liberal. Also, the populist anger that had spelled the decline of the legislative caucus, the rise of the nomination convention, and the first primaries led, in 1972, to the first Presidential nominating caucuses. (Iowa was the first state to hold them.) More significant, a Commission on Party Structure and Delegate Selection established new rules to include more women, minorities, and younger people (a response to their lack of representation during the 1968 Democratic National Convention, and the attendant protests). It led, as well, to a huge rise in the number of states that conducted primaries. And then there was, after 1972, a feeling of grim dismay about American party politics, a new kind of cynicism, and even a new kind of political reporting, drunk with anti-establishment swagger. "It was just before midnight when I left Cambridge and headed north on U.S. 93 toward Manchester—driving one of those big green rented Auto/Stick Cougars," Hunter S. Thompson wrote, in "Fear and Loathing on the Campaign Trail '72," about travelling north to report on the New Hampshire primary, "running late, as usual: left hand on the wheel and the other on the radio dial, seeking music, and a glass of iced Wild Turkey spilling into my crotch on every turn." (My worry, on the drive, was whether I'd remembered to put the lasagna in the oven for my kids.) The year 1972 is even taken, sometimes, as not only the end of the fifth party system but the end of the two-party system altogether. "The Party's Over" was the title that the political columnist David Broder gave to a polemic published in 1972, which was also the year that a despairing Arthur M. Schlesinger, Jr., wrote the introduction to a four-volume "History of U.S. Political Parties," in which he declared, of the system, "Its prospects have rarely appeared more clouded than they do today." No one's ever published volume five.

Less convincingly, some scholars have suggested that the sixth party system began in 1980. "Without parties there can be no organized and coherent politics," the Committee for Party Renewal, a bipartisan group of political scientists, proclaimed that year, just before the Reagan revolution realized what Goldwater had only promised, and cable guys began knocking on American doors. Reagan, the Great Communicator, led the G.O.P. at the dawn of a new era of political communication. The F.C.C. abandoned the Fairness Doctrine in 1987, leading to the creation of a new breed of partisan political communicators. "The Rush Limbaugh Show" was heard nationally for the first time in 1988. A fair argument can be made for the significance of 1996, too. That was the start of the first Web browser—during his campaign, Bob Dole famously provided voters with his Web site, but gave them the wrong address—and the first year of Fox News and MSNBC, which were equally keen to animate the party base. A new party system, a new age of news.

"I'M SO GLAD TO BE BACK with so many friends, so many patriots, so many lovers of liberty," Ted Cruz said to a packed auditorium at Elm Street Middle School, in Nashua, New Hampshire, on Wednesday, the night after Rubio spoke at the Exeter town hall and Clinton at Winnacunnet High School. I'd driven to Nashua in the rain, and parked on a residential street behind the school. When I got out of my car, in the dark, I walked straight into a big, boxy television set that had been left on the sidewalk, to be hauled away with the trash.

In the auditorium, Cruz's stage had two American flags flanking his campaign banner: "TRUS**TED**." Cruz was introduced by Jeff Kuhner, the host of a political talk show on AM radio in Boston. He led the crowd in the Pledge of Allegiance, facing a third flag, held by Gary Dipiero, a Cruz supporter from Saugus, Massachusetts, who was carrying a "Hillary for Prison" sign. (Dipiero told me that he expects this of a Cruz Presidency: "He's going to prosecute her and throw her in jail.") "As many of you know, I'm an American historian," Kuhner, who was a graduate student at Ohio University, said. "And what I can tell you now, with one-hundred-per-cent absolute certainty, is we are now at a fundamental crossroads. This election—and I know it's a cliché, but it's true—this election is the most important election in our lifetimes." Dipiero waved his flag. The crowd rose to its feet. Kuhner said, "Senator Ted Cruz, I honestly believe, is a Latino Reagan."

Cruz strode onstage. He was wearing a navy sweater, bluejeans, and rugged boots. He reminded his audience that, in 1980, Reagan won the New Hampshire primary. With their votes that year, he said, Granite Staters had made the world safe for democracy: "Because of the men and women of New Hampshire, we won the Cold War and we tore the Berlin Wall to the ground." The smartphones came out: portrait for the candidate, landscape for the stage.

Apart from the bluejeans and the boots, which Reagan liked to wear, too, very little about Ted Cruz is reminiscent of Ronald Reagan. Where Reagan was warm and prided himself on being welcoming, Cruz is cold: he likes to make threats. Also, Cruz is a product of political disequilibrium rather than a creator of it. Howard Dean's MoveOn.org-fuelled campaign, in 2004, was, in hindsight, a dry run. Facebook launched in 2004, YouTube in 2005, Twitter in 2006, the iPhone in 2007. By 2008, Twitter had a million users, and only about one in six Americans had a smartphone. Today, Twitter has more than three hundred million users, and two out of three Americans own smartphones. These have become political tools, a hand-held pollster, lobbyist, donor, and, maybe one day, voter. Trump, the Kardashian candidate, has six million Twitter followers, which is more than five times the population of New Hampshire. "What is this Snapshot thing and why do I only get ten seconds?" Sanders tweeted in November, joking, the day he signed up. He now has the biggest Snapchat following in this campaign.

At the Cruz rally, I talked to a fellow from Nashua named Paul Fortier, forty-six, who was there with his daughter. He thinks that once people get to know Cruz better they won't like him. Fortier considers Trump to be the only true outsider: "He's the only candidate that can turn Washington upside down." Fair enough. Trump is likely to turn a lot of things upside down; he already has. But, while his gambit is anti-establishment, his success is entirely due to the establishment: his. The G.O.P. and the Democratic Party are reeling in the disequilibrium created by the latest communications revolution, the membership careering out of the party leaders' control. It didn't help that the Republican National Committee and the Democratic National Committee presumed that Jeb Bush and Hillary Clinton would win the party nominations, despite each candidate's known weaknesses. But Trump is the last person to credibly claim to be an outsider. He is a media emperor, tweeting from his Tower.

It is rare to meet a non-supporter at an event like Cruz's. Fortier had managed to wander in; his fourteen-year-old son had a basketball game in the gym down the hall. Cruz's night at the Elm Street School, like Rubio's evening in Exeter, was billed as a "town hall," an invocation of a long-standing democratic institution, in which ordinary citizens get to ask candidates questions and weigh their answers. But, really, these gatherings are rallies for supporters (Cruz's was advertised on and sponsored by Kuhner's show), performances as much for the Internet as for the audience. Some Republican candidates deny press passes to journalists they consider to be part of the "liberal media," preferring to bypass the press in favor of a direct feed. Trump's decision to sit out the last debate in Iowa before the caucuses took this one step further, but in the very same direction. "Reporters want Hillary to win," Cruz said in an interview on Fox News last month. "The answer is to do what Reagan did, go over the head of the media." But, as Cruz pointed out, that's a lot easier today than it was when Reagan was running. "We don't live anymore in a world of three networks that have a stranglehold on information," Cruz went on. "We have got the Internet. We have got the Drudge Report. We have got talk radio. We have got social media. We've got the ability to go directly around, and directly to the people."

"WHAT'S WRONG WITH A REVOLUTION?" Anderson Cooper asked Hillary Clinton at CNN's Democratic Town Hall, in the three-hundred-and-fifty-seat Derry Opera House. "Well, that's for Senator Sanders to explain," she said. "I think the progress that we have made, and particularly the Democratic Party has made, has been hard fought for, hard won, and must be defended."

There will not be a revolution, but this election might mark the beginning of the seventh party system. The Internet, like all new communications technologies, has contributed to a period of political disequilibrium, one in which, as always, party followers have been revolting against party leaders. So far, neither the R.N.C. nor the D.N.C., nor any of their favored candidates, has been able to grab the wheel. Trump, meanwhile, is barrelling down the highway toward the White House, ignoring every road sign, a man without a party.

The fate of the free world does not hinge on this election. But the direction of the party system might. And that's probably worth thinking about, slowly and deeply. Parties, while not written into the U.S. Constitution, do sustain our system of government. As the political scientist V. O. Key pointed out, half a century ago, "They perform an essential function in the management of succession to power, as well as in the process of obtaining popular consent to the course of public policy. They amass sufficient support to buttress the authority of governments; or, on the contrary, they attract or organize discontent and dissatisfaction sufficient to oust the government. In either case, they perform the function of the articulation of the interests and aspirations of a substantial segment of the citizenry, usually in ways contended to be promotive of the national weal."

The American party system is not only a creation of the press; it is dependent on it. It is currently fashionable, indispensable, even, to malign the press, whether liberal or conservative. "That's the media game," Sanders said, dismissing a question that Cooper had asked him during CNN's town hall. "That's what the media talks about. Who cares?" But when the press is in the throes of change, so is the party system. And the national weal had better watch out. It's unlikely, but not impossible, that the accelerating and atomizing forces of this latest communications revolution will bring about the end of the party system and the beginning of a new and wobblier political institution. With our phones in our hands and our eyes on our phones, each of us is a reporter, each a photographer, unedited and ill judged, chatting, snapping, tweeting, and posting, yikking and yakking. At some point, does each of us become a party of one?

I watched Wednesday night's Democratic Town Hall from inside the Halligan Tavern, an Irish pub housed in an old brick fire station across the street from the Derry Opera House. CNN had reserved the entire restaurant for the press, since there was no room inside the dollhouse-size opera house. CNN played on screens above the bar and on the walls. More than a hundred reporters huddled with their laptops at tables, upstairs and down. A few people followed the response on #DemTownHall. On side tables, fried chicken, macaroni and cheese, and potato skins were served from platters warmed by cans of Sterno, their blue flames flickering. Power strips rested on every table, like so many centerpieces. The coffee was free. So was the Wi-Fi. The password was the date, 02032016.

Six days later, New Hampshire voters went to the polls. Sanders beat Clinton; Trump beat everyone else. Rubio had been demoted to a meme: a talking machine. Cruz had wobbled. Kasich gained strength; Bush got out the vote. But, among both Republicans and Democrats, even the second-place candidates lagged behind the winners by double digits. The party had been crashed; the system had been hacked.

—2016

BAD NEWS

I N T H E 1 9 3 0 S , O N E I N F O U R A M E R I C A N S G O T T H E I R
news from William Randolph Hearst, who lived in a cas-
tle and owned twenty-eight newspapers in nineteen cities. Hearst's
papers were all alike: hot-blooded, with leggy headlines. Page 1 was
supposed to make a reader blurt out, "Gee whiz!" Page 2: "Holy
Moses!" Page 3: "God Almighty!" Still, you can yank people around
for only so long. Wonder ebbs. Surprise is fleeting. Even rage abates.
In 1933, Hearst turned seventy. He started to worry. How would the
world remember him when he could no longer dictate the headlines?
Ferdinand Lundberg, a reporter for the *New York Herald Tribune,* was
beginning work on a book about him; no one expected it to be
friendly. Hearst therefore did what many a rich, aging megalomaniac
has done before and since: he hired a lackey to write an authorized
biography, preemptively.

In 2010, one in four Americans got the news from Fox News.
That year, Roger Ailes, its head, turned seventy. Gabriel Sherman,
an editor and reporter for *New York* magazine, was beginning work
on a book about him. Sherman interviewed more than six hundred
people for *The Loudest Voice in the Room.* Ailes, who is known for
menace, was not among them. "Take your best shot at me," Ailes is
said to have told another *New York* writer, "and I'll have the rest of
my life to go after you." Unwilling to sit down for an interview with
Sherman, Ailes met instead with Zev Chafets, a former columnist
for the *Daily News,* a contributor to the *New York Times Magazine,*
and the author of a biography of Rush Limbaugh. Chafets shadowed
Ailes at Fox News; watched his son play basketball; walked with
him, flanked by his bodyguard; and visited his home, in Garrison,
New York, where Ailes has bought up not only the land around his

nine-thousand-square-foot mansion but also the local newspaper, to
which he named, as publisher, his wife.

"I got a closer, more prolonged look at Roger Ailes than any journalist ever has," Chafets writes in *Roger Ailes: Off Camera*, which
appeared, preemptively, a year before Sherman's book. Ailes, Chafets
says, looks like "a small-town banker in a Frank Capra movie." That
sounds disapproving, but in this particular Bedford Falls we are meant
to admire Mr. Potter and each of his little witticisms. Ailes on Gingrich: "Newt's a prick." Biden: "He's dumb as an ashtray." Maddow:
"Rachel is good and she will get even better when she discovers that
there are people on earth who don't share every one of her beliefs."
Krugman: "He's a dope but nobody wants to say it because he's won
awards." There's plenty of obloquy in Chafets's book. There's also
a great deal of what might be termed the testicular imagination.
Rupert Murdoch says, of meeting Ailes, "I thought, Either this man
is crazy or he has the biggest set of balls I've ever seen." Chafets adds,
by way of aside, "Ailes was thinking pretty much the same thing."
Holy Moses.

WILLIAM RANDOLPH HEARST NEEDED A MOUTHPIECE;
he couldn't trust an actual biographer—he was convinced that most
people who wrote serious books for a living were communists. In the
fall of 1934, he ordered his editors to send reporters posing as students to college campuses, to find out which members of the faculty
were Reds. Many of the people Hearst thought were communists
thought Hearst was a fascist. This charge derived, in part, from the
fact that Hearst had professed his admiration for Hitler and Mussolini. It was easy to despise Hearst. It was also lazy. Hating some
crazy old loudmouth who is a vindictive bully and lives in a castle is
far less of a strain than thinking about the vulgarity and the preju-
dices of his audience. In 1935, the distinguished war correspondent
and radio broadcaster Raymond Gram Swing observed, "People who
are not capable of disliking the lower middle class in toto, since it is
a formidable tax on their emotions, can detest Hearst instead." Ailes
haters, take note.

Swing despaired over what had happened to journalism under Hearst, and said so, which took courage. Hearst attacked his critics in his papers relentlessly and ferociously. Some fought back. "Only cowards can be intimidated by Hearst," the historian Charles Beard said. Beard had resigned from Columbia in 1917, after the university began firing professors who opposed U.S. involvement in the war. (Beard himself favored American involvement; what he opposed was the university's assault on intellectual freedom.) He'd been elected president of the American Political Science Association in 1925 and, in 1933, president of the American Historical Association. He wasn't someone Hearst could easily crush, or daunt. In February of 1935, Beard addressed an audience of nine hundred schoolteachers in Atlantic City. "William Randolph Hearst has pandered to depraved tastes and has been an enemy of everything that is noblest and best in the American tradition," he said. "No person with intellectual honesty or moral integrity will touch him with a ten-foot pole." The crowd gave Beard a standing ovation.

To write the story of his life, Hearst turned to a woman named Cora Baggerly Older. Her husband, Fremont Older, was one of Hearst's editors; the Olders had often visited Hearst at his 165-room castle, San Simeon. In December of 1935, Older, at work on the biography, alerted Hearst's office that she had learned "that a hostile book called THE LORD OF SAN SIMEON written by Oliver Carlson and Ernest Sutherland Bates is soon to be published by the Viking Press." Lundberg's biography was about to come out, too. It was called *Imperial Hearst*. A preface was supplied by Charles Beard.

ROGER AILES WAS BORN IN WARREN, OHIO, in 1940. He has hemophilia, which didn't stop his father from beating him with an electrical cord. A story Ailes has told—"his Rosebud story," according to Stephen Rosenfield, who worked with Ailes in the 1970s—is about a lesson he learned in his bedroom as a boy. His father, holding out his arms, told him to jump off the top bunk and then deliberately failed to catch him, saying, "Don't ever trust anybody."

Ailes went to Ohio University, where he majored in television and radio, and worked for the campus radio station, WOUB. While he was in college, his parents divorced; his mother told the court that her husband had threatened to kill her. After graduation, Ailes took a job at KYW-TV, in Cleveland, working for *The Mike Douglas Show.*

"Roger Ailes was a legend at a very young age," according to Marvin Kalb, and by all accounts Ailes was an exceptionally talented television producer. In 1967, he met Joe McGinniss, then a columnist for the *Philadelphia Inquirer,* who wrote about him in *The Selling of the President 1968,* an account of Nixon's presidential campaign, and catapulted him to celebrity. The book's turning point comes when, one day in 1967, in the greenroom of *The Mike Douglas Show,* Nixon says to Ailes, "It's a shame a man has to use gimmicks like this to get elected." Ailes says, "Television is not a gimmick." Ailes became Nixon's television producer. In McGinniss's telling, Ailes more or less got Nixon elected.

After the election, Ailes moved to New York and worked as a television consultant, talent agent, and Off Broadway producer. Entertainment slid into politics, politics into entertainment. Ailes began making issue ads and advising candidates. One of his clients was Philip Morris. Ailes insisted that he had no partisan loyalties. "I don't have this burning thing to elect all Republicans," he told the *Washington Post* in 1972. That year, he helped run the North Carolina gubernatorial campaign of Jim Holshouser Jr., a Republican who supported busing. "If you don't do an antibusing spot on TV, you will lose the election," Ailes told Holshouser. "Now, if I were you, I'd do the fucking spot, win the election, and then, once you're in office, do whatever you think is right." Holshouser did the spot and won. ("And what did he do about busing?" Chafets asks Ailes. Ailes answers, "I have no idea.")

In 1974, Ailes was hired as a consultant for Television News Inc., or TVN, a news service funded by Joseph Coors. Six months later, he became TVN's news director. "He didn't know anything about news," Reese Schonfeld, a TVN executive and, later, a cofounder of CNN, told Sherman. "He knew television." In 1975, the *Columbia Journalism Review* called Ailes "the only man in history to run a national news organization while owning an entertainment industry consulting firm." TVN folded later that year.

In the 1980s, Ailes's politics grew more conservative, as did the GOP. Between 1980 and 1986, Ailes helped get thirteen Republican senators and eight members of Congress elected, including Dan Quayle and Mitch McConnell. He also played a crucial role in the presidential campaigns of Ronald Reagan and George H. W. Bush. He urged Reagan to disarm Walter Mondale in debate by promising not to make age an issue. "I am not going to exploit, for political purposes, my opponent's youth and inexperience," Reagan said. Ailes calmed Bush's nerves before his first debate against Michael Dukakis. "If you get in trouble out there, just call him an animal fucker," Ailes whispered. According to a team of reporters from *Newsweek*, Ailes had proposed an ad, which never ran, called "Bestiality." It would have featured a screen of text—"In 1970, Governor Michael Dukakis introduced legislation in Massachusetts to repeal the ban on sodomy and bestiality"—shown over a soundtrack of barnyard animals, bleating.

"HAVE NOT SEEN BOOK BUT JACKET IS COLOR OF SAN SIMEONS INDOOR POOL," Cora Baggerly Older wrote in a telegram to Hearst on February 7, 1936, the day *William Randolph Hearst: American* appeared. The reviews were not kind. One critic observed, "Mrs. Older writes an authorized biography, and the result is about what one would look for." Chafets compares Ailes to Rudyard Kipling and Teddy Roosevelt. "Likenesses between William Randolph Hearst and Napoleon, Charlemagne, the Louis of France and the Popes of Rome are noted in Mr. Hearst's official biography," a reviewer remarked about Older's book, "yet it is possible that Mrs. Fremont Older, the biographer, is amazed at her own moderation."

Both Carlson and Bates's and Lundberg's Hearst biographies appeared a couple of months later, in April 1936. Carlson was a historian of journalism, Bates an English professor; their account is a story of Hearst's life as a decline into a savage cynicism, to the point that his "so-called 'news' papers are little more than a

gigantic chain-store, selling political patent medicines and adulter-
ated economics." Lundberg called for a congressional inquiry into
Hearst's enterprises. *The New Yorker* called Beard's introduction "as
juicy a piece of invective as you will find in several months of
Sundays." Beard had, in fact, got rather exercised. "Hearst's fate is
ostracism by decency in life, and oblivion in death," he wrote. "It
goes with him to the vale of shadows." He was badly provoked, of
course. Still, one prefers, as a rule, to stop short of cursing a man to
eternal damnation.

IN 1988, Ailes cowrote a book called *You Are the Message*. Its
premise is that everyone, at every moment, is not so much communicating as broadcasting. You have only seven seconds to be likable
before someone changes the channel. "It's what I call the like factor,"
the book explains. (Today, this hooey has gone online: Like me!
Follow me!)

Ailes met Limbaugh in 1991. Limbaugh was the host of the nation's
most successful right-wing radio talk show, an entertainment genre
made possible by Reagan's 1987 repeal of the FCC's Fairness Doctrine,
which had been established in 1949. Ailes began producing a Limbaugh
television show. In 1994, Ailes launched America's Talking, an affiliate
of NBC's cable outlet, CNBC. Its twelve-hour all-talk lineup included
a call-in show called *Am I Nuts?* and *Pork*, a program about government waste. As Sherman tells it, among the factors that contributed to
its demise, less than two years later, was Ailes's tendency to insult his
colleagues. On the radio, he said of Mary Matalin and Jane Wallace,
the hosts of a show called *Equal Time*, that they were "girls who if you
went into a bar around seven, you wouldn't pay a lot of attention but
get to be tens around closing time." In a meeting, Ailes allegedly called
his CNBC associate David Zaslav "a little fucking Jew prick." NBC
commissioned an investigation, which concluded that Ailes had a "history of abusive, offensive, and intimidating statements/threats and personal attacks made to and upon a number of other people."

Ailes called the charges "false and despicable" (and Zaslav later
recanted), but in November 1995, Ailes agreed to NBC's stipulation

that he would "not engage in conduct that a reasonable employee would perceive as intimidating or abusive." A month later, NBC and Microsoft announced the creation of MSNBC, which was assigned the slot that America's Talking had occupied on the cable dial. Zaslav was hired to help launch it.

Fox News, owned by Murdoch and run by Ailes, got its start in 1996. "I left politics a number of years ago," Ailes said at a press conference. "We expect to do fine, balanced journalism." CNN had sixty million subscribers. MSNBC had twenty-five million. Fox News debuted in October 1996, with seventeen million.

The best thing that ever happened to Fox News was the Monica Lewinsky story, which, together with other Clinton scandals, led to a 400 percent increase in prime-time ratings. Much of Fox's lineup was already in place, but when the Lewinsky scandal broke, early in 1998, Ailes launched Brit Hume's 6:00 p.m. newscast, *Special Report*, and moved *The O'Reilly Report* to 8:00 p.m. By the beginning of 1999, Fox News was beating MSNBC.

During the 2000 election, Ailes relied on John Ellis, a first cousin of George W. Bush, to head Fox News's "decision desk." "Jebbie says we got it!" Ellis said at around 2:10 a.m. on Election Night, after getting off the phone with the governor of Florida. Fox called the election for Bush. Later, before a House subcommittee, Ailes was asked if there had been anything inappropriate in his employing Ellis. "Quite the contrary," he said. "I see this as a good journalist talking to his very high-level sources on Election Night."

Fox News's coverage of 9/11 and the war in Iraq improved its ratings, demonstrated its influence, and intensified the controversy over its practices. Critics charged that Fox News didn't report the war; it promoted it. When CBS's Morley Safer questioned Fox News about the flag pins worn by its anchors and reporters, Ailes said, "I'm a little bit squishy on killing babies, but when it comes to flag pins I'm pro-choice." By January of 2002, Fox was beating CNN.

In the years since, Fox News has steered the conservative movement. "That's a hard-hitting ad," Sean Hannity said, airing the attack on John Kerry by the Swift Boat Veterans for Truth, in 2004. In

2009, Glenn Beck's show, which debuted the day before Obama's inauguration, helped boost the channel's ratings and fueled the Tea Party movement.

"You don't get me," Ailes told Sherman, when they met at a party. "You don't get me" is what Fox News viewers across the country have been saying to the Washington press corps since the channel started, and fair enough. Still, in the end, the overturning of American journalism hasn't served their interests, or anyone's. Well-reported news is a public good; bad news is bad for everyone.

Sherman sees Ailes as a kingmaker, which isn't entirely convincing. Ailes is an entertainer. He's also a bogeyman. Raymond Gram Swing noticed that Hearst was largely a projection of his readers: "If he ever indulges in introspection his tragedy must be in seeing that for all his power, for all his being the biggest publisher in the world, he is not a leader, never has been a leader and never could be a leader." Hearst died in 1951. Between 1952 and 1988, an era marked by the Fairness Doctrine (and, according to conservatives, a liberal media), Republicans won seven out of ten presidential elections. Between 1988 and 2012, during the ascendancy of conservative media, Republicans won only three out of seven presidential elections. When Mitt Romney lost, Ailes blamed the party. "The GOP couldn't organize a one-car funeral," he said. Another explanation is that the conservative media drove the party into a graveyard.

No one reads Mrs. Older anymore. Hearst endures, instead, in *Citizen Kane*, a 1941 film that bears enough of a resemblance to Lundberg's book that Lundberg sued. "I had never seen or heard of the book *Imperial Hearst* by Mr. Lundberg," Orson Welles insisted in a deposition. A trial ended in a hung jury; the case was settled out of court.

Lundberg's evidence was good, but Welles made a persuasive argument that Kane wasn't a character; he was a type—an American sultan. If Xanadu looked like San Simeon, that's because men like Kane always wall themselves off in "one of those enormous imitation feudal kingdoms." A man like Kane, Welles said, believes that "politics as the means of communication, and indeed the nation itself, is all there for his personal pleasuring." The audience he craves he also hates. "Such men as Kane always tend toward the newspaper and entertainment world," Welles said. "They combine a morbid pre-occupation with the public with a devastatingly low opinion of the public mentality and moral character."

Nothing could be more natural than that a man like that would attempt to dictate his place in history. And nothing could be more unavailing. History is the shadow cast by the dead. So long as there's light, the shadow will fall.

—2014

Postscript: In 2016, six women who had worked at Fox News, including two prominent anchors, filed sexual harassment charges against Ailes. He resigned in 2017 and died later that year.

AFTER THE FACT

T ED CRUZ'S CAMPAIGN AUTOBIOGRAPHY IS CALLED *A Time for Truth.* "This guy's a liar," Donald Trump said at a 2016 GOP debate, pointing at Cruz. Trump thought a lot of people were liars, especially politicians (Jeb Bush: "Lying on campaign trail!") and reporters ("Too bad dopey @megynkelly lies!"). Not for nothing was he called the Human Lie Detector. And not for nothing was he called a big, fat Pinocchio with his pants on fire by the fact-checking teams at the *Times*, the *Washington Post*, and PolitiFact, whose careful reports apparently had little influence on the electorate, because, as a writer for *Politico* admitted, "Nobody but political fanatics pays much mind to them." "You lied," Marco Rubio said to Trump during another truth-for-tat debate. Cruz tried to break in, noting that Rubio had called him a liar, too. Honestly, there was so much loudmouthed soothsaying that it was hard to tell who was saying what. A line from the transcript released by CNN reads:

UNIDENTIFIED MALE: I tell the truth, I tell the truth.

Eat your heart out, Samuel Beckett.

On the one hand, not much of this is new. "Gen. Jackson is incapable of deception," Andrew Jackson's supporters insisted, in 1824. "Among all classes in Illinois the *sobriquet* of 'honest Abe' is habitually used by the masses," a Republican newspaper reported of Lincoln, in 1860. The tweets at #DumpTrump—"This man is a hoax!"— don't quite rise to the prose standard of the arrows flung at supporters of John Adams, who Jeffersonians said engaged in "every species of villainous deception, of which the human heart, in its last stage of depravity is capable."

"When a president doesn't tell the truth, how can we trust him to lead?" a Mitt Romney ad asked in 2012, during an election season in which the Obama campaign assembled a so-called Truth Team to point out Romney's misstatements of fact. Remember the Swift Boat Veterans for Truth, from 2004? This kind of thing comes and goes, and, then again, it comes. Cast back to Nixon: *Among all classes, the sobriquet of "Tricky Dick" was habitually used by the masses.* "Liar" isn't what opponents generally called Ford or Carter or the first George Bush, but a Bob Dole ad, in 1996, charged that "Bill Clinton is an unusually good liar," and much the same was said of Hillary Clinton, dubbed "a congenital liar" by William Safire. A Bernie Sanders campaign ad referred to him, pointedly, as "an honest leader"; his supporters were less restrained. At a rally in Iowa, they chanted, "She's a liar!"

On the other hand, some of this actually is new. When a sitting member of Congress called out "You lie!" during the president's remarks before a joint session in 2009, that, for instance, was new. ("That's not true," Obama replied.) John Oliver's #MakeDonaldDrumpfAgain campaign is both peerless and unprecedented. On HBO, Oliver checked Trump's facts, called Trump a "litigious serial liar," and dared him to sue. Also newish in 2016 was the rhetoric of unreality, the insistence, chiefly by Democrats, that some politicians were incapable of perceiving the truth because they had an epistemological deficit: they no longer believed in evidence, or even in objective reality.

To describe this phenomenon, Democrats in 2016 went very often to the Orwellian well: "The past was erased, the erasure was forgotten, the lie became truth." Hillary Clinton had a campaign ad called "Stand for Reality." "I'm just a grandmother with two eyes and a brain," she says, which is an awfully strange thing for a former First Lady, U.S. senator, and secretary of state to say. But what she meant, I guess, was that even some random old lady can see what Republican aspirants for the Oval Office can't: "It's hard to believe there are people running for president who still refuse to accept the settled science of climate change."

The past has not been erased, its erasure has not been forgotten, the lie has not become truth. But the past of proof is strange and, on its uncertain future, much in public life turns. In the end, it comes down to this: the history of truth is cockamamie, and during the 2016 U.S. presidential campaign, it got cockamamier.

MOST OF WHAT IS WRITTEN ABOUT TRUTH is the work of philosophers, who explain their ideas by telling little stories about experiments they conduct in their heads, like the time Descartes tried to convince himself that he didn't exist, and found that he couldn't, thereby proving that he did. Michael P. Lynch is a philosopher of truth. His fascinating book *The Internet of Us: Knowing More and Understanding Less in the Age of Big Data* begins with a thought experiment: "Imagine a society where smartphones are miniaturized and hooked directly into a person's brain." As thought experiments go, this one isn't much of a stretch. ("Eventually, you'll have an implant," Google's Larry Page promised, "where if you think about a fact it will just tell you the answer.") Now imagine that, after living with these implants for generations, people grow to rely on them, to know what they know and forget how people used to learn—by observation, inquiry, and reason. Then picture this: overnight, an environmental disaster destroys so much of the planet's electronic communications grid that everyone's implant crashes. It would be, Lynch says, as if the whole world had suddenly gone blind. There would be no immediate basis on which to establish the truth of a fact. No one would really know anything anymore, because no one would know how to know. I Google, therefore I am not.

Lynch thought we were frighteningly close to this point: blind to proof, no longer able to know. After all, we were already no longer able to agree about how to know. (See: climate change, above.) Lynch wasn't terribly interested in how we got here. He began at the arrival gate. But altering the flight plan would seem to require going back to the gate of departure.

Historians don't rely on thought experiments to explain their ideas, but they do like little stories. When I was eight or nine years old, a rotten kid down the street stole my baseball bat, a Louisville Slugger that I'd bought with money I'd earned delivering newspapers, and on whose barrel I'd painted my last name with my mother's nail polish, peach-plum pink. "Give it back," I told that kid when I stomped over to his house, where I found him practicing his swing in the back yard. "Nope," he said. "It's mine." Ha, I scoffed. "Oh, yeah? Then why does it have my name on it?" Here he got wily. He said that my last name was also the name of his baseball team in the town in Italy that he was from, and that everyone there had bats like this. It was a dumb story. "You're a liar," I pointed out. "It's mine." "Prove it," he said, poking me in the chest with the bat.

The law of evidence that reigns in the domain of childhood is essentially medieval. "Fight you for it," the kid said. "Race you for it," I countered. A long historical precedent stands behind these judicial methods for the establishment of truth, for knowing how to know what's true and what's not. In the West, for centuries, trial by combat and trial by ordeal—trial by fire, say, or trial by water— served both as means of criminal investigation and as forms of judicial proof. Kid jurisprudence works the same way: it's an atavism. As a rule, I preferred trial by bicycle. If that kid and I had raced our bikes and I'd won, the bat would have been mine, because my victory would have been God-given proof that it had been mine all along: in such cases, the outcome is itself evidence. Trial by combat and trial by ordeal place judgment in the hands of God. Trial by jury places judgment in the hands of men. It requires a different sort of evidence: facts.

A "fact" is, etymologically, an act or a deed. It came to mean something established as true only after the church effectively abolished trial by ordeal in 1215, the year that King John pledged, in Magna Carta, "No free man is to be arrested, or imprisoned . . . save by the lawful judgment of his peers or by the law of the land." In England, the abolition of trial by ordeal led to the adoption of trial by jury for criminal cases. This required a new doctrine of evidence and a new method of inquiry, and led to what the historian Barbara Shapiro called "the culture of fact": the idea that an observed or witnessed act or thing—the substance, the *matter*, of fact—is the basis of truth and the only kind of evidence that's admissible not only in court but also in other realms where truth is arbitrated. Between the thirteenth century and the nineteenth, the fact spread from law outward to science, history, and journalism.

What were the facts in the case of the nail-polished bat? I didn't want to fight, and that kid didn't want to race. I decided to wage a battle of facts. I went to the library. Do they even have baseball in Italy? Sort of. Is my name the name of a baseball team? Undeterminable, although in Latin it means "hare," a fact that, while not dispositive, was so fascinating to me that I began to forget why I'd looked it up.

I never did get my bat back. Forget the bat. The point of the story is that I went to the library because I was trying to pretend that I was a grownup, and I had been schooled in the ways of the Enlightenment. Empiricists believed they had deduced a method by which they could discover a universe of truth: impartial, verifiable knowledge. But the movement of judgment from God to man wreaked epistemological havoc. It made a lot of people nervous, and it turned out that not everyone thought of it as an improvement. For the length of the eighteenth century and much of the nineteenth, truth seemed more knowable, but after that it got murkier. Somewhere in the middle of the twentieth century, fundamentalism and postmodernism, the religious right and the academic left, met up: either the only truth is the truth of the divine or there is no truth; for both, empiricism is an error. That epistemological havoc has never ended: much of contemporary discourse and pretty much all of American politics is a dispute over evidence. An American presidential debate has a lot more in common with trial by combat than with trial by jury, which is what people are talking about when they say these debates seem "childish": the outcome is the evidence. The ordeal endures.

THEN CAME THE INTERNET. The era of the fact is coming to an end: the place once held by "facts" is being taken over by "data." This is making for more epistemological mayhem, not least because the collection and weighing of facts require investigation, discernment, and judgment, while the collection and analysis of data are outsourced to machines. "Most knowing now is Google-knowing—knowledge acquired online," Lynch wrote in *The Internet of Us* (his title is a riff on the ballyhooed and bewildering Internet of Things). We now only rarely discover facts, Lynch observes; instead, we download them. Of course, we also upload them: with each click and keystroke, we hack off tiny bits of ourselves and glom them onto a data leviathan.

"The Internet didn't create this problem, but it is exaggerating it," Lynch wrote, and it's an important and understated point. Blaming the internet is shooting fish in a barrel—a barrel that is floating in the sea of history. It's not that you don't hit a fish; it's that the issue is the ocean. No matter the bigness of the data, the vastness of the web, the freeness of speech, nothing could be less well settled in the twenty-first century than whether people know what they know from faith or from facts, or whether anything, in the end, can really be said to be fully proved.

Lynch has been writing about this topic for a long time, and passionately. The root of the problem, as he saw it, is a well-known paradox: reason can't defend itself without resort to reason. In his 2012 book *In Praise of Reason*, Lynch identified three sources of skepticism about reason: the suspicion that all reasoning is rationalization, the idea that science is just another faith, and the notion that objectivity is an illusion. These ideas have a specific intellectual history, and none of them are on the wane. Their consequences, he believed, are dire: "Without a common background of standards against which we measure what counts as a reliable source of information, or a reliable method of inquiry, and what doesn't, we won't be able *to agree on the facts,* let alone values. Indeed, this is precisely the situation we seem to be headed toward in the United States." Hence, truthiness. "I'm no fan of dictionaries or reference books: they're elitist," Stephen Colbert said in 2005, when he coined "truthiness" while lampooning George W. Bush. "I don't trust books. They're all fact, no heart. And that's exactly what's pulling our country apart today."

The origins of no other nation are as wholly dependent on the empiricism of the Enlightenment, as answerable to evidence. "Let facts be submitted to a candid world," Thomas Jefferson wrote in the Declaration of Independence. Or, as James Madison asked, "Is it not the glory of the people of America, that whilst they have paid a decent regard to the opinions of former times and other nations, they have not suffered a blind veneration for antiquity, for custom, or for names, to overrule the suggestions of their own good sense, the knowledge of their own situation, and the lessons of their own experience?" When we Google-know, Lynch argued, we no longer take responsibility for our own beliefs, and we lack the capacity to see how bits of facts fit into a larger whole. Essentially, we forfeit our reason and, in a republic, our citizenship. You could see how this works every time you tried to get to the bottom of a story by reading the news on your smartphone. Or you could see it in a GOP debate when Rubio said that Trump had hired Polish workers, undocumented immigrants, and Trump called him a liar:

TRUMP: That's wrong. That's wrong. Totally wrong.
RUBIO: That's a fact. People can look it up. I'm sure people are googling it right now. Look it up. "Trump Polish workers," you'll see a million dollars for hiring illegal workers on one of his projects.

In the hour after the debate, Google Trends reported a 700 percent spike in searches for "Polish workers." "We rate Rubio's claim Half True," PolitiFact reported. But what you saw when you Google "Polish workers" was a function of, among other things, your language, your location, and your personal web history. Reason can't defend itself. Neither can Google.

TRUMP DIDN'T REASON. He was a lot like that kid who stole my bat. He wanted combat. Cruz's appeal was to the judgment of God. "Father God, please . . . awaken the body of Christ, that we might pull back from the abyss," he preached on the campaign trail. Rubio's appeal was to Google.

Is there another appeal? People who care about civil society have two choices: find some epistemic principles other than empiricism on which everyone can agree or else find some method other than reason with which to defend empiricism. Lynch suspected that doing the first of these things is not possible, but that the second might be. He thought the best defense of reason is a common practical and ethical commitment. I believe he means popular sovereignty. That, anyway, is what Alexander Hamilton meant in *The Federalist Papers*, when he explained that the United States is an act of empirical inquiry: "It seems to have been reserved to the people of this country, by their conduct and example, to decide the important question, whether societies of men are really capable or not of establishing good government from reflection and choice, or whether they are forever destined to depend for their political constitutions on accident and force." The evidence is not yet in.

—2016

Postscript: Trump won the nomination and the election in 2016, and when he lost in 2020, his former Republican challengers failed to dispute his claim, a lie, that he had, in fact, won.

THE DISRUPTION MACHINE

I N THE LAST YEARS OF THE 1980S, I WORKED NOT AT startups but at what might be called finish-downs. Tech companies that were dying would hire temps—college students and new graduates—to do what little was left of the work of the employees they'd laid off. This was in Cambridge, near MIT. I'd type users' manuals, save them onto 5.25-inch floppy disks, and send them to a line printer that yammered like a set of prank-shop chatter teeth, but, by the time the last perforated page coiled out of it, the equipment whose functions those manuals explained had been discontinued. We'd work a month here, a week there. There wasn't much to do. Mainly, we sat at our desks and wrote wishy-washy poems on keyboards manufactured by Digital Equipment Corporation, left one another sly messages on pink While You Were Out sticky notes, swapped paperback novels—Kurt Vonnegut, Margaret Atwood, Gabriel García Márquez, that kind of thing—and, during lunch hour, had assignations in empty, unlocked offices. At Polaroid, I once found a Bantam Books edition of *Steppenwolf* in a clogged sink in an employees' bathroom, floating like a raft. "In his heart he was not a man, but a wolf of the steppes," it said on the bloated cover. The rest was unreadable.

Not long after that, I got a better assignment: answering the phone for Michael Porter, a professor at Harvard Business School. I was an assistant to his assistant. In 1985, Porter had published a book called *Competitive Advantage*, in which he elaborated on the three strategies—cost leadership, differentiation, and focus—that he'd described in his 1980 book, *Competitive Strategy*. I almost never saw Porter, and when I did, he was dashing, affably, out the door, suitcase in hand. My job was to field inquiries from companies that wanted to book him for speaking engagements. *The Competitive Advantage of Nations* appeared in 1990. Porter's ideas about business strategy reached executives all over the world.

Porter was interested in how companies succeed. The scholar who in some respects became his successor, Clayton M. Christensen, entered a doctoral program at Harvard Business School in 1989 and joined the faculty in 1992. Christensen was interested in why companies fail. In his 1997 book, *The Innovator's Dilemma*, he argued that, very often, it isn't because their executives made bad decisions but because they made good decisions, the same kind of good decisions that had made those companies successful for decades. (The "innovator's dilemma" is that "doing the right thing is the wrong thing.") As Christensen saw it, the problem was the velocity of history, and it wasn't so much a problem as a missed opportunity, like a plane that takes off without you, except that you didn't even know there was a plane, and had wandered onto the airfield, which you thought was a meadow, and the plane ran you over during takeoff. Manufacturers of mainframe computers made good decisions about making and selling mainframe computers and devising important refinements to them in their R&D departments—"sustaining innovations," Christensen called them—but, busy pleasing their mainframe customers, one tinker at a time, they missed what an entirely untapped customer wanted, personal computers, the market for which was created by what Christensen called "disruptive innovation": the selling of a cheaper, poorer-quality product that initially reaches less profitable customers but eventually takes over and devours an entire industry.

Ever since *The Innovator's Dilemma*, everyone is either disrupting or being disrupted. There are disruption consultants, disruption conferences, and disruption seminars. In 2014, the University of Southern California is opening a new program: "The degree is in disruption," the university announced. "Disrupt or be disrupted," the venture capitalist Josh Linkner warns in a new book, *The Road to Reinvention*, in which he argues that "fickle consumer trends, friction-free markets, and political unrest," along with "dizzying speed, exponential complexity, and mind-numbing technology advances," mean that the time has come to panic as you've never panicked before. Larry Downes and Paul Nunes, who blog for *Forbes*, insist that we have entered a new and even scarier stage: "big bang disruption." "This isn't disruptive innovation," they warn. "It's devastating innovation."

Things you own or use that are now considered to be the product of disruptive innovation include your smartphone and many of its apps, which have disrupted businesses from travel agencies and record stores to mapmaking and taxi dispatch. Much more disruption, we are told, lies ahead. Christensen has cowritten books urging disruptive innovation in higher education (*The Innovative University*), public schools (*Disrupting Class*), and health care (*The Innovator's Prescription*). His acolytes and imitators, including no small number of hucksters, have called for the disruption of more or less everything else. If the company you work for has a chief innovation officer, it's because of the long arm of *The Innovator's Dilemma*. If your city's public school district has adopted an Innovation Agenda, which has disrupted the education of every kid in the city, you live in the shadow of *The Innovator's Dilemma*. If you saw the episode of the HBO sitcom *Silicon Valley* in which the characters attend a conference called TechCrunch Disrupt 2014 (which is a real thing), and a guy from the stage, a Paul Rudd look-alike, shouts, "Let me hear it, *DISSS-RUPPTTT!*," you have heard the voice of Clay Christensen, echoing across the valley.

In 2014, days after the *Times*'s publisher, Arthur Sulzberger Jr., fired Jill Abramson, the paper's executive editor, the *Times*'s "Innovation" report was leaked. It included graphs inspired by Christensen's *Innovator's Dilemma*, along with a lengthy, glowing summary of the book's key arguments. The report explains, "Disruption is a predictable pattern across many industries in which fledgling companies use new technology to offer cheaper and inferior alternatives to products sold by established players (think Toyota taking on Detroit decades ago). Today, a pack of news startups are hoping to 'disrupt' our industry by attacking the strongest incumbent—The New York Times."

A pack of attacking startups sounds something like a pack of ravenous hyenas, but, generally, the rhetoric of disruption—a language of panic, fear, asymmetry, and disorder—calls on the rhetoric of another kind of conflict, in which an upstart refuses to play by the established rules of engagement, and blows things up. Don't think of Toyota taking on Detroit. Startups are ruthless and leaderless and unrestrained, and they seem so tiny and powerless, until you realize, but only after it's too late, that they're devastatingly dangerous: *Bang! Ka-boom!* Think of it this way: the *Times* is a nation-state; *BuzzFeed* is stateless. Disruptive innovation is competitive strategy for an age seized by terror.

EVERY AGE HAS A THEORY of rising and falling, of growth and decay, of bloom and wilt: a theory of nature. Every age also has a theory about the past and the present, of what was and what is, a notion of time: a theory of history. Theories of history used to be supernatural: the divine ruled time; the hand of God, a special providence, lay behind the fall of each sparrow. If the present differed from the past, it was usually worse: supernatural theories of history tend to involve decline, a fall from grace, the loss of God's favor, corruption. Beginning in the eighteenth century, as the intellectual historian Dorothy Ross once pointed out, theories of history became secular; then they started something new—historicism, the idea "that all events in historical time can be explained by prior events in historical time." Things began looking up. First there was that, then there was this, and this is *better* than that. The eighteenth century embraced the idea of progress; the nineteenth century had evolution; the twentieth century had growth and then innovation. Our era has disruption, which, despite its futurism, is atavistic. It's a theory of history founded on a profound anxiety about financial collapse, an apocalyptic fear of global devastation, and shaky evidence.

Most big ideas have loud critics. Not disruption. Disruptive innovation as the explanation for how change happens has been subject to little serious criticism, partly because it's headlong, while critical inquiry is unhurried; partly because disrupters ridicule doubters by charging them with fogyism, as if to criticize a theory of change were identical to decrying change; and partly because, in its modern usage, innovation is the idea of progress jammed into a criticism-proof jack-in-the-box.

The idea of progress—the notion that human history is the history of human betterment—dominated the worldview of the West between the Enlightenment and the First World War. It had critics from the start, and, in the last century, even people who cherish the idea of progress, and point to improvements like the eradication of contagious diseases and the education of girls, have been hard-pressed to hold on to it while reckoning with two world wars, the Holocaust and Hiroshima, genocide and global warming. Replacing "progress" with "innovation" skirts the question of whether a novelty is an improvement: the world may not be getting better and better but our devices are getting newer and newer.

The word "innovate"—to make new—used to have chiefly negative connotations: it signified excessive novelty, without purpose or end. Edmund Burke called the French Revolution a "revolt of innovation"; Federalists declared themselves to be "enemies to innovation." George Washington, on his deathbed, was said to have uttered these words: "Beware of innovation in politics." Noah Webster warned in his dictionary, in 1828, "It is often dangerous to innovate on the customs of a nation."

The redemption of innovation began in 1939, when the economist Joseph Schumpeter, in his landmark study of business cycles, used the word to mean bringing new products to market, a usage that spread slowly, and only in the specialized literatures of economics and business. (In 1942, Schumpeter theorized about "creative destruction"; Christensen, retrofitting, believes that Schumpeter was really describing disruptive innovation.) "Innovation" began to seep beyond specialized literatures in the 1990s, and gained ubiquity only after 9/11. One measure: between 2011 and 2014, *Time*, the *Times Magazine*, *The New Yorker*, *Forbes*, and even *Better Homes and Gardens* published special "innovation" issues—the modern equivalents of what, a century ago, were known as "sketches of men of progress."

The idea of innovation is the idea of progress stripped of the aspirations of the Enlightenment, scrubbed clean of the horrors of the twentieth century, and relieved of its critics. Disruptive innovation goes further, holding out the hope of salvation against the very damnation it describes: disrupt, and you will be saved.

DISRUPTIVE INNOVATION AS A THEORY of change is meant to serve both as a chronicle of the past (this has happened) and as a model for the future (it will keep happening). The strength of a prediction made from a model depends on the quality of the historical evidence and on the reliability of the methods used to gather and interpret it. Historical analysis proceeds from certain conditions regarding proof. None of these conditions have been met.

The Innovator's Dilemma consists of a set of handpicked case studies, beginning with the disk drive industry, which was the subject of Christensen's doctoral thesis, in 1992. "Nowhere in the history of business has there been an industry like disk drives," Christensen writes, which makes it a very odd choice for an investigation designed to create a model for understanding other industries. The first hard disk drive, which weighed more than a ton, was invented at IBM in 1955, by a team that included Alan Shugart. Christensen is chiefly concerned with an era, beginning in the late 1970s, when disk drives decreased in size from 14 inches to 8, then from 8 to 5.25, from 5.25 to 3.5, and from 3.5 to 2.5 and 1.8. He counts 116 new technologies, and classes 111 as sustaining innovations and 5 as disruptive innovations.

Each of these five, he says, introduced "smaller disk drives that were slower and had lower capacity than those used in the mainstream market," and each company that adopted them was an entrant firm that toppled an established firm. In 1973, Alan Shugart founded Shugart Associates, which introduced a 5.25-inch floppy disk drive in 1976; the company was bought by Xerox the next year. In 1978, Shugart Associates developed an 8-inch hard disk drive; Christensen, who is uninterested in the floppy disk drive industry, classes the company as an entrant firm and credits it with disrupting established firms that manufactured 14-inch hard drives.

In 1979, Alan Shugart founded Shugart Technology, which changed its name to Seagate Technology after Xerox threatened

THE DISRUPTION MACHINE 109

to sue. In 1980, Seagate Technology introduced the first 5.25-inch hard disk drive; Christensen, at this point, classes Seagate as an entrant firm, and Shugart Associates as a failed incumbent, even though Shugart Associates was shifting its focus to what was then its very profitable floppy disk drive business. In the mid-eighties, Seagate—here considered by Christensen to be an established firm—delayed manufacturing 3.5-inch drives, which were valued by producers of portable computers and laptops, because its biggest customer, IBM, didn't want them; IBM wanted a better and faster version of the 5.25-inch drive for its full-sized desktop computers. Seagate didn't start shipping 3.5-inch drives until 1988, and by then, Christensen argues, it was too late.

In his original research, Christensen established the cutoff for measuring a company's success or failure as 1989 and explained that "'successful firms' were arbitrarily defined as those which achieved more than fifty million dollars in revenues in constant 1987 dollars in any single year between 1977 and 1989—even if they subsequently withdrew from the market." Much of the theory of disruptive innovation rests on this arbitrary definition of success.

In fact, Seagate Technology was not felled by disruption. Between 1989 and 1990, its sales doubled, reaching $2.4 billion, "more than all of its U.S. competitors combined," according to an industry report. In 1997, the year Christensen published *The Innovator's Dilemma*, Seagate was the largest company in the disk drive industry, reporting revenues of nine billion dollars. In 2013, Seagate shipped its two-billionth disk drive. Most of the entrant firms celebrated by Christensen as triumphant disrupters, on the other hand, no longer exist, their success having been in some cases brief and in others illusory. (The fleeting nature of their success is, of course, perfectly consistent with his model.) Between 1982 and 1984, Micropolis made the disruptive leap from 8-inch to 5.25-inch drives through what Christensen credits as the "Herculean managerial effort" of its CEO, Stuart Mahon. ("Mahon remembers the experience as the most exhausting of his life," Christensen writes.) But shortly thereafter, Micropolis, unable to compete with companies like Seagate, failed.

MiniScribe, founded in 1980, started out selling 5.25-inch drives and saw quick success. "That was MiniScribe's hour of glory," the company's founder later said. "We had our hour of infamy shortly after that." In 1989, MiniScribe was investigated for fraud and soon collapsed; a report charged that the company's practices included fabricated financial reports and "shipping bricks and scrap parts disguised as disk drives."

As striking as the disruption in the disk drive industry seemed in the 1980s, more striking, from the vantage of history, are the continuities. Christensen argues that incumbents in the disk drive industry were regularly destroyed by newcomers. But today, after much consolidation, the divisions that dominate the industry are divisions that led the market in the 1980s. (In some instances, what shifted was their ownership: IBM sold its hard disk division to Hitachi, which later sold its division to Western Digital.) In the longer term, victory in the disk drive industry appears to have gone to the manufacturers that were good at incremental improvements, whether or not they were the first to market the disruptive new format. Companies that were quick to release a new product but not skilled at tinkering have tended to flame out.

Other cases in *The Innovator's Dilemma* are equally murky. In his account of the mechanical excavator industry, Christensen argues that established companies that built cable-operated excavators were slow to recognize the importance of the hydraulic excavator, which was developed in the late 1940s. "Almost the entire population of mechanical shovel manufacturers was wiped out by a disruptive technology—hydraulics—that the leaders' customers and their economic structure had caused them initially to ignore," he argues. Christensen counts thirty established companies in the 1950s and says that, by the 1970s, only four had survived the entrance into the industry of thirteen disruptive newcomers, including Caterpillar, O&K, Demag, and Hitachi. But, in fact, many of Christensen's "new entrants" had been making cable-operated shovels for years. O&K, founded in 1876, had been making them since 1908; Demag had been building excavators since 1925, when it bought a company that built steam shovels; Hitachi, founded in 1910, sold cable-operated shovels before the Second World War. Manufacturers that were genuinely new to excavation equipment tended to sell a lot of hydraulic excavators, if they had a strong distribution network, and then not do so well. And some established companies disrupted by hydraulics didn't do half as badly as Christensen suggests. Bucyrus is the old-line shovel-maker he writes about most. It got its start in Ohio, in 1880, built most of the excavators that dug the Panama Canal, and became Bucyrus-Erie in 1927, when it bought the Erie Steam Shovel Company. It acquired a hydraulics equipment firm in 1948, but, Christensen writes, "faced precisely the same problem in marketing its hydraulic backhoe as Seagate had faced with its 3.5-inch drives."

Unable to persuade its established consumers to buy a hydraulic excavator, Bucyrus introduced a hybrid product, called the Hydro-hoe, in 1951—a merely sustaining innovation. Christensen says that Bucyrus "logged record profits until 1966—the point at which the disruptive hydraulics technology had squarely intersected with customers' needs," and then began to decline. "This is typical of industries facing a disruptive technology," he explains. "The leading firms in the established technology remain financially strong until the disruptive technology is, in fact, in the midst of their mainstream market."

But actually, between 1962 and 1979 Bucyrus's sales grew sevenfold and its profits grew twenty-five-fold. Was that so bad? In the 1980s, Bucyrus suffered. The whole construction equipment industry did: it was devastated by recession, inflation, the oil crisis, a drop in home building, and the slowing of highway construction. (Caterpillar sustained heavy losses, too.) In the early 1990s, after a disastrous leveraged buyout handled by Goldman Sachs, Bucyrus entered Chapter 11 protection, but it made some sizable acquisitions when it emerged, as Bucyrus International, and was a leading maker of mining equipment, just as it had been a century earlier. Was it a failure? Caterpillar didn't think so when, in 2011, it bought the firm for nearly nine billion dollars.

Christensen's sources are often dubious and his logic questionable. His single citation for his investigation of the "disruptive transition from mechanical to electronic motor controls," in which he identifies the Allen-Bradley Company as triumphing over four rivals, is a book called *The Bradley Legacy*, an account published by a foundation established by the company's founders. This is akin to calling an actor the greatest talent in a generation after interviewing his publicist. "Use theory to help guide data collection," Christensen advises.

He finds further evidence of his theory in the disruption of the department store by the discount store. "Just as in disk drives and excavators," he writes, "a few of the leading traditional retailers— notably S. S. Kresge, F. W. Woolworth, and Dayton Hudson—saw the disruptive approach coming and invested early." In 1962, Kresge (which traces its origins to 1897) opened Kmart; Dayton-Hudson (1902) opened Target; and Woolworth (1879) opened Woolco. Kresge and Dayton-Hudson ran their discount stores as independent organizations; Woolworth ran its discount store in-house. Kmart and Target succeeded; Woolco failed. Christensen presents this story as yet more evidence of an axiom derived from the disk drive industry: "two models for how to make money cannot peacefully coexist within a single organization." In the mid-1990s, Kmart closed more than two hundred stores, a fact that Christensen does not include in his account of the industry's history. (Kmart filed for bankruptcy in 2002.) Only in a footnote does he make a vague allusion to Kmart's troubles—"when this book was being written, Kmart was a crippled company"—and then he dismisses this piece of counterevidence by fiat: "Kmart's present competitive struggles are unrelated to Kresge's strategy in meeting the original disruptive threat of discounting."

In his discussion of the steel industry, in which he argues that established companies were disrupted by the technology of minimilling (melting down scrap metal to make cheaper, lower-quality sheet metal), Christensen writes that U.S. Steel, founded in 1901, lowered the cost of steel production from "nine labor-hours per ton of steel produced in 1980 to just under three hours per ton in 1991," which he attributes to the company's "ferociously attacking the size of its workforce, paring it from more than 93,000 in 1980 to fewer than 23,000 in 1991," in order to point out that even this accomplishment could not stop the coming disruption. Christensen tends to ignore factors that don't support his theory. Factors having effects on both production and profitability that Christensen does not mention are that, between 1986 and 1987, twenty-two thousand workers at U.S. Steel did not go to work, as part of a labor action, and that U.S. Steel's workers are unionized and have been for generations, while minimill manufacturers, with their newer workforces, are generally non-union. Christensen's logic here seems to be that the industry's labor arrangements can have played no role in U.S. Steel's struggles—and are not even worth mentioning—because U.S. Steel's struggles must be a function of its having failed to build minimills. U.S. Steel's struggles have been and remain grave, but its failure is by no means a matter of historical record. Today, the largest U.S. producer of steel is—U.S. Steel.

THE THEORY OF DISRUPTION is meant to be predictive. On March 10, 2000, Christensen launched a $3.8 million Disruptive Growth Fund, which he managed with Neil Eisner, a broker in St. Louis. Christensen drew on his theory to select stocks. Less than a year later, the fund was quietly liquidated: during a stretch of time when the Nasdaq lost 50 percent of its value, the Disruptive Growth Fund lost 65 percent. In 2007, Christensen told *BusinessWeek* that "the prediction of the theory would be that Apple won't succeed with the iPhone," adding, "History speaks pretty loudly on that." In its first five years, the iPhone generated a hundred and fifty billion dollars of revenue. In the preface to the 2011 edition of "The Innovator's Dilemma," Christensen reports that, since the book's publication, in 1997, "the theory of disruption continues to yield predictions that are quite accurate." This is less because people have used his model to make accurate predictions about things that haven't happened yet than because disruption has been sold as advice, and because much that happened between 1997 and 2011 looks, in retrospect, disruptive. Disruptive innovation can reliably be seen only after the fact. History speaks loudly, apparently, only when you can make it say what you want it to say. The popular incarnation of the theory tends to disavow history altogether. "Predicting the future based on the past is like betting on a football team simply because it won the Super Bowl a decade ago," Josh Linkner writes in *The Road to Reinvention*. His first principle: "Let go of the past." It has nothing to tell you. But unless you already believe in disruption, many of the successes that have been labeled disruptive innovation look like something else, and many of the failures that are often seen to have resulted from failing to embrace disruptive innovation look like bad management.

Christensen has compared the theory of disruptive innovation to a theory of nature: the theory of evolution. But among the many differences between disruption and evolution is that the advocates of disruption have an affinity for circular arguments. If an established company doesn't disrupt, it will fail, and if it fails it must be because it didn't disrupt. When a startup fails, that's a success, since epidemic failure is a hallmark of disruptive innovation. ("Stop being afraid of failure and start embracing it," the organizers of FailCon, an annual conference, implore, suggesting that, in the era of disruption, innovators face unprecedented challenges. For instance: maybe you made the wrong hires?) When an established company succeeds, that's only because it hasn't yet failed. And, when any of these things happen, all of them are only further evidence of disruption.

The handpicked case study, which is Christensen's method, is a notoriously weak foundation on which to build a theory. But if the handpicked case study is the approved approach, it would seem that efforts at embracing disruptive innovation are often fatal. Morrison-Knudsen, an engineering and construction firm, got its start in 1905 and helped build more than a hundred and fifty dams all over the world, including the Hoover. Beginning in 1988, a new CEO, William Agee, looked to new products and new markets, and, after Bill Clinton's election, in 1992, bet on mass transit, turning to the construction of both commuter and long-distance train cars through two subsidiaries, MK Transit and MK Rail. These disruptive businesses proved to be a disaster. Morrison-Knudsen announced in 1995 that it had lost three hundred and fifty million dollars, by which point the company had essentially collapsed—not because it didn't disruptively innovate but because it did. Time Inc., founded in 1922, auto-disrupted, too. In 1994, the company launched Pathfinder, an early new-media venture, an umbrella website for its magazines, at a cost estimated to have exceeded a hundred million dollars; the site was abandoned in 1999. Had Pathfinder been successful, it would have been greeted, retrospectively, as evidence of disruptive innovation. Instead, as one of its producers put it, "it's like it never existed."

In the late 1990s and early 2000s, the financial services industry innovated by selling products like subprime mortgages, collateralized debt obligations, and mortgage-backed securities, some to a previously untapped customer base. At the time, Ed Clark was the CEO of Canada's TD Bank, which traces its roots to 1855. Clark, who earned a PhD in economics at Harvard with a dissertation on public investment in Tanzania, forswore Canada's version of this disruptive innovation, asset-backed commercial paper. The decision made TD Bank one of the strongest banks in the world. Between 2002 and 2012, TD Bank's assets increased from $278 billion to $806 billion. Since 2005, TD Bank has opened thirteen hundred branches in the United States, bought Commerce Bank for $8.5 billion, in 2008, and adopted the motto "America's Most Convenient Bank." With the money it earned by expanding its traditional banking services—almost four billion dollars a year during the height of the financial crisis, according to the Canadian business reporter Howard Green—it set about marketing itself as the bank with the longest hours, the best teller services, and free dog biscuits.

When the financial services industry disruptively innovated, it led to a global financial crisis. Like the bursting of the dot-com bubble, the meltdown didn't dim the fervor for disruption; instead, it fueled it, because these products of disruption contributed to the panic on which the theory of disruption thrives.

DISRUPTIVE INNOVATION AS AN EXPLANATION for how change happens is everywhere. Ideas that come from business schools are exceptionally well marketed. Faith in disruption is the best illustration, and the worst case, of a larger historical transformation having to do with secularization, and what happens when the invisible hand replaces the hand of God as explanation and justification. Innovation and disruption are ideas that originated in the arena of business but which have since been applied to arenas whose values and goals are remote from the values and goals of business. People aren't disk drives. Public schools, colleges and universities, churches, museums, and many hospitals, all of which have been subjected to disruptive innovation, have revenues and expenses and infrastructures, but they aren't industries in the same way that manufacturers of hard disk drives or truck engines or dry goods are industries. Journalism isn't an industry in that sense, either.

Doctors have obligations to their patients, teachers to their students, pastors to their congregations, curators to the public, and journalists to their readers—obligations that lie outside the realm of earnings, and are fundamentally different from the obligations that a business executive has to employees, partners, and investors. Historically, institutions like museums, hospitals, schools, and universities have been supported by patronage, donations made by individuals or funding from church or state. The press has generally supported itself by charging subscribers and selling advertising. (Underwriting by corporations and foundations is a funding source of more recent vintage.) Charging for admission, membership, subscriptions and, for some, earning profits are similarities these institutions have with businesses. Still, that doesn't make them industries, which turn things into commodities and sell them for gain.

In *The Innovative University*, written with Henry J. Eyring, who used to work at the Monitor Group, a consulting firm cofounded by Michael Porter, Christensen subjected Harvard, a college founded by seventeenth-century theocrats, to his case study analysis. "Studying the university's history," Christensen and Eyring wrote, "will allow us to move beyond the forlorn language of crisis to hopeful and practical strategies for success." On the basis of this research, Christensen and Eyring's recommendations for the disruption of the modern university include a "mix of face-to-face and online learning." The publication of *The Innovative University*, in 2011, contributed to a frenzy for massive open online courses, or MOOCs, at colleges and universities across the country, including a collaboration between Harvard and MIT, which was announced in May of 2012. Shortly afterward, the University of Virginia's panicked board of trustees attempted to fire the president, charging her with jeopardizing the institution's future by failing to disruptively innovate with sufficient speed; the vice-chair of the board forwarded to the chair a *Times* column written by David Brooks, "The Campus Tsunami," in which he cited Christensen.

Christensen and Eyring's recommendation of a "mix of face-to-face and online learning" was drawn from an investigation that involves a wildly misguided attempt to apply standards of instruction in the twenty-first century to standards of instruction in the seventeenth. One table in the book, titled "Harvard's Initial DNA, 1636–1707," looks like this:

Initial Traits	Implications
Small, face-to-face classes	High faculty-student intimacy Low instructional efficiency
Classical, religious instruction	High moral content in the curriculum Narrow curriculum with low practicality for non-pastors
Nonspecialized faculty	Dogmatic instruction High faculty empathy for learners Low faculty expertise

In 2014, there were twenty-one thousand students at Harvard. In 1640, there were thirteen. The first year classes were held, Harvard students and their "nonspecialized faculty" (one young schoolmaster, Nathaniel Eaton), enjoying "small, face-to-face classes" (Eaton's wife, who fed the students, was accused of putting "goat's dung in their hasty pudding") with "high faculty empathy for learners" (Eaton conducted thrashings with a stick of walnut said to have been "big enough to have killed a horse"), could have paddled together in a single canoe. That doesn't mean good arguments can't be made for online education. But there's nothing factually persuasive in this account of its historical urgency and even inevitability, which relies on a method well outside anything resembling plausible historical analysis.

Christensen and Eyring also urge universities to establish "heavyweight innovation teams": Christensen thinks that R&D departments housed within a business and accountable to its executives are structurally unable to innovate disruptively—they are preoccupied with pleasing existing customers through incremental improvement. Christensen argues, for instance, that if Digital Equipment Corporation, which was doing very well making minicomputers in the 1960s and '70s, had founded, in the '80s, a separate company at another location to develop the personal computer, it might have triumphed. The logic of disruptive innovation is the logic of the startup: establish a team of innovators, set a whiteboard under a blue sky, and never ask them to make a profit, because there needs to be a wall of separation between the people whose job is to come up with the best, smartest, and most creative and important ideas and the people whose job is to make money by selling stuff. Interestingly, a similar principle has existed, for more than a century, in the press. The "heavyweight innovation team"? That's what journalists used to call the "newsroom."

It's readily apparent that, in a democracy, the important business interests of institutions like the press might at times conflict with what became known as the "public interest." That's why, a very long time ago, newspapers like the *Times* and magazines like this one established a wall of separation between the editorial side of affairs and the business side. (The metaphor is to the Jeffersonian wall between church and state.) "The wall dividing the newsroom and business side has served The Times well for decades," according to the *Times*'s 2014 "Innovation" report, "allowing one side to focus on readers and the other to focus on advertisers," as if this had been, all along, simply a matter of office efficiency. But the notion of a wall should be abandoned, according to the report, because it has "hidden costs" that thwart innovation. Shortly before the release of the report, the *Times* tried to recruit, as its new head of audience development, Michael Wertheim, the former head of promotion at the disruptive media outfit Upworthy. Wertheim turned the *Times* job down, citing its wall as too big an obstacle to disruptive innovation. The recommendation of the "Innovation" report is to understand that both sides, editorial and business, share, as their top priority, "Reader Experience," which can be measured, following Upworthy, in "Attention Minutes." Vox Media, a digital-media disrupter that is mentioned ten times in the *Times* report and is included, along with *BuzzFeed*, in a list of the *Times*'s strongest competitors (few of which are profitable), called the report "brilliant," "shockingly good," and an "insanely clear" explanation of disruption, but expressed the view that there's no way the *Times* will implement its recommendations, because "what the report doesn't mention is the sobering conclusion of Christensen's research: companies faced with disruptive threats almost never manage to handle them gracefully."

DISRUPTIVE INNOVATION IS A THEORY about why businesses fail. It's not more than that. It doesn't explain change. It's not a law of nature. It's an artifact of history, an idea, forged in time; it's the manufacture of a moment of upsetting and edgy uncertainty. Transfixed by change, it's blind to continuity. It makes a very poor prophet.

The upstarts who work at startups don't often stay at any one place for very long. (Three out of four startups fail. More than nine out of ten never earn a return.) They work a year here, a few months there—zany hours everywhere. They wear jeans and sneakers and ride scooters and share offices and sprawl on couches like Great Danes. Their coffee machines look like dollhouse-size factories.

They are told that they should be reckless and ruthless. Their investors, if they're like Josh Linkner, tell them that the world is a terrifying place, moving at a devastating pace. "Today I run a venture capital firm and back the next generation of innovators who are, as I was throughout my earlier career, dead-focused on eating your lunch," Linkner writes. His job appears to be to convince a generation of people who want to do good and do well to learn, instead, remorselessness. Forget rules, obligations, your conscience, loyalty, a sense of the common-weal. If you start a business and it succeeds, Linkner advises, sell it and take the cash. Don't look back. Never pause. Disrupt or be disrupted.

But they do pause and they do look back, and they wonder. Mean-while, they tweet, they post, they tumble in and out of love, they ponder. They send one another sly messages, touching the screens of sleek, soundless machines with a worshipful tenderness. They swap novels: David Foster Wallace, Chimamanda Ngozi Adichie, Zadie Smith. *Steppenwolf* is still available in print, five dollars cheaper as an e-book. He's a wolf, he's a man. The rest is unreadable. So, as ever, is the future.

—2014

THE ROBOT CARAVAN

T HE ROBOTS ARE COMING. HIDE THE WD-40. LOCK up your nine-volt batteries. Build a booby trap out of giant magnets; dig a moat as deep as a grave. "Ever since a study by the University of Oxford predicted that 47 percent of U.S. jobs are at risk of being replaced by robots and artificial intelligence over the next fifteen to twenty years, I haven't been able to stop thinking about the future of work," Andrés Oppenheimer writes, in *The Robots Are Coming: The Future of Jobs in the Age of Automation.* No one is safe. Chapter 4: "They're Coming for Bankers!" Chapter 5: "They're Coming for Lawyers!" They're attacking hospitals: "They're Coming for Doctors!" They're headed to Hollywood: "They're Coming for Entertainers!" I gather they have not yet come for the manufacturers of exclamation points.

The old robots were blue-collar workers, burly and clunky, the machines that rusted the Rust Belt. But according to the economist Richard Baldwin, in *The Globotics Upheaval: Globalization, Robotics, and the Future of Work,* the new ones are "white-collar robots," knowledge workers and quinoa-and-oat-milk globalists, the machines that will bankrupt Brooklyn. Mainly, they're algorithms. Except when they're immigrants. Baldwin calls that kind "remote intelligence," or RI: they're not exactly robots but, somehow, they fall into the same category. They're people from other countries who can steal your job without ever really crossing the border: they just hop over, by way of the internet and apps like Upwork, undocumented, invisible, ethereal. Between artificial intelligence and remote intelligence, Baldwin warns, "this international talent tidal wave is coming straight for the good, stable jobs that have been the foundation of middle-class prosperity in the US and Europe, and other high-wage economies."

Change your Wi-Fi password. Clear your browser history. Ask HR about early retirement. The globots are coming.

How can you know if you're about to get replaced by an invading algorithm or an augmented immigrant? "If your job can be easily explained, it can be automated," Anders Sandberg, of Oxford's Future of Humanity Institute, tells Oppenheimer. "If it can't, it won't." (Rotten luck for people whose job description is "Predict the future.") Baldwin offers three-part advice: (1) avoid competing with AI and RI; (2) build skills in things that only humans can do, in person; and (3) "realize that humanity is an edge not a handicap." What all this means is hard to say, especially if you've never before considered being human to be a handicap. As for the future of humanity, Oppenheimer offers another cockamamie rule of three: "Society will be divided into three general groups. The first will be members of the elites, who will be able to adapt to the ever-changing technological landscape and who will earn the most money, followed by a second group made up primarily of those who provide personalized services to the elite, including personal trainers, Zumba class instructors, meditation gurus, piano teachers, and personal chefs, and finally a third group of those who will be mostly unemployed and may be receiving a universal basic income as compensation for being the victims of technological unemployment."

Readers of Douglas Adams will recognize this sort of hooey from *The Hitchhiker's Guide to the Galaxy*. Long ago, in a galaxy not at all far away, the people of the planet Golgafrincham were divided into three groups: A, "all the brilliant leaders, the scientists, the great artists, you know, all the achievers"; B, "hairdressers, tired TV producers, insurance salesmen, personnel officers, security guards, public relations executives, management consultants" (the group that everyone else considers to be "a bunch of useless idiots"); and, C, "all the people who did the actual work, who made things and did things." The B people, told they must lead an expedition to colonize another planet, rocket away in a starship, having been led to believe that their planet is doomed. "Apparently it was going to crash into the sun or something," the B ship's captain tells Arthur Dent, vaguely wondering why the other ships never followed. "Or maybe it was that the moon was going to crash into us. Something of the kind. Absolutely terrifying prospect whatever it was." Dent inquires, "And they made sure they sent you lot off first, did they?"

This time, notwithstanding Elon Musk's ambition to colonize Mars, no one's trying to persuade the B people to board a spaceship, because the B people—the hairdressers and the Zumba-class instructors, the meditation gurus and the personal trainers—are supposed to stick around to cater to the A people. No, this time it's the C people, the people who make and do things—things that can now be made and done faster and cheaper by robots—who are being flushed down the cosmic toilet. The historian and sometime futurist Yuval Noah Harari has a name for the C people: he calls them the "useless class." Some futurists suggest that, in our Asimov-y future, these sort of people might wind up spending their empty days playing video games. Otherwise, they'll wage a revolution, an eventuality that the self-proclaimed "cognitive elite"—the A people, who believe themselves to be cleverer than the cleverest robots—intend to wait out in fortified lairs. (Peter Thiel owns nearly five hundred acres of land in New Zealand, complete with its own water supply.) More popular is the proposal to pay the C people for doing nothing, in order to avert the revolution. "It's going to be necessary," Musk said during a summit in Dubai two years ago, joining a small herd of other billionaires, including Mark Zuckerberg, of Facebook, and Stewart Butterfield, of Slack, who endorse universal basic income. It's either that or build a wall.

FEAR OF A ROBOT INVASION IS the obverse of fear of an immigrant invasion, a partisan coin: heads, you're worried about robots; tails, you're worried about immigrants. There's just the one coin. Both fears have to do with jobs, whose loss produces suffering, want, and despair, and whose future scarcity represents a terrifying prospect. Misery likes a scapegoat: heads, blame machines; tails, foreigners. But is the present alarm warranted? Panic is not evidence of danger; it's evidence of panic. Stoking fear of invading robots and of invading immigrants has been going on for a long time, and the predictions of disaster have, generally, been bananas. Oh, but this time it's different, the robotomizers insist.

This thesis has been rolling around like a marble in the bowl of a lot of people's brains for a while now, and many of those marbles were handed out by Martin Ford, in his 2015 book, *Rise of the Robots: Technology and the Threat of a Jobless Future*. In the book, and in an essay in *Confronting Dystopia: The New Technological Revolution and the Future of Work*, Ford acknowledges that all other earlier robot-invasion panics were unfounded. In the nineteenth century, people who worked on farms lost their jobs when agricultural processes were mechanized, but they eventually earned more money working in factories. In the twentieth century, automation of industrial production led to warnings about "unprecedented economic and social disorder." Instead, displaced factory workers moved into service jobs. Machines eliminate jobs; rising productivity creates new jobs.

"Given this long record of false alarms, contemporary economists are generally dismissive of arguments that technological progress might lead to unemployment as well as falling wages and soaring income inequality," Ford admits. After all, "history shows that the economy has consistently adjusted to advancing technology by creating new employment opportunities and that these new jobs often require more skills and pay higher wages."

That was then. The reason that things will be different this time, Ford argues, has to do with the changing pace of change. The transformation from an agricultural to an industrial economy was linear; the current acceleration is exponential. The first followed Newton's law; the second follows Moore's. The employment apocalypse, when it comes, will happen so fast that workers won't have time to adjust by shifting to new employment sectors, and, even if they did have time to adjust, there would be no new employment sectors to go to, because robots will be able to do just about everything.

It is quite possible that this thesis is correct; it is not possible to know that it is correct. Ford, an advocate of universal basic income, is neither a historian nor an economist. He is a futurist, a modern-day shaman, with an MBA. Everybody thinks about the future; futurists do it for a living. Policymakers make plans; futurists read omens. The robots-are-coming omen-reading borrows as much from the conventions of science fiction as from those of historical analysis. It uses "robot" as a shorthand for everything from steam-powered looms to electricity-driven industrial assemblers and artificial intelligence, and thus has the twin effects of compressing time and conflating one thing with another. It indulges in the supposition that work is something the wealthy hand out to the poor, from feudalism to capitalism, instead of something people do, for reasons that include a search for order, meaning, and purpose. It leaves out of its accounting the largest source of labor in the United States before the Civil War, people held in bondage, and fails to consider how the rise of wage labor left women's work uncompensated. And it ignores the brutal truth that, in American history, panic about technological change is almost always tangled up with panic about immigration. Nineteenth-century populists, those farmers left behind by the industrial revolution, wanted railroad companies to be taxed, but they also wanted to bar African Americans and Asian immigrants from full citizenship. They raged against the machine; they fought for the color line.

FUTURISTS FORETELL INEVITABLE OUTCOMES by conjuring up inevitable pasts. People who are in the business of selling predictions need to present the past as predictable—the ground truth, the test case. Machines are more predictable than people, and in histories written by futurists the machines just keep coming; depicting their march as unstoppable certifies the futurists' predictions. But machines don't just keep coming. They are funded, invented, built, sold, bought, and used by people who could just as easily not fund, invent, build, sell, buy, and use them. Machines don't drive history; people do. History is not a smart car.

In *Temp: How American Work, American Business, and the American Dream Became Temporary*, the historian Louis Hyman argues that in the course of the past century management consultants, taking the wheel, reinvented work by making employers more like machines, turning work into the kind of thing that robots could do long before there were any robots able to do it. His story begins in the 1920s, with the rise of management consulting, and takes a turn in the '50s, with the first major wave of automation, a word coined in 1948. "Machines should be used instead of people whenever possible," a staffer for the National Office Managers Association advised in 1952. To compete, workers had to become as flexible as machines: able to work on a task basis; ineligible for unions; free at night; willing to work any shift; requiring no health care or other benefits, not so much as a day off at Christmas; easy to hire; and easier to fire.

"The rise of computers and the rise of temps went hand in hand," Hyman writes. By 1958, Elmer Winter had founded Manpower Inc., and companies all over the country had come to rely on the services of management consultants to trim their employment costs. Hyman argues, "Beginning in the midst of the postwar boom in the 1950s, American jobs were slowly remade from top to bottom: consultants supplanted executives at the top, temps replaced office workers in the middle, and day laborers pushed out union workers at the bottom. On every step of the ladder, work would become more insecure as it became more flexible."

Gradually, Hyman says, "the key features of the postwar corporation—stable workforce, retained earnings, and minimized risk—became liabilities rather than assets." Beginning in the 1970s, Harvard Business School's Michael Porter introduced the logic underlying outsourcing. By the 1980s, corporations had to get "lean." (I worked for Porter in those days, as a Manpower temp.) By the 1990s, they needed to "downsize." If businesses exist not to make things and employ people but instead to maximize profits for investors, labor can be done by temps, by poorly paid workers in other countries, or by robots, whichever is cheapest.

The robots, though, were mainly for show. In the 1980s, Apple called its headquarters the Robot Factory. "To understand the electronics industry is simple: every time someone says 'robot,' simply picture a woman of color," Hyman advises. One in five electronics companies used no automation at all, and the rest used very little. Seagate's disk drives were assembled by women in Singapore. Hewlett-Packard hired so many temporary workers that it started its own temp agency. The most important technology in the electronics industry, as Hyman points out, was the fingernail.

In the 1980s, the sociologist Patricia Fernandez-Kelly conducted a study of the electronics and garment industries in Southern California. More than 70 percent of the labor force was women of color, and more than 70 percent of those women were Hispanic. In San Diego, Fernandez-Kelly interviewed a woman she called Fermina Calero (a pseudonym, to protect her from deportation). Calero was born in Mexico. In 1980, when she was twenty-one, she began working in Tijuana, soldering filaments of metal for sixty-five cents an hour. In 1983, Calero crossed into the United States, illegally, to work at Kaypro, the maker of the Kaypro II, a personal computer that briefly rivaled the Apple II. In the 1960s and '70s, Andrew Kay, the company's founder, had hired management consultants to help him reimagine his labor force. In the '80s, when people speaking English responded to the company's newspaper Help Wanted ads, they were told that there were no openings; when people speaking Spanish called, they were invited to apply. By the time Calero started working for Kaypro, its workforce consisted of seven hundred people, nearly all undocumented Mexican immigrants. The company's general manager said, "They are reliable; they work hard; they don't make trouble." At Kaypro, Calero earned nearly five dollars an hour. When the Immigration and Naturalization Service raided the factory, she hid in a supply closet. She was not a robot.

IN 1984, THE YEAR THAT CALERO HID in a closet at Kaypro, computer scientists at the annual meeting of the American Association for Artificial Intelligence began warning about the coming of an "AI winter": artificial intelligence had been overhyped by a credulous press and overfunded by incautious investors, and, given these wild and wide-eyed expectations, it had underdelivered. The hype was about to die down, and the funding to dry up. The AI winter lasted for years.

Skeptics of the current robots-are-coming argument predict the arrival of another AI winter. "We have not moved a byte forward in understanding human intelligence," Zia Chishti wrote in the *Financial Times*. "We have much faster computers, thanks to Moore's law, but the underlying algorithms are mostly identical to those that powered machines 40 years ago." That goes back to the time of the Kaypro.

A lot has changed in those forty years, not least in the availability of enormous sets of data that artificial intelligences can use to study and learn. Still, the economist Robert J. Gordon is unconvinced that the robots are coming. In his 2016 book, *The Rise and Fall of American Growth*, he argued that a century of economic expansion that began in 1870—driven by developments like electricity, a public water supply, and the interstate highway system—ended in 1970, and that, since then, inventions have been merely incremental. The telephone was patented in 1876. It changed people's lives, and contributed to a huge rise in productivity. The cell phone, Gordon argues, just isn't that different from a telephone. In a 2016 essay, "Why Robots Will Not Decimate Human Jobs," Gordon points out that the uses to which smartphones get put are "not a part of the market economy that creates jobs and pays wages." Robots have altered manufacturing, he concedes, but he doesn't think that they've altered the economy, or that they're about to. "I play a game called 'find the robot,'" he writes. "In my daily strolls in and out of supermarkets, restaurants, doctor and dentist offices, my nearby hospital, offices in my own university, and the vast amount of employment involving elementary and secondary teachers, personal trainers, and old age caretakers, I have yet to find a robot."

STILL, EVEN IF THE HYPE about robots is mostly unwarranted, the worry about jobs is real. If the latest jobs numbers look good, the longer-term trends look bad, especially for Americans without a high school diploma, a population whose real wages have been falling for decades. In a downward compression of the labor market, these jobs have been taken not so much by robots as by college graduates: as much as 40 percent of college graduates work at jobs that do not require a college degree, Ellen Ruppel Shell reports, in *The Job: Work and Its Future in a Time of Radical Change.* Four out of every five children born in the United States in 1950 went on to earn more than their parents. For children born in 1980, that ratio had fallen to one in two. Lately, it's down to one in three. Estimates range from the cautious to the entirely hysterical, but one reasonable study predicts that, by 2050, one in four working-age American men will be unemployed, having been replaced by some form of automation. Most imminently threatened are the millions of people who work as drivers of cars and trucks, allegedly soon to be replaced by fleets of self-driving vehicles.

Economic inequality produces political instability and partisan death matches. Everyone worries about jobs, but people who worry about robots and people who worry about immigrants propose very different solutions. Either way, much writing in this field is, essentially, fantasy. In *The Globotics Upheaval*, Baldwin predicts that the march of the robots will have four stages: transformation, upheaval, backlash, and resolution. The resolution will involve what he calls "shelterism." Once white-collar workers realize that their jobs are on the line, too, they'll find ways to protect themselves by "sheltering" certain activities, things that only humans can do. He explains, "This will mean that our work lives will be filled with far more caring, sharing, understanding, creating, empathizing, innovating, and managing people who are actually in the same room. This is a logical inevitability—everything else will be done by globots." The catch is that, historically, caring for, sharing, understanding, and empathizing with people who are in the same room as you are has been the work of women, and is therefore either unpaid, and not recognized as work, or paid very badly. Childcare, elementary school teaching, nursing, geriatric care, and social work will not suddenly become high-paying, high-prestige professions simply because everything else is done by robots. If that were going to happen, it would already be happening, because we already know that these jobs require beings who are human. Instead, something darker is going on, mirrored in the feminizing of robots, from the male robots of the 1960s and '70s—Hal, R2-D2, C-3PO, and Mr. Robinson's robot on *Lost in Space*—to the fembots and sexbots of *Her* and *Ex Machina*, and, not least, the sexy and slavish Alexa. Female workers aren't being paid more for being human; instead, robots are selling better when they're female.

The economist Oren Cass, the author of *The Once and Future Worker: A Vision for the Renewal of Work in America*, much of which originally appeared in *National Review*, is fed up with the robot hysteria. "Technological innovation and automation have always been integral to our economic progress, and in a well-functioning labor market, they should produce gains for all types of workers," he insists. He has no patience with advocates of universal basic income, either. "We have reached a point where the rich think paying everyone else to go away represents compassionate thinking," he writes.

Like Hyman, Cass blames mid-twentieth-century economic thinkers for the current malaise, though he blames different thinkers. In the middle decades of the twentieth century, he argues, economic policymakers abandoned workers and the health of the labor market in favor of a commitment to overall economic growth, with redistribution as an adjustment and consumerism as its objective. That required quantifying prosperity, hence the GDP, a measure that Cass, along with other writers, finds to be disastrous, not least because it values consumers above producers. Cass sees universal basic income as the end-stage scenario of every other redistribution program, whose justification is that the poor will be fine without work as long as they can buy things. Here he mocks the advocates of the current economic arrangement, who are prone to note that the poor are not actually starving, "and so many people have iPhones!"

Reporters are suckers for the hype, Cass maintains, pointing out that after a 2017 study by the National Bureau of Economic Research suggested that, in the next hundred years, robots might eliminate as many manufacturing jobs as were lost in 2001 (presumably, a tolerable loss), the *Times* ran a story with the headline "Evidence That Robots Are Winning the Race for American Jobs," while the *Washington Post* titled its story "We're So Unprepared for the

Robot Apocalypse." Cass offers a careful criticism of the robots-are-stealing-our-jobs theory. He cites four of its errors. It overestimates twenty-first-century innovations and underestimates the innovations of earlier centuries. It miscalculates the pace of change. It assumes that automation will not create new sectors. (3D printing might replace a lot of manufacturing workers, but it could also create a lot of new small businesses.) And it fails to appreciate the complexity of many of the jobs it thinks robots can do. The 2013 Oxford study that kept Andrés Oppenheimer up at night Cass finds to be mostly silly. Its authors, Carl Frey and Michael Osborne, rated 702 occupations from least "computerizable" to most. Highly vulnerable are school bus drivers, and, while a self-driving school bus does not seem technically too far off, Cass points out, few parents can imagine putting their kids on a bus without a grownup to make sure they don't bash one another the whole way to school.

Cass's own policy proposals center, very reasonably, on the importance of work and family, but he fails to demonstrate how his proposals—lowering environmental regulations and establishing academic tracking in high schools—will achieve his objectives. And though *The Once and Future Worker* offers a rousing call for an honest reckoning with American economic policy, it also indulges in its own sleight of hand. "The story goes that 'automation' or the 'knowledge economy,' not bad public policy, is to blame," Cass writes. "Historically, economists and policy makers have led the effort to explain that technological innovation is good for workers throughout the economy, even as its 'creative destruction' causes dislocation for some. So why, suddenly, are they so eager to throw robots and programmers under the bus?" One answer might be that, given the current state of American political polarization, it's either throw the robots under the bus or throw the immigrants. Cass, not surprisingly, advocates restricting immigration.

DONALD TRUMP RAN FOR PRESIDENT on a promise to create twenty-five million new jobs in a decade. "My economic plan rejects the cynicism that says our labor force will keep declining, that our jobs will keep leaving, and that our economy can never grow as it did once before," he said in September 2016. Many economists mocked his plan, which included protecting American jobs by imposing tariffs on imports. The *Economist* announced a new political fault line, not between left and right but between open and closed: "Welcome immigrants or keep them out? Open up to foreign trade or protect domestic industries? Embrace cultural change, or resist it?" Barack Obama was an opener. Openers tend to talk about robots. "The next wave of economic dislocation won't come from overseas," Obama said in his Farewell Address, in January 2017, days before Trump's inauguration. "It will come from the relentless pace of automation that makes many good, middle-class jobs obsolete."

Trump is a closer. Closers tend to talk about immigrants. "We're going to fight for every last American job," he promised from the floor of a Boeing plant in South Carolina, weeks after taking office. "I don't want companies leaving our country," he said. "There will be a very substantial penalty to be paid when they fire their people and move to another country, make the products, and think that they are going to sell it back over what will soon be a very, very strong border." That June, Boeing laid off nearly two hundred employees from the South Carolina plant, as part of a 40 percent reduction in its production of 777s. Over the year 2017, the company laid off nearly six thousand workers.

Trump's administration mocked fears of a robot invasion. Closers usually do. "I'm not worried at all," Secretary of the Treasury Steve Mnuchin said two years ago. Nevertheless, some think tankers suggested that Trump's election was "secretly about automation." And a study published in 2018 in the *Oxford Review of Economic Policy*—whose lead author, Carl Frey, is the same guy who made the list of the 702 most computerizable jobs—argued that the robot caravan got Trump elected. Measuring the density of robots and comparing them with election returns, Frey and his colleagues found that "electoral districts that became more exposed to automation during the years running up to the election were more likely to vote for Trump." Indulging in a counterfactual, they suggest that a less steeply rising increase in exposure to robots would have tipped both Pennsylvania and Wisconsin toward voting for Hillary Clinton. According to this line of thinking, Twitter bots and fake Facebook news didn't elect Donald Trump, but robots really might have. Or maybe it was all the talk about the wall.

Heads, the robots are coming! Accept the inevitability of near-universal unemployment! Tails, the Mexicans are coming! Close the borders! So far, the only other choice, aside from helplessly watching the rise of extremism, is to mint a new coin. Heat a forge. Smelt a blank. Engrave two dies. Put your blank in between them. Strike the whole thing with a hammer. Anyone can do it.

—2019

THE WOMAN CARD

"*I*T MEANS FREEDOM FOR WOMEN TO VOTE AGAINST THE *party this donkey represents*" read the sign on a donkey named Woodrow who, wearing a bow, was paraded through Denver by the National Woman's Party during its campaign against the Democratic incumbent, President Wilson, in 1916. Twenty sixteen, the hundredth anniversary of the Woman's Party arrived, unnoticed, on June 5th. Two days later, Hillary Clinton became the first woman to claim the Presidential nomination of a major party: the Democratic Party.

If elected, Clinton will become the first female President in the nation's history. She will also join John Quincy Adams, James Monroe, Martin Van Buren, and James Buchanan as the only Presidents to have served both in the Senate and as Secretary of State. If she loses the election to Donald Trump, he will be the first man elected President who has never served the public either in government or in the military. Trump wants to make America great again; Clinton wants to make history. That history is less about the last glass ceiling than about a party realignment as important as the Nixon-era Southern Strategy, if less well known. Call it the Female Strategy.

For the past century, the edges of the parties have been defined by a debate about the political role and constitutional rights of women. This debate is usually reduced to cant, as if the battle between the parties were a battle between the sexes. Republicans and Democrats are "just like men and women," Trent Lott liked to say: Democrats might be from Venus, but the G.O.P. is "the party of Mars." Democrats have talked about a Republican "war on women"; Trump says, of Clinton, "The only card she has is the woman card." She polls better among women; he polls better among men. The immediacy and starkness of the contrast between the candidates obscures the historical realignment hinted at in their own biographies: she used to be a Republican and he used to be a Democrat. This election isn't a battle between the sexes. But it is a battle between the parties, each hoping to win the votes of women without losing the votes of men. It's also marked by the sweeping changes to American politics caused by women's entry into public life. Long before women could vote, they carried into the parties a political style they had perfected first as abolitionists and then as prohibitionists: the moral crusade. No election has been the same since.

FOR A VERY LONG TIME, the parties had no idea what to do with women. At the nation's founding, women made an argument for female citizenship based on their role as mothers: in a republic, the civic duty of women is to raise sons who will be virtuous citizens. Federalists doffed their top hats, and no more. In the eighteen-twenties and thirties, Jacksonian democracy involved a lot of brawls: women were not allowed. When the social reformer Fanny Wright spoke at a political meeting in 1836, she was called a "female man." Instead, women entered public affairs by way of an evangelical religious revival that emphasized their moral superiority, becoming temperance reformers and abolitionists: they wrote petitions. "The right of petitioning is the only political right that women have," Angelina Grimké pointed out in 1837.

The Whig Party was the first to make use of women in public, if ridiculously: in 1840, Tennessee women marched wearing sashes that read "Whig Husbands or None." Because neither the Whig nor the Democratic Party was able to address the question of slavery, a crop of new parties sprang up. Fuelled by antislavery arguments, and adopting the style of moral suasion favored by female reformers, these parties tended to be welcoming to women, and even to arguments for women's rights.

The Republican Party was born in 1854, in Ripon, Wisconsin, when fifty-four citizens founded a party to oppose the Kansas-Nebraska Act, which threatened to create two new slave states. Three of those citizens were women. Women wrote Republican campaign literature, and made speeches on behalf of the Party. Its first Presidential nominee, in 1856, was John Frémont, but more than one Republican observed that his wife, Jessie Benton Frémont, "would have been the better candidate." One of the Party's most popular and best-paid speakers was Anna Dickinson, who became the first woman to speak in the Hall of the House of Representatives.

The women's-rights movement was founded in 1848. "It started right here in New York, a place called Seneca Falls," Clinton said in her victory speech on June 7th, after effectively clinching the Democratic nomination. Advocates of women's rights were closely aligned with the Republican Party, and typically fought to end slavery and to earn for both black men and all women political equality with white men. In 1859, Elizabeth Cady Stanton wrote to Susan B. Anthony, "When I pass the gate of the celestials and good Peter asks me where I wish to sit, I will say, 'Anywhere so that I am neither a negro nor a woman. Confer on me, great angel, the glory of White manhood, so that henceforth I may feel unlimited freedom.' "

After Lincoln signed the Emancipation Proclamation, Stanton and Anthony gathered four hundred thousand signatures on petitions demanding the Thirteenth Amendment. They then began fighting for the Fourteenth Amendment, which they expected to guarantee the rights and privileges of citizenship for all Americans. Instead, they were told that "this is the Negro's hour," and that the amendment would include the word "male," so as to specifically exclude women. "Do you believe the African race is composed entirely of males?" Stanton asked Wendell Phillips. And then she warned, "If that word 'male' be inserted, it will take us a century at least to get it out."

The insertion of the word "male" into the Fourteenth Amendment had consequences that have lasted well into this year's Presidential election. At the time, not everyone bought the argument that it was necessary to disenfranchise women in order to secure ratification. "Can any one tell us why the great advocates of Human Equality . . . forget that when they were a weak party and needed all the womanly strength of the nation to help them on, they always united the words 'without regard to sex, race, or color'?" one frustrated female supporter of the Republican Party asked. She could have found an answer in an observation made by Charles Sumner: "We know how the Negro will vote, but are not so sure of the women."

This election, many female voters, especially younger ones, resent being told that they should support Hillary Clinton just because she's a woman. It turns out that women don't form a political constituency any more than men do; like men, women tend to vote with their families and their communities. But, in 1865, how women would vote was impossible to know. Would black women vote the way black men voted? Would white women vote like black women? The parties, led by white men, decided they'd just as soon not find out.

Women tried to gain the right to vote by simply seizing it, a plan that was known as the New Departure. Beginning in 1868, black and white women went to the polls all over the country and got arrested. Sojourner Truth tried to vote in Battle Creek, Michigan. Five black women were arrested for voting in South Carolina in 1870, months before Victoria Woodhull became the first woman to run for President. She announced that women already had the right to vote, under the privileges-and-immunities clause of the Constitution, and, in 1871, she made this argument before the House Judiciary Committee. Anthony was arrested for voting in 1872—not for Woodhull but for the straight Republican ticket—and, in the end, the Supreme Court ruled against Woodhull's interpretation of the Constitution. Thus ended the New Departure.

Prevented from entering the electorate, women who wanted to influence public affairs were left to plead with men. For decades, these women had very little choice: whatever fight they fought, they had only the weapons of the nineteenth-century religious revival: the sermon, the appeal, the conversion, the crusade. The full measure of the influence of the female campaign on the American political style has yet to be taken. But that influence was felt first, and longest, in the Republican Party.

At the Republican nominating convention in 1872, the Party split into two, but neither faction added a suffrage plank to its platform. "We recognize the equality of all men before the law," the

Liberal Republicans declared, specifically discounting women. Stanton called the position taken by the regular Republicans—"the honest demand of any class of citizens for additional rights should be treated with respectful consideration"—not a plank but a splinter. Still, a splinter was more than suffragists ever got from the Democratic Party. In 1880, Anthony wrote a speech to deliver at the Democratic National Convention. It began, "To secure to twenty millions of women the rights of citizenship is to base your party on the eternal principles of justice." Instead, her statement was read by a male clerk, while Anthony looked on, furious, after which, as the *Times* reported, "No action whatever was taken in regard to it, and Miss Anthony vexed the Convention no more."

Close elections seemed to be good for the cause because, in a tight race, both parties courted suffragists' support, but women soon discovered that this was fruitless: if they allied with Republicans, Democrats campaigned against Republicans by campaigning against suffrage. This led to a certain fondness for third parties—the Equal Rights Party, the Prohibition Party, the Home Protection Party. J. Ellen Foster, an Iowa lawyer who had helped establish the Woman's Christian Temperance Union, spoke at a Republican rally and cautioned that a third party rewards women's support with nothing more than flattery: "It gives to women seats in conventions and places their names on meaningless committees and tickets impossible of success." In 1892, Foster founded the Women's National Republican Association, telling the delegates at the Party's Convention that year, "We are here to help you. And we have come to stay."

IN THE SECOND DECADE of the twentieth century, anticipating the ratification of the Nineteenth Amendment, the parties scrambled to secure the loyalty of voters who would double the size of the electorate, no less concerned than Sumner had been about how women would vote. "With a suddenness and force that have left observers gasping women have injected themselves into the national campaign this year in a manner never before dreamed of in American politics," the New York *Herald* reported in 1912. When Theodore Roosevelt founded the Progressive Party, it adopted a suffrage plank, and he aggressively courted women. He considered appointing Jane Addams to his cabinet. At the Progressive Party's Convention, Addams gave the second nominating speech. Then she grabbed a "Votes for Woman" flag and marched it across the platform and up and down the auditorium. Roosevelt had tried to win the Republican nomination by bribing black delegates, who were then shut out of the Progressive Party's Convention. When Addams got back to Chicago, she found a telegram from a black newspaper editor: "Woman suffrage will be stained with Negro Blood unless women refuse all alliance with Roosevelt."

Alice Paul, a feminist with a Ph.D. from the University of Pennsylvania who'd been arrested for fighting for suffrage in England, decided that American women ought to form their own party. "The name Woman's Party is open to a quite natural misunderstanding," Charlotte Perkins Gilman admitted, introducing the National Woman's Party in 1916. It wasn't a party, per se; it was a group of women whose strategy was to protest the existing parties, on the theory that no party could be trusted to advance the interests of women.

Terrified by the very idea of a party of women, the D.N.C. formed a "Women's Division" in 1917, the R.N.C. in 1918. The G.O.P. pursued a policy of "complete amalgamation," its chairman pledging "to check any tendency toward the formation of a separate women's party." White women worked for both parties; black women worked only for the G.O.P., to fight the Democratic Party, which had become the party of Southern whites. "The race is doomed unless Negro Women take an active part in local, state and national politics," the National League of Republican Colored Women said.

After 1920, Carrie Chapman Catt, the longtime head of the National American Woman Suffrage Association, turned it into the League of Women Voters, providing voter education and other aids to good government. Meanwhile, she told women to join the parties: "The only way to get things in this country is to find them on the inside of the political party." Inside those parties, women fought for equal representation. The Women's Division of the D.N.C.

implemented a rule mandating an equal number of male and female delegates, in 1920. In 1923, the Republican National Committee introduced rule changes—billed as "seats for women"—that added bonus delegates for states that had voted Republican in the previous election. But the Democrats' fifty-fifty rule was observed only in the breach, and, as both Catherine E. Rymph and Melanie Gustafson have pointed out in their rich histories of women in the Republican Party, the real purpose of adding the new G.O.P. seats was to reduce the influence of black Southern delegates.

The League of Women Voters was nonpartisan, but the National Woman's Party remained antipartisan. It focussed on securing passage of an Equal Rights Amendment, drafted by Paul, who had lately earned a law degree, and first introduced into Congress in 1923. Yet, for all the work of the Woman's Party, the G.O.P. was the party of women or, rather, of white women, for most of the twentieth century. In the late nineteen-twenties and thirties, black men and women left the Republican Party, along with smaller numbers of white women, eventually forming a New Deal coalition of liberals, minorities, labor unionists, and, from the South, poor whites. F.D.R. appointed Molly Williams Dewson the director of the D.N.C.'s Women's Division, which grew to eighty thousand members.

In 1937, determined to counter the efforts of the lady known as "More Women" Dewson, the R.N.C. appointed Marion Martin its assistant chairman; during her tenure, she founded a national federation of women's clubs whose membership grew to four hundred thousand. Martin, thirty-seven and unmarried, had a degree in economics and had served a combined four terms in the Maine legislature. She led a moral crusade against the New Deal. In 1940, she also got the R.N.C. to pass its own fifty-fifty rule and to endorse the Equal Rights Amendment, formally, in its platform. This went only so far. In 1946, Martin argued that party women needed more power. "We need it not because we are feminists but because there are a great many non-partisan women's organizations that do wield an influence in this country," she said. Five days later, she was forced to resign.

Hillary Rodham was born in Chicago in 1947. In 1960, when Richard Nixon ran against J.F.K., she checked voter lists for the G.O.P. By then, the majority of Republican Party workers were female. During the Cold War, the G.O.P. boasted about "the women who work on the home front, ringing the doorbells, filling out registration cards, and generally doing the housework of government." As the historian Paula Baker has pointed out, party work is just like other forms of labor; women work harder, are paid less, are rarely promoted, and tend to enter a field when men begin to view it as demeaning. The elephant was the right symbol for the Party, one senator said, because it has "a vacuum cleaner in front and a rug beater behind."

Betty Farrington, one of Martin's successors, turned the women's federation into a powerhouse of zealous crusaders. After Truman defeated Dewey, in 1948, Farrington wanted the G.O.P. to find its strongman:

How thankful we would have been if a leader had appeared to show us the path to the promised land of our hope. The world needs such a man today. He is certain to come sooner or later. But we cannot sit idly by in the hope of his coming. Besides his advent depends partly on us. The mere fact that a leader is needed does not guarantee his appearance. People must be ready for him, and we, as Republican women, in our clubs, prepare for him.

That man, many Republican voters today appear to believe, is Donald J. Trump, born in New York in 1946.

POLITICAL PARTIES MARRY INTERESTS to constituencies. They are not defined by whether they attract women, particularly. Nor are they defined by their positions on equal rights for women and men. But no plausible history of American politics can ignore, first, the influence of a political style perfected, over a century, by citizens who, denied the franchise, were forced to plead, and, second, the effects of the doubling of the size of the electorate.

The Republican Party that is expected to nominate Trump was built by housewives and transformed by their political style, which men then made their own. The moral crusade can be found among

nineteenth-century Democrats—William Jennings Bryan, say—
but in the twentieth century it became the hallmark of the conservative wing of the Republican Party; it is the style, for instance,
of Ted Cruz. This began in 1950, when the Republican Wom-
en's Club of Ohio County, West Virginia, invited as its principal
speaker for Lincoln Day Senator Joseph McCarthy. It was during
this speech that McCarthy said he had a list of subversives working at the State Department. "The great difference between our
Western Christian world and the atheistic Communist world is not
political—it is moral," McCarthy said. His rhetoric was that of the
nineteenth-century women's crusade. The great crusader Barry
Goldwater said in 1955, "If it were not for the National Federation
of Republican Women, there would not be a Republican Party."
That year, Republican women established Kitchen Cabinets,
appointing a female equivalent to every member of Eisenhower's
cabinet; their job was to share "political recipes on G.O.P. accomplishments with the housewives of the nation," by sending monthly
bulletins on "What's Cooking in Washington." One member of
the Kitchen Cabinet was Phyllis Schlafly.

In 1963, Schlafly nominated Goldwater to speak at a celebration
marking the twenty-fifth anniversary of the National Federation of
Republican Women. In a straw poll taken after Goldwater delivered
his speech, 262 out of 293 Federation delegates chose him. Meanwhile, Margaret Chase Smith was drafted into the race, a liberal alternative. As the historian Ellen Fitzpatrick recounts in a terrific new
book, "The Highest Glass Ceiling," Smith was the first woman elected
on her own to the Senate and the first woman to serve in both houses
of Congress. Asked why she agreed to run against Goldwater, she once
said, "There was nowhere to go but the Presidency." She was the first
and boldest member of the Senate to oppose McCarthy, in a speech she
made from the floor, known as the Declaration of Conscience: "I don't
want to see the Republican Party ride to political victory on the Four
Horsemen of Calumny—Fear, Ignorance, Bigotry, and Smear." At the
Convention in 1964, she refused to endorse Goldwater, and denied
him her delegates.

Young Trump had little interest in politics. He liked the movies. In 1964, he graduated from military school, where he'd been known as a ladies' man, and thought about going to the University of Southern California, to study film. Hillary Rodham was a "Goldwater Girl." But Smith was her hero. She decided to run for president of her high-school class, against a field of boys, and lost, "which did not surprise me," she wrote in her memoir, "but still hurt, especially because one of my opponents told me I was 'really stupid if I thought a girl could be elected president.' "

It's right about here that the G.O.P. began to lose Hillary Rodham. In 1965, as a freshman at Wellesley, she was president of the Young Republicans; she brought with her to college Goldwater's "The Conscience of a Conservative." But Goldwater's defeat led to a struggle for the future of the Party, and that struggle turned on Schlafly. In 1966, Elly Peterson, a Michigan state party chairman and supporter of George Romney, tried to keep Schlafly from becoming the president of the National Federation. "The nut fringe is beautifully organized," Peterson complained. At a three-thousand-woman Federation convention in 1967, Schlafly was narrowly defeated. Three months later, she launched her monthly newsletter. Rejecting the nascent women's-liberation movement, she nevertheless blamed sexism for the G.O.P.'s failure to fully embrace its most strenuous conservatives:

The Republican Party is carried on the shoulders of the women who do the work in the precincts, ringing doorbells, distributing literature, and doing all the tiresome, repetitious campaign tasks. Many men in the Party frankly want to keep the women doing the menial work, while the selection of candidates and the policy decisions are taken care of by the men in the smoke-filled rooms.

In the summer of 1968, Trump graduated from Wharton, where, he later said, he spent most of his time reading the listings of foreclosures on federally financed housing projects. That September, in Atlantic City, feminists staged a protest at the Miss America pageant, the sort of pageant that Trump would one day buy, run, and cherish. They carried signs reading "Welcome to the Cattle Auction."

Rodham, a twenty-year-old Capitol Hill intern, attended the Republican National Convention in Miami as a supporter of the anti-war candidate, Nelson Rockefeller. For the first time since 1940, the G.O.P. dropped from its platform its endorsement of equal rights. Rodham went home to see her family, and, hiding the fact from her parents, drove downtown to watch the riots outside the Democratic National Convention. One month too young to vote, she'd supported the antiwar Democrat, Eugene McCarthy, before the Convention, but later said she would probably have voted for the Party's nominee, Hubert Humphrey.

In 1969, Rodham, senior class president at Wellesley, became the first student invited to deliver a commencement address, a speech that was featured in *Life*. In 1970, a leader of her generation, a student at Yale Law School, and wearing a black armband mourning the students killed at Kent State, she spoke about her opposition to the Vietnam War at a convention of the League of Women Voters, on the occasion of its fiftieth anniversary. She had become a feminist, and a Democrat.

WHAT FOLLOWED IS MORE FAMILIAR. Between 1964 and 1980, Schlafly's arm of the Party steadily gained control of the G.O.P., which began courting evangelical Christians, including white male Southern Democrats alienated by their party's civil-rights agenda. In the wake of Roe v. Wade, and especially after the end of the Cold War, the Republican Party's new crusaders turned their attention from Communism to abortion. The Democratic Party became the party of women, partly by default. For a long time, it could have gone another way.

In 1971, Hillary Rodham met Bill Clinton, Donald Trump took over the family business, and Gloria Steinem, Tanya Melich, Bella Abzug, and Shirley Chisholm helped found the National Women's Political Caucus, which, like the National Woman's Party, sought to force both parties to better represent women and to gain passage of the Equal Rights Amendment. At the 1972 G.O.P. Convention, in Miami, Republican feminists demanded that the Party restore its

E.R.A. plan to the platform. They won, but at a cost. After the Convention, Schlafly founded *STOP ERA.*

The Democratic Party, meanwhile, was forging a new coalition. "A new hat, or rather a bonnet, was tossed into the Democratic Presidential race today," Walter Cronkite said on CBS News, when Chisholm, the first black woman to be elected to Congress, announced her bid. She went all the way to the Convention. Chisholm said, "You can go to that Convention and you can yell, 'Woman power! Here I come!' You can yell, 'Black power! Here I come!' The only thing those hard-nosed boys are going to understand at that Convention: 'How many delegates you got?' " She got a hundred and fifty-two.

By 1973, Trump was making donations to the Democratic Party. "The simple fact is that contributing money to politicians is very standard and accepted for a New York City developer," he explains in "The Art of the Deal." He also appeared, for the first time, in a story in the *Times,* with the headline *"Major Landlord Accused of Antiblack Bias in City."* The Department of Justice had charged Trump and his father with violating the 1968 Fair Housing Act. "We never have discriminated," Trump told the *Times,* "and we never would."

In 1974, Rodham moved to Washington, D.C., where she worked for the special counsel preparing for the possible impeachment of Richard Nixon. The next year, she married Bill Clinton, though she didn't take his name. The G.O.P., weakened by Watergate, and thinking to stanch the flow of departing women, elected as party chair Mary Louise Smith, an ardent feminist. In 1975, some thirty G.O.P. feminists formed the Republican Women's Task Force to support the E.R.A., reproductive rights, affirmative action, federally funded child care, and the extension of the Equal Pay Act.

The shift came in 1976. Rodham went to the Democratic Convention, at Madison Square Garden. Schlafly went to the Republican Convention, in Kansas City, where, as the political scientist Jo Freeman has argued, feminists won the battle but lost the war. For the nomination, Ford, a supporter of the E.R.A., defeated Reagan, an opponent, but the platform committee defeated the E.R.A. by a single vote.

In 1980, Republican feminists knew they'd lost when Reagan won the nomination; even so moderate a Republican as George Romney called supporters of the E.R.A. "moral perverts," and the platform committee urged a constitutional ban on abortion. Tanya Melich, a Republican feminist, began talking about a "Republican War against Women," a charge Democrats happily made their own. Mary Crisp, a longtime R.N.C. co-chair, was forced out, and declared of the party of Lincoln and of Anthony, "We are reversing our position and are about to bury the rights of over a hundred million American women under a heap of platitudes."

Buried they remain. Until 1980, during any Presidential election for which reliable data exist and in which there had been a gender gap, the gap had run one way: more women than men voted for the Republican candidate. That changed when Reagan became the G.O.P. nominee; more women than men supported Carter, by eight percentage points. Since then, the gender gap has never favored a G.O.P. Presidential candidate. The Democratic Party began billing itself as the party of women. By 1987, Trump had become a Republican.

In the Reagan era, Republican strategists believed that, in trading women for men, they'd got the better end of the deal. As the Republican consultant Susan Bryant pointed out, Democrats "do so badly among men that the fact that we don't do quite as well among women becomes irrelevant." And that's more or less where it lies.

With the end of the E.R.A., whose chance at ratification expired in 1982, both parties abandoned a political settlement necessary to the stability of the republic. The entrance of women into politics on terms that are, fundamentally and constitutionally, unequal to men's has produced a politics of interminable division, infused with misplaced and dreadful moralism. Republicans can't win women; when they win, they win without them, by winning with men. Democrats need to win both the black vote and the female vote. Trump and Clinton aren't likely to break that pattern. Trump, with his tent-revival meetings, is crusading not only against Clinton and against

Obama but against immigrants, against Muslims, and, in the end, against every group of voters that has fled the Republican Party, as he rides with his Four Horsemen: Fear, Ignorance, Bigotry, and Smear.

"This is a movement of the American people," Trump wrote in an e-mail to supporters. "And the American people *never* lose." It took a very long time, and required the work of the Republican Party, to change the meaning of "the American people" to include everyone. It hasn't taken very long at all for Trump to change it back. The next move is Clinton's, and her party's.

—2016

THE WAR AND THE ROSES

CLEVELAND

They perched on bar stools, their bodies long and lean, like eels, the women in sleeveless dresses the color of flowers or fruit (marigold, tangerine), the men in fitted suits the color of embers (charcoal, ash). Makeshift television studios lined the floor and the balcony of the convention hall: CNN, Fox, CBS, Univision, PBS. MSNBC built a pop-up studio on East Fourth Street, a square stage raised above the street, like an outdoor boxing ring. "Who won today? Who will win tomorrow?" the networks asked. The guests slumped against the ropes and sagged in their seats, or straightened their backs and slammed their fists. The hosts narrowed their eyes, the osprey to the fish: "Is America over?"

Americans had been assassinating one another, in schools and in churches, in cars and in garages, in bars, parks, and streets, insane with hate—hate whites, hate Blacks, hate Christians, hate Muslims, hate gays, hate police. A certain number of Americans, bearing arms, had lost their minds, their souls, the feel of the earth beneath their feet. Dread fell, and lingered, like mud after rain. At the 2016 Republican National Convention, in Cleveland, Ohio, gas masks were banned, body armor was allowed. "Write any or all emergency phone numbers somewhere on your body using a pen," a security memo urged reporters. "Best to write your name, too," came a whisper over a stall in a women's room, a Sharpie skittering along the tiled floor, as if it had traveled all the way from 1862, when twenty-one-year-old Oliver Wendell Holmes Jr., wounded at Antietam and afraid he was about to die, scratched a note and pinned it to his uniform, Union blue: "I am Capt. O. W. Holmes," hoping his body would find its way home.

"Has America ever before been so divided?" the television hosts asked their guests on street-side sets, while the American people, walking by, stopped, watched, and listened, a tilt of the head, a frown, a selfie. "Wash yourselves! Make yourselves clean!" evangelicals advised, by megaphone, placard, and pamphlet. "Judgment is coming!" T-shirts stating the significance of life came in black and blue or pink (for fetuses). Past the chain-link gate at the entrance to the Quicken Loans Arena, a line of delegates and reporters snaked across an empty parking lot and into security tents—conveyor belts, wands, please place your laptop in the bin—as if we were about to board an airplane, take off, and fly to another country, a terrible country, a land of war. "There are a lot of people who think the whole purpose of all this turmoil is to create martial law," Hal Wick, a delegate from South Dakota, told me, musing darkly on the shootings. Wick doesn't believe that the United States will last much longer if Hillary Clinton is elected. "If you do the research and the reading," he said, "you find out that, if you get to a point where more than half the people are on the dole, the country doesn't exist. It descends into anarchy." It won't take as long as four years. "I give it two or three," Wick said. "Tops."

A parking garage attached to the arena had been converted into a media production center, cubbies for radio and television and Snapchat and Twitter, like cabins on a ship, the floor a tangle of cables like the ropes on deck. Don King stood astride its bow, dressed like a Reagan-era Bruce Springsteen (faded jean jacket; swatches of red, white, and blue). He'd wanted to speak at the convention, but he'd been snubbed; this was his chance to testify. An audience of reporters and photographers flocked around him, seagulls to a mast. He drew himself up. He threw his head back. He roared, as if he were introducing a matchup: "Donald Trump is for *the people!*"

Every tyrant from Mao to Perón rules in the name of the people; his claim does not lessen their suffering. Every leader of every democracy rules in the name of the people, too, but their suffering, if they suffer, leads to his downfall, by way of their votes (which used to be called their "voices"). Still, "the voice of the People" is a figure of speech. "Government requires make-believe," the historian

Edmund S. Morgan once gently explained. "Make believe that the king is divine, make believe that he can do no wrong or make believe that the voice of the people is the voice of God. Make believe that the people *have* a voice or make believe that the representatives of the people *are* the people."

Cast back to a time long past. In the thirteenth century, the king of England summoned noblemen to court and demanded that they pledge to obey his laws and pay his taxes, and this they did. But then they, along with other men, sent by counties and towns, began pretending that they weren't making these pledges for themselves alone but that they represented the interests of other people, that they parleyed, that they *spoke* for them; in 1377, they elected their first "Speaker." In the 1640s, many of those men, a Parliament, wished to challenge the king, who claimed that he was divine and that his sovereignty came from God. No one really believed that; they only pretended to believe it. To counter that claim, men in Parliament began to argue that they represented the People, that the People were sovereign, and that the People had granted them authority to represent them, in some time immemorial. Royalists pointed out that this was absurd. How can "the People" rule when "they which are the people this minute, are not the people the next minute"? Who even are they? Also, when, exactly, did they grant Parliament their authority?

In 1647, the Levellers, hoping to remedy this small defect, drafted An Agreement of the People, with the idea that every freeman would assent to it, granting to his representatives the power to represent him. That never quite came to pass, but when, between 1649 and 1660, England had no king, and became a commonwealth, it got a little easier to pretend that there existed such a thing as the People, and that they were the sovereign rulers of . . . themselves. This seed, planted in American soil, under an American sun, sprouted and flourished, fields of wheat, milled to grain, the daily bread. ("The fiction that replaced the divine right of kings is our fiction," Morgan wrote, "and it accordingly seems less fictional to us.") When Parliament then said, "We, the People, have decided to tax you," the colonists, meeting in their own assemblies, answered, "No, *we're* the People." By 1776, what began as make-believe had become self-evident; by 1787, it had become the American creed.

We the people are, apparently, grievously vexed. Around the corner from Don King, NBC News was running a promotional stunt called Election Confessions ("Tell us what you really think"), asking passersby to write on colored sticky notes and shove them in a ballot box; the confessions were displayed, anonymously, on a wall monitor. Blue: "I can't believe it got this far." Orange: "I get to vote for the first time, and now I don't want to." Green: "THESE ARE OUR CHOICES?" I wandered down an aisle and sat next to Johnny Shull, a delegate from North Carolina who used to teach economics at the Charles Koch Institute and helps run a conservative talk-radio hour, *The Chad Adams Show*. Sitting beside him was Susan Phillips, a warm and friendly woman who was a guest that day on the show. I told Shull what Wick had said, about the end of America. "That's silly," he said. Shull had originally supported Rand Paul and was now a Trump delegate. He thinks America is resilient and will bounce back, no matter who wins. Phillips agrees with Wick. She loves Trump because he says all the things she wants to say and can't; because he speaks her thoughts about the half of America that's living off the other half, and about the coming lawlessness. (Mitt Romney's "47 percent," which is the same figure that the Nixon campaign complained about in 1972, has very lately risen, in the populist imagination, to 49 percent.) I asked Phillips what happens if Trump loses. She said, "Then we've got to build our compounds, get our guns ready, and prepare for the worst." Half of the people believe that they know how the other half lives, and deem them enemies.

WE THE PEOPLE WELCOME YOU TO CLEVELAND, banners declared, hanging from street lamps along the road to the city's Public Square, a granite-and-steel plaza with fountains and patches of grass, trough and pasture. Parts of Ohio used to belong to Connecticut, and the New Englanders who settled Cleveland, in the eighteenth century, set aside land for a commons, a place for grazing sheep and cattle and for arguing about politics: the public square, the people's park.

"God hates America!" a wiry man was shouting from the sound-stage. "America is doomed!" Most of the protesters came in ones and twos. Oskar Mosco, who told me that he was a pedicab driver from California, carried a poster board on which he'd written, WHY VOTE? He said, "Democracy, lately, is just a fiction." *Make believe the people rule.* I sat down on a step next to Amy Thie, a twenty-two-year-old student at the University of Cincinnati. She'd made a T-shirt that read, "I know shirts. I make the best shirts. Mexico will pay for them. It's terrific. Everyone agrees I have baby hands," to which she'd affixed a pair of pink plastic doll hands, one clutching a miniature American flag. "Some people really hate Trump," she said. "I don't hate him. I think he's bringing to light aspects of our society that need to come to light." She's worried about the world, but she's not that worried about Trump. "People are too reasonable for this movement to win."

Thie's faith in the people is a faith in the future. It dates to the era of Andrew Jackson, when the idea of the people got hitched to the idea of progress, especially technological progress—the steam engine, the railroad, the telegraph. Ralph Waldo Emerson, awed by the force of American ideas, American people, and American machines, called the United States "the country of the future." If the people can be trusted to be reasonable, all things are possible, the historian George Bancroft argued, in an 1835 speech called "The Office of the People." Bancroft was writing at a time when poor men were newly enfranchised, and a lot of his friends thought that these men were too stupid to vote. Bancroft offered reassurance. If you lock a man in a dark dungeon for his whole life and finally let him out, he may be blinded by the light, but that doesn't mean he lacks the faculty of sight; one day, he will see. Let him add his voice:

> Wherever you see men clustering together to form a party, you may
> be sure that however much error may be there truth is there also.
> Apply this principle boldly, for it contains a lesson of candor and a

voice of encouragement. There never was a school of philosophy nor a clan in the realm of opinion but carried along with it some important truth. And therefore every sect that has ever flourished has benefited Humanity, for the errors of a sect pass away and are forgotten; its truths are received into the common inheritance.

The voice of the People became a roar and a rumpus. Year after year, the People convened, to write and revise and ratify state constitutions, to vote on party rules and platforms, to pick candidates. The men who drafted the Constitution had been terrified of an unchecked majority; events in France had hardly quieted their concerns. John Adams and James Madison, old men, hobbled into constitutional conventions in Massachusetts and Virginia, where they sat, stiffly, and endured the declamations of long-whiskered shavers and strivers, the lovers of the People. Americans had grown convention-mad. In 1831, they even began nominating candidates for the presidency in convention halls. The People must exist: they climbed the rafters.

By the time I got to my seat in the Quicken Loans Arena, the chairman of the Republican National Committee, Reince Priebus, was ordering delegates to file out, sending them off to this committee meeting or that: Rules, Platform, Credentials. When he stepped down from the podium, the jumbo teleprompter that he'd been reading from flickered, went black, and then turned back on. I stared, wide-eyed. "They put that up there whenever the stage is empty," a reporter from *The Nation* told me, helpfully. Up there, in LED, was the Gettysburg Address. *Four score and seven years ago our fathers brought forth on this continent, a new nation, conceived in liberty, and dedicated to the proposition that all men are created equal. Now we are engaged in a great civil war, testing whether that nation, or any nation so conceived and so dedicated, can long endure.*

Lincoln stopped in Cleveland in 1861, on the way to his inauguration as the first Republican president. Down on the convention floor, George Engelbach, a delegate from Missouri, was dressed as Lincoln: top hat and suit, whiskers. I asked him why he admired Lincoln. "If it were not for him, we would have a divided country," he said. Engelbach has been a Trump supporter from the start, because "Trump's the only one who can put it back together again." That night, the speakers at the convention talked about dead bodies: the bodies of Americans killed by undocumented immigrants, of Americans killed by terrorists in Benghazi, of Americans killed by men who supported Black Lives Matter. A grieving mother blamed Hillary Clinton for her son's death. Soldiers described the corpses of their fallen comrades. "I pulled his body armor off and checked for vitals," one said. "There were no signs of torture or mutilation," another said. *We have come to dedicate a portion of that field, as a final resting place for those who here gave their lives that that nation might live.* But this wasn't Gettysburg. This battle isn't over. "Our own city streets have become the battleground," the Homeland Security Committee chair, Mike McCaul, said. The Milwaukee County sheriff, David A. Clarke Jr., said, "I call it anarchy."

The next day, in Public Square, Vets vs. Hate took the stage. "Please stop using our veterans as props," Alexander McCoy, an ex-marine, begged the Trump-Pence campaign. I went to see a ten-foot-tall American bald eagle, made entirely out of red-white-and-blue Duck Brand duct tape, on display in a parking lot. (Hope is, always, the thing with feathers.) Then I got a ride out to the Cleveland History Center, where Lauren R. Welch gave me a tour of a collection of memorabilia from earlier GOP conventions, the buttons and the bunting. Welch, twenty-eight and African American, has lived in Cleveland nearly all her life. She's an activist, a supporter of Black Lives Matter. I asked whether either of the two major presidential candidates could bring about a better future. "Even Obama couldn't bring people together," she said, searchingly. No, she said. "Hope comes from the people."

After the Civil War, the idea of the People and the idea of progress got uncoupled, an engine careering away from its train. This was the work of the late nineteenth-century People's Party, a left-wing movement of farmers and workers who found out the hard way that progress sometimes mows men down; they wanted to use democracy to limit certain kinds of technological progress, for the sake of equality. Historians have tended to consider Populism muddleheaded: America looked forward, Populists looked backward. "The utopia of the Populists was in the past, not the future," Richard Hofstadter wrote, disapprovingly. Many historians have said the same thing about conservatism, especially the Trump variety, whose followers, like their leftier, Populist forebears, have found out the hard way that progress mows some men down. I talked to Jimmy Sengenberger, a young conservative who thinks a lot about this question. "Looking back at the founding principles of this country is the best way to look forward," he told me. Sengenberger, twenty-five, was an alternate delegate from Colorado. He's polite and ambitious, a Jimmy Olsen look-alike. He works in a law office during the week and hosts a talk-radio show on Saturday nights. "Progressivism is regressive," he said. "Conservatism is the only truly forward-looking political philosophy."

Newt Gingrich is a historian, so on the third day of the convention, before he was due to speak, I figured I'd ask him whether he was worried that the right had ceded all talk of progress to the left. "No. Listen to my speech," he told me. "I'm going to talk about safety." When I suggested that making America safe again isn't exactly forward-looking, he assured me that he was going to talk about the future. Back inside the convention hall, after yet another speech by yet another made-for-television Trump child, Ted Cruz was doing a mic check, not by reading the Gettysburg Address from the teleprompter, as others did, but by reciting Dr. Seuss: "I do not like green eggs and ham, I do not like them, Sam-I-am"; ode to an ornery man. That night, Cruz was booed off the stage. Gingrich, who followed him, did talk about the future: he warned of a coming apocalypse.

ON THE LAST DAY of the GOP convention, I went back to Public Square. They came and they came, the protesters, one by one, and two by two. A mother of nine named Samia Assed wandered by. She owns two New York–style delis in Santa Fe. Her family is originally from Palestine. She had driven to Cleveland in a caravan organized by the Grassroots Global Justice Alliance. I asked her if she thought that either Trump or Clinton could bridge the divide. She looked at me as if I were nuts. "They *are* the divide," she said. Erika Husby, another protester, had blond hair piled in a messy bun and was wearing a poncho painted to look like a brick wall. It read WALL OFF TRUMP. She's twenty-four and from Chicago, where she teaches English as a second language. She liked Sanders but was willing to vote for Clinton. Black Lives Matter is "changing the country for the better," she said. Joshua Kaminski, twenty-eight, originally from Michigan, was wearing a Captain America T-shirt and a silver cross on a silver chain. He works for Delta Airlines. He and Oskar Mosco got to talking, each keen, each curious. "I've seen conservatism and Christianity separate," Kaminski told Mosco. "I'm not going to vote against my morals anymore." He's pretty sure he'll vote for Johnson-Weld. Meanwhile, he was giving out water bottles labeled ELECT JESUS.

The rule inside the convention was: Incite fear and division in order to call for safety and union. I decided that the rule outside the convention was: No kidding, it's really awfully nice out here, in a beautiful city park, on a sunny day in July, where a bunch of people are arguing about politics and nothing could possibly be more interesting, and the Elect Jesus people are giving out free water, icy cold, and the police are playing Ping-Pong with the protesters, and you can take a nap in the grass if you want, and you will dream that you are on a farm because the grass smells kind of horsy, and like manure, because of all the mounted police from Texas, wearing those strangely sexy cowboy hats; and, yes, there are police from all over the country here, and if you ask for directions one of them will say to you, "Girl, I'm from Atlanta!" and you have to know that, if they weren't here, who knows what would happen; there are horrible people shouting murderous things and tussling, that's what they came here for, and anything can blow up in an instant; and, yes, there are civilians carrying military-style weapons, but, weirdly, they are less scary here than they are online; they look ridiculous, honestly, and this one lefty guy is a particular creep, don't get cornered; but, also, there's a little Black girl in the fountain rolling around, getting soaked, next to some white guy who's sitting there, just sitting there, in the water, his legs kicked out in front of him, holding a cardboard sign that reads TIRED OF THE VIOLENCE.

I climbed up the steps of the park's Civil War Soldiers' and Sailors' Monument, not far from the spot where Lincoln's casket was put on display, in 1865, on his way home. It was as if he had pinned a note to his suit: *We here highly resolve that these dead shall not have died in vain—that this nation, under God, shall have a new birth of freedom, and that government of the people, by the people, for the people, shall not perish from the earth.*

I trudged back to the arena for the final night's speakers.

"No one has more faith in the American people than my father," Ivanka Trump said. She called him "the people's champion." She was wearing a sleeveless dress the color of a grapefruit, the pinkest of peonies.

Trump took the stage, in a suit as black as cinder. "The American people will come first again," he thundered.

"*I am your voice,*" he said. His face turned as red-hot as the last glowing ember of a fire, dying.

PHILADELPHIA

Welcome to the city of love. "What love, what care, what service, and what travail hath there been to bring thee forth," William Penn said, in 1684, praying for a tiny, frail settlement huddled along the banks of the Delaware River. "O that thou mayest be kept from the evil that would overwhelm thee." In the Wells Fargo Center, LOVE TRUMPS HATE signs fluttered on the floor of the convention hall like the pages of a manuscript scattered by a fierce wind. It was a book of antonyms: the future, not the past; love, not hate. "We are the party of tomorrow!" John Lewis hollered to the crowd. "What the world needs now is love," the Democrats sang, holding hands, leaning, listing. And still the signs fluttered and scattered, the book of antonyms ripped up by Sanders delegates, who tore at its pages and yanked at its

binding, its brittle glue. Anne Hamilton, a delegate from North Carolina, got out a marker and doctored her LOVE TRUMPS HATE sign to
read LOVE BERNIE OR TRUMP WINS. She was determined. "They said
they were going to replace me with an alternate," she told me. "And
I just kept repeating, 'Freedom of speech, freedom of speech!'" And
a future under Clinton or Trump? "It's like a windshield after a rock
hits it," she said. "The glass looks like a spider's web, and you can see
through it, but not really, and then, all at once, in a flash, it cracks,
and it shatters, and there's nothing left." Slivers of glass and the rush
of an unshielded wind.

Philadelphia was to Cleveland the zig to its zag, the other half
of the zipper. The Democrats recycle. They provide compost bins.
They speak Spanish in the security lines. They serve kosher food.
They offer a "Gluten-Free Section." They have blue-curtained
breastfeeding and pumping areas. The Democrats run out of coffee.
They run out of seats. They run out of food. They run out of *water.*
They talk for too long; they run out of time. During breaks between
speakers, the Republicans played the Knack's "My Sharona" ("When
you gonna give me some time, Sharona / Ooh, you make my motor
run"); the Democrats played Prince's "Let's Go Crazy" ("Dearly
beloved / We are gathered here today / To get through this thing
called 'life'"). Try to get through a night at a Democratic convention, early in the week, with nothing more than M&M's and the
voice of the People to jolt you awake. It's like being at a sleepover and
trying to stay up until midnight for the candlelit séance, the conjuring of a spirit: *Speak, speak!*

Dearly beloved. "There is tension and dissension in the land,"
Cynthia Hale, of the Ray of Hope Christian Church, in Decatur,
Georgia, said, leading the invocation on the convention's first day.
And there was tension and dissension in the hall. "It's time that the
people took the power back," Rebecca Davies, a delegate from Illinois, told me. I asked her if she supported Clinton. "God, no!" she
said, mock-affronted. She was wearing a pointy hat, made of green
felt, with a red feather tucked in its brim. She'd got the hat at a gathering that morning, when Sanders tried to persuade his followers

to support Clinton, and they balked. People all over the arena were wearing Robin Hood hats, as if it were 1937 and Warner Bros. was holding auditions for an Errol Flynn film. Davies was cheerful, but she was disappointed; the People, spurned.

The proceedings began. But when Barney Frank got up to speak the crowd booed him. "Thank you, or not, as the case may be," Frank said, grimly. Frank, no fan of Bernie Sanders, co-chaired the Rules Committee, whose decisions Sanders supporters had protested—a protest strengthened by the release, the day before, of hacked Democratic National Committee emails. (Hacked by Russia? Hack more! Trump taunted.) The People had been betrayed by the party, corrupted. "The DNC thinks it's better to keep people ignorant," Robyn Sumners told me, angry, astonished. She was a precinct inspector in California's District 29, where Sanders lost by a smidgen. She blames the press and the DNC. "They don't want people involved," she said. "They don't trust us. They're afraid of Bernie because you know what Bernie does? He wakes people up. I learned in this election: They don't want us to vote." Some Sanders people covered their mouths with blue tape, on which they'd written SILENCED. The People, muffled, stifled, muzzled, unloved.

Carl Davis, a delegate from Texas, works in the mayor's office in Houston. He's African American and a long-standing Clinton supporter. He was a Clinton delegate in 2008, too. "The Democratic Party brings hope to this nation," he told me. "We, we are the ones looking out for the people of this country." Not Trump, not Trump, not Trump. "My name isn't Sucker Boone," Emily Boone, a Kentucky delegate, snapped, when I asked her what she thought of the Republican nominee. When Democrats on the floor talked about Trump, wincing, shuddering, they tended to talk about a political apocalypse possibly even darker than the one conjured by Trump supporters when they imagined a Clinton presidency: fascism, the launch codes, the end of days.

"Donald Trump knows that the American people are angry—a fact so obvious he can see it from the top of Trump Tower," Elizabeth Warren said from the lectern, undertaking the sober, measured work of arguing that Trump did not speak for the American people, that he had misjudged if he thought that he could make the American people angry with one another. "I've got news for Donald Trump," Warren said. "The American people are not falling for it!"

The People are easy to invoke but impossible to curb. A spirit can't be bottled. "If you look at our platform, all the way through it talks about trying to lift people up, people who have been left behind," Chris McCurry told me. This was McCurry's first convention. He was a delegate from South Carolina, where he works as an IT guy in the state's Department of Transportation. He was wearing a hat decorated with red-white-and-blue tinsel and a vest pinned with eleven Hillary buttons. "She's spent her whole life trying to lift up women and children, and when we do that we lift up the nation, when you do that you get gay rights, you fight racism," he said. "You *always* progress."

The Democratic Party's argument is that it is the only party that contains multitudes. What happens when the people are sovereign? "The dangerous term, as it turned out, was not sovereignty," as the historian Daniel T. Rogers once put it. "It was the People." When white men said, "We are the People and therefore we rule," how were they to deny anyone else the right to rule, except by denying their very peoplehood? "We, too, are people!" shouted women, Blacks, immigrants, the poorest of the poor. And, lo, the People did say, "No, you are not people!" That worked for only so long. And, when it failed, the People passed new immigration and citizenship laws, and restricted voting rights, and made corporations honorary people, to give themselves more power. And, lo, a lot of Americans got to worrying about what viciousness, what greed, and what recklessness the People were capable of. These people called themselves Progressives.

In the early decades of the twentieth century, the left lost its faith in the People but kept its faith in progress. Progressives figured that experts, with the light of their science, ought to guide the government in developing the best solutions to political and economic problems. In the 1940s, populism began to move from the left to the right, not sneakily or stealthily but in the shadows all the same, unnoticed, ignored, demeaned. In Christopher Lasch's grumpiest book, *The True and Only Heaven*, from 1991, he argued that a big problem with postwar liberalism was liberals' failure to really listen to the continuing populist criticism of the idea of progress. "Their confidence in being on the winning side of history made progressive people unbearably smug and superior," Lasch wrote, "but they felt isolated and beleaguered in their own country, since it was so much less progressive than they were." That went on for decades.

In 1992, the year Bill Clinton was elected, a letter to the editor appeared in a small newspaper in upstate New York. "The American Dream of the middle class has all but disappeared, substituted with people struggling just to buy next week's groceries," the letter writer argued. "What is it going to take to open up the eyes of our elected officials? AMERICA IS IN SERIOUS DECLINE." It was written by a young Timothy McVeigh.

And still, after Oklahoma City, and Waco, and the militia movement, all through the 1990s, progressive politicians and intellectuals continued to ignore the right-wing narrative of decline, even as it became the hallmark of conservative talk radio. And they ignored Sanders's warnings about decline, too, when he talked about the growing economic divide, the widening gap between the rich and the poor, and the stranglehold of corporate interests over politics. "There is a war going on in this country," Sanders said, in an eight-and-a-half-hour speech from the floor of the Senate, in 2010. "I am talking about a war being waged by some of the wealthiest and most powerful people against working families, against the disappearing and shrinking middle class of our country." He spoke alone. Progressives and liberals talked about growth, prosperity, globalization, innovation.

Dearly beloved. "Don't let anyone ever tell you that this country isn't great," Michelle Obama said, in an uplifting speech on the first night of the Democratic convention. But then Sanders got up and said it: "This election is about ending the forty-year decline of our middle class, the reality that forty-seven million men, women, and children live in poverty." A sea of blue signs waved at him, as if in rebuke: A FUTURE TO **BELIEVE IN**. Sanders, and only Sanders, talked that way about decline and suffering. Meanwhile, outside, a sudden summer storm battered the city, the rain falling like dread.

FUTURE IS BRIGHT was stamped in white on hot-pink sunglasses that Planned Parenthood gave out to volunteers. Cecile Richards, the head of the Planned Parenthood Action Fund, sat next to Bill Clinton the night Michelle Obama addressed the convention. "Look, it was amazing to be there," Richards said, when I talked to her the next morning. "The passing of the torch, from one incredible woman to another incredible woman." Richards thinks that the Republicans are fighting a kind of progress they can't stop. "If I were trying to lead a party that believed in rolling back LGBTQ rights and women's rights, and denying climate change, that would be a very tough agenda to sell to young people in this country," she said. Downtown, a dozen volunteers wearing pink pinnies gathered in front of a Planned Parenthood clinic on Locust Street to help escort women into the clinic, intending to steer them clear of pro-life protesters, who never turned up. The idea that love conquers all entered American political rhetoric by way of the gay rights and the same-sex-marriage movements, in which activists, following the model of the civil rights and the reproductive rights movements, largely bypassed the People and took their case, instead, to the Supreme Court. A few blocks down Locust Street, hundreds of people had gathered for the Great Wall of Love, a rally for unity in front of the Mazzoni Center, an LGBTQ clinic. They sang "Seasons of Love," from *Rent*. They waved white placards that read, in rainbow-colored letters, LOVE WINS.

That night, Sanders, seated with the delegation from Vermont, called for Clinton's nomination by acclamation. The People shouted, but not with one voice. Hundreds of Sanders delegates and supporters rose from their seats and walked out. "We will not yield," Alyssa DeRonne, a delegate from Asheville, North Carolina, said. "I want to see my children philosophizing and inventing new things, not blowing up another country." Anne Hamilton walked out, too. So did Sanders delegates from Hawaii. Carolyn Golojuch, a seventy-year-old Clinton delegate from Honolulu, was disgusted by the walkout. "I have stood on the streets by the state capitol for eighteen years, working for same-sex-marriage rights, for my son, for everyone," she told me. "I have lost jobs. I have fought and I have fought. These Sanders people, they haven't learned how to compromise. And you know what? They don't own the word 'progressive.'" Golojuch's husband, Mike, was wearing a rainbow ALL YOU NEED IS LOVE button, but neither of them had any illusions that love always wins.

What wins? I asked Elizabeth Warren. "The last three or four years that I have been in the Senate, it's been like climbing a sheer rock wall," she said. "And all I do is try to find a finger hole or a toe hole, somewhere, somewhere." People are right to be angry, she said. They should be angry. They're not wrong that the system is rigged. "The rich and the powerful have all kinds of money and all kinds of weapons, to make the country, and the government, just the way they want it," she said. "And the rest of us? All we've got are our voices and our votes, and the only way those have any strength is if we use them together and aim them perfectly."

Two protests were happening by LOVE Park, across the street from city hall, in the shadow of a thirty-foot-tall sculpture called *Government of the People*: naked bodies smushed into the shape of a clenched fist. If you stood in the middle of the park, you could listen to both protests at the same time:

> "We, the people, can solve our ills, if we work together—"
> "—patriarchy is woven into the fabric—"
> "Yesterday we took some action—"
> "That is fucked up!"

At one end of the park, a very small audience listened to the Revolution Club; at the other end, by the main stage, hundreds of people, including a lot of Sanders delegates, had gathered for an Occupy DNC rally. They were young, and they were mad, and they were undaunted.

They wore Bernie masks and waved Bernie puppets. They chanted, "Hell no, DNC, we won't vote for Hillary." They were waiting for the Green Party's Jill Stein to come and speak. "Jill not Hill," they cried. A woman in a red-white-and-blue cowboy hat raised a sign to the sky: THIS IS NOT A RIOT. They wanted to boycott the Democratic Party. They wanted to ban the oligarchy. "I need that 'Power to the People' right now!" Bruce Carter, of Black Men for Bernie, called from the Occupy stage. "We ain't in no dance mode, we in a fighting mode," he said. "I don't want to dance right now. I want to be mad as hell." The music started. *Power to the people, power to the people, power to the people.* The people began to sway.

Something was slipping away, leaching out, like rainwater. The People had lost their footing, their common ground, muddied. Maybe it was a problem that the Levellers had never managed to get everyone in seventeenth-century England to sign on to that Agreement of the People, because the people I talked to in Cleveland and Philadelphia didn't quite seem to believe in representation anymore. Either they were willing to have Trump speak in their stead ("*I am your voice*"), the very definition of a dictator, or else they wanted to speak for themselves, because the system was rigged, because the establishment could not be trusted, or because no one, no one, could understand them, their true, particular, Instagram selves. They hated and were hated; they wanted to love and be loved. They could see, even through a broken windshield, that the future wasn't all dark and it wasn't all bright; it was as streaked as a sky at twilight.

"Let love rule," Lenny Kravitz sang, a choir behind him, the night before the Democratic convention ended. "We are not a fragile people," President Obama insisted, in a beautiful speech as boundless in its optimism as Trump's was in its pessimism. And, when he has faltered, Obama said, something, someone, an idea, had always picked him up. "It's been you," he said. "The American people."

The next morning, Trump's campaign instructed his supporters not to watch Clinton's speech and, instead, to send money, heaps of it, promising that Hillary would hear the amount by 8:00 p.m., so that "before she steps on stage, she'll have stuck in the back of her mind exactly what's coming for her this November: THE AMERICAN PEOPLE!"

That night, the Democrats told a love story. "We are reviving the heart of our democracy," said the Reverend William Barber II, a North Carolina minister, while the people climbed to the rafters. "We must shock this nation with the power of love."

Ivanka Trump had introduced her father; Chelsea Clinton introduced her mother. Daughters are the new political wives. Chelsea wore a red dress with a heart-shaped neckline. She introduced the presidential nominee as a grandmother. "I hope that my children will someday be as proud of me as I am of my mom," she said. Mother love is the corsage pinned to every dress, right or left. "I'm a mom!" said everyone who was one, at both conventions, from Laura Ingraham to Kirsten Gillibrand. "We all hope for a better tomorrow," Morgan Freeman intoned, in his voice-over to a Clinton campaign film. "Every parent knows that your dream for the future beats in the heart of your child." And here, at last, was the resolution, shaky and cynical, of the argument between the people and progress. People + progress = children. In an age of atrocity, the unruliness of the people and a fear of the future have combined with terror, naked terror, to make the love of children an all-purpose proxy for each fraying bond, each abandoned civic obligation, the last, lingering devotion.

Hillary Clinton took the stage in a suit of paper-white. "I am so proud to be your mother," she said to her daughter, addressing the American people not as citizens but as objects of love. "I will carry all of your voices and stories with me to the White House," she promised, the words like lace. "We begin a new chapter tonight." The balloons fell.

And the nation clenched its teeth, the top and the bottom of a jaw, and waited for November.

—2016

IN EVERY DARK HOUR

T HE LAST TIME DEMOCRACY NEARLY DIED ALL OVER the world and almost all at once, Americans argued about it, and then they tried to fix it. "The future of democracy is topic number one in the animated discussion going on all over America," a contributor to the *New York Times* wrote in 1937. "In the Legislatures, over the radio, at the luncheon table, in the drawing rooms, at meetings of forums and in all kinds of groups of citizens everywhere, people are talking about the democratic way of life." People bickered and people hollered, and they also made rules. "You are a liar!" one guy shouted from the audience during a political debate heard on the radio by ten million Americans, from Missoula to Tallahassee. "Now, now, we don't allow that," the moderator said, calmly, and asked him to leave.

In the 1930s, you could count on the Yankees winning the World Series, dust storms plaguing the prairies, evangelicals preaching on the radio, Franklin Delano Roosevelt residing in the White House, people lining up for blocks to get scraps of food, and democracies dying, from the Andes to the Urals and the Alps.

In 1917, Woodrow Wilson's administration had promised that winning the Great War would "make the world safe for democracy." The peace carved nearly a dozen new states out of the former Russian, Ottoman, and Austrian Empires. The number of democracies in the world rose; the spread of liberal-democratic governance began to appear inevitable. But this was no more than a reverie. Infant democracies grew, toddled, wobbled, and fell: Hungary, Albania, Poland, Lithuania, Yugoslavia. In older states, too, the desperate masses turned to authoritarianism. Benito Mussolini marched on Rome in 1922. It had taken a century and a half for European monarchs who ruled by divine right and brute force to be replaced by constitutional democracies and the rule of law. Now fascism and communism toppled these governments in a matter of months, even before the stock market crash of 1929 and the misery that ensued.

"Epitaphs for democracy are the fashion of the day," the soon-to-be Supreme Court justice Felix Frankfurter wrote, dismally, in 1930. The *annus horribilis* that followed differed from every other year in the history of the world, according to the British historian Arnold Toynbee: "In 1931, men and women all over the world were seriously contemplating and frankly discussing the possibility that the Western system of Society might break down and cease to work." When Japan invaded Manchuria, the League of Nations condemned the annexation, to no avail. "The liberal state is destined to perish," Mussolini predicted in 1932. "All the political experiments of our day are anti-liberal." By 1933, the year Adolf Hitler came to power, the American political commentator Walter Lippmann was telling an audience of students at Berkeley that "the old relationships among the great masses of the people of the earth have disappeared." What next? More epitaphs: Greece, Romania, Estonia, and Latvia. Authoritarians multiplied in Portugal, Uruguay, Spain. Japan invaded Shanghai. Mussolini invaded Ethiopia. "The present century is the century of authority," he declared, "a century of the Right, a Fascist century."

American democracy, too, staggered, weakened by corruption, monopoly, apathy, inequality, political violence, hucksterism, racial injustice, unemployment, even starvation. "We do not distrust the future of essential democracy," FDR said in his first inaugural address, telling Americans that the only thing they had to fear was fear itself. But there *was* more to be afraid of, including Americans' own declining faith in self-government. "What Does Democracy Mean?" NBC radio asked listeners. "Do we Negroes believe in democracy?" W. E. B. Du Bois asked the readers of his newspaper column. Could it happen here? Sinclair Lewis asked in 1935. Americans suffered, and hungered, and wondered. The historian Charles Beard, in the inevitable essay on "The Future of Democracy in the

United States," predicted that American democracy would endure, if only because "there is in America, no Rome, no Berlin to march on." Some Americans turned to communism. Some turned to fascism. And a lot of people, worried about whether American democracy could survive past the end of the decade, strove to save it.

"It's not too late," Jimmy Stewart pleaded with Congress, rasping, exhausted, in *Mr. Smith Goes to Washington*, in 1939. "Great principles don't get lost once they come to light." It wasn't too late. It's still not too late.

THERE'S A KIND OF LIKENESS you see in family photographs, generation after generation. The same ears, the same funny nose. Sometimes now looks a lot like then. Still, it can be hard to tell whether the likeness is more than skin-deep.

In the 1990s, with the end of the Cold War, democracies grew more plentiful, much as they had after the end of the First World War. As ever, the infant mortality rate for democracies was high: baby democracies tend to die in their cradles. Starting in about 2005, the number of democracies around the world began to fall, as it had in the 1930s. Authoritarians rose to power: Vladimir Putin in Russia, Recep Tayyip Erdoğan in Turkey, Viktor Orbán in Hungary, Jarosław Kaczyński in Poland, Rodrigo Duterte in the Philippines, Jair Bolsonaro in Brazil, and Donald J. Trump in the United States.

"American democracy," as a matter of history, is democracy with an asterisk, the symbol A-Rod's name would need if he were ever inducted into the Hall of Fame. Not until the 1964 Civil Rights Act and the 1965 Voting Rights Act can the United States be said to have met the basic conditions for political equality requisite in a democracy. All the same, measured not against its past but against its contemporaries, American democracy in the twenty-first century is withering. The Democracy Index rates 167 countries, every year, on a scale that ranges from "full democracy" to "authoritarian regime." In 2006, the U.S. was a "full democracy," the seventeenth most democratic nation in the world. In 2016, the index for the first time rated the United States a "flawed democracy," and since then American democracy has gotten only more flawed. True, the United States still doesn't have a Rome or a Berlin to march on. That hasn't saved the nation from misinformation, tribalization, domestic terrorism, human rights abuses, political intolerance, social-media mob rule, white nationalism, a criminal president, the nobbling of Congress, a corrupt presidential administration, assaults on the press, crippling polarization, the undermining of elections, and an epistemological chaos that is the only air that totalitarianism can breathe.

Nothing so sharpens one's appreciation for democracy as bearing witness to its demolition. Mussolini called Italy and Germany "the greatest and soundest democracies which exist in the world today," and Hitler liked to say that, with Nazi Germany, he had achieved a "beautiful democracy," prompting the American political columnist Dorothy Thompson to remark of the fascist state, "If it is going to call itself democratic we had better find another word for what we have and what we want." In the 1930s, Americans didn't find another word. But they did work to decide what they wanted, and to imagine and to build it. Thompson, who had been a foreign correspondent in Germany and Austria and had interviewed the führer, said, in a column that reached eight million readers, "Be sure you know what you prepare to defend."

It's a paradox of democracy that the best way to defend it is to attack it, to ask more of it, by way of criticism, protest, and dissent. American democracy in the 1930s had plenty of critics, left and right, from Mexican Americans who objected to a brutal regime of forced deportations to businessmen who believed the New Deal to be unconstitutional. W. E. B. Du Bois predicted that, unless the United States met its obligations to the dignity and equality of all its citizens and ended its enthrallment to corporations, American democracy would fail: "If it is going to use this power to force the world into color prejudice and race antagonism; if it is going to use it to manufacture millionaires, increase the rule of wealth, and break down democratic government everywhere; if it is going increasingly to stand for reaction, fascism, white supremacy and imperialism; if it is going to promote war and not peace; then America will go the way of the Roman Empire."

The historian Mary Ritter Beard warned that American democracy would make no headway against its "ruthless enemies—war, fascism, ignorance, poverty, scarcity, unemployment, sadistic criminality, racial persecution, man's lust for power and woman's miserable trailing in the shadow of his frightful ways"—unless Americans could imagine a future democracy in which women would no longer be barred from positions of leadership: "If we will not so envisage our future, no Bill of Rights, man's or woman's, is worth the paper on which it is printed."

If the United States hasn't gone the way of the Roman Empire and the Bill of Rights is still worth more than the paper on which it's printed, that's because so many people have been, ever since, fighting the fights Du Bois and Ritter Beard fought. There have been wins and losses. The fight goes on.

Could no system of rule but extremism hold back the chaos of economic decline? In the 1930s, people all over the world, liberals, hoped that the United States would be able to find a middle road, somewhere between the malignity of a state-run economy and the mercilessness of laissez-faire capitalism. Roosevelt campaigned in 1932 on the promise to rescue American democracy by way of a "new deal for the American people," his version of that third way: relief, recovery, and reform. He won forty-two of forty-eight states, and trounced the incumbent, Herbert Hoover, in the Electoral College 472–59. Given the national emergency in which Roosevelt took office, Congress granted him an almost entirely free hand, even as critics raised concerns that the powers he assumed were barely short of dictatorial.

New Dealers were trying to save the economy; they ended up saving democracy. They built a new America; they told a new American story. On New Deal projects, people from different parts of the country labored side by side, constructing roads and bridges and dams, everything from the Lincoln Tunnel to the Hoover Dam, joining together in a common endeavor, shoulder to the wheel, hand to the forge. Many of those public works projects, like better transportation and better electrification, also brought far-flung communities, down to the littlest town or the remotest farm, into a national culture, one enriched with new funds for the arts, theater, music, and storytelling. With radio, more than with any other technology of communication, before or since, Americans gained a sense of their shared suffering, and shared ideals: they listened to one another's voices.

This didn't happen by accident. Writers and actors and directors and broadcasters made it happen. They dedicated themselves to using the medium to bring people together. Beginning in 1938, for instance, FDR's Works Progress Administration produced a twenty-six-week radio drama series for CBS called *Americans All, Immigrants All*, written by Gilbert Seldes, the former editor of the *Dial*. "What brought people to this country from the four corners of the earth?" a pamphlet distributed to schoolteachers explaining the series asked. "What gifts did they bear? What were their problems? What problems remain unsolved?" The finale celebrated the American experiment: "The story of magnificent adventure! The record of an unparalleled event in the history of mankind!"

There is no twenty-first-century equivalent of Seldes's *Americans All, Immigrants All*, because it is no longer acceptable for a serious artist to write in this vein, and for this audience, and for this purpose. (In some quarters, it was barely acceptable even then.) Love of the ordinary, affection for the common people, concern for the commonweal: these were features of the best writing and art of the 1930s. They are not so often features lately.

Americans reelected FDR in 1936 by one of the widest margins in the country's history. American magazines continued the trend from the twenties, in which hardly a month went by without their taking stock: "Is Democracy Doomed?" "Can Democracy Survive?" (Those were the past century's versions of more recent titles, such as *How Democracy Ends*, *Why Liberalism Failed*, *How the Right Lost Its Mind*, and *How Democracies Die*. The same ears, that same funny nose.) In 1934, the *Christian Science Monitor* published a debate called "Whither Democracy?," addressed "to everyone who has been thinking about the future of democracy—and who hasn't." It staked, as adversaries, two British scholars: Alfred Zimmern, a historian from Oxford, on the right, and Harold Laski, a political theorist from the London School of Economics, on the left. "Dr. Zimmern says in effect that where democracy has failed it has not been really tried," the editors explained. "Professor Laski sees an irrepressible conflict between the idea of political equality in democracy and the fact of economic inequality in capitalism, and expects at least a temporary resort to Fascism or a capitalistic dictatorship." On the one hand, American democracy is safe; on the other hand, American democracy is not safe.

Zimmern and Laski went on speaking tours of the United States, part of a long parade of visiting professors brought here to prognosticate on the future of democracy. Laski spoke to a crowd three thousand strong, in Washington's Constitution Hall. "Laski Tells How to Save Democracy," the *Washington Post* reported. Zimmern delivered a series of lectures titled "The Future of Democracy," at the University of Buffalo, in which he warned that democracy had been undermined by a new aristocracy of self-professed experts. "I am no more ready to be governed by experts than I am to be governed by the ex-Kaiser," he professed, expertly.

The year 1935 happened to mark the centennial of the publication of Alexis de Tocqueville's *Democracy in America*, an occasion that elicited still more lectures from European intellectuals coming to the United States to remark on its system of government and the character of its people, close on Tocqueville's heels. Heinrich Brüning, a scholar and a former chancellor of Germany, lectured at Princeton on "The Crisis of Democracy"; the Swiss political theorist William Rappard gave the same title to a series of lectures he delivered at the University of Chicago. In "The Prospects for Democracy," the Scottish historian and later BBC radio quiz-show panelist Denis W. Brogan offered little but gloom: "The defenders of democracy, the thinkers and writers who still believe in its merits, are in danger of suffering the fate of Aristotle, who kept his eyes fixedly on the city-state at a time when that form of government was being reduced to a shadow by the rise of Alexander's world empire." Brogan hedged his bets by predicting the worst. It's an old trick.

The endless train of academics were also called upon to contribute to the nation's growing number of periodicals. In 1937, *The New Republic*, arguing that "at no time since the rise of political democracy have its tenets been so seriously challenged as they are today," ran a series on "The Future of Democracy," featuring pieces by the likes of Bertrand Russell and John Dewey. "Do you think that political democracy is now on the wane?" the editors asked each writer. The series' lead contributor, the Italian philosopher Benedetto Croce, took issue with the question, as philosophers, thankfully, do. "I call this kind of question 'meteorological,'" he grumbled. "It is like asking, 'Do you think that it is going to rain today? Had I better take my umbrella?'" The trouble, Croce explained, is that political problems are not external forces beyond our control; they are forces within our control. "We need solely to make up our own minds and to act."

Don't ask whether you need an umbrella. Go outside and stop the rain.

HERE ARE SOME OF THE SORTS OF PEOPLE who went out and stopped the rain in the 1930s: schoolteachers, city councillors, librarians, poets, union organizers, artists, precinct workers, soldiers, civil rights activists, and investigative reporters. They knew what they were prepared to defend and they defended it, even though they also knew that they risked attack from both the left and the right. Charles Beard (Mary Ritter's husband) spoke out against the newspaper tycoon William Randolph Hearst, the Rupert Murdoch of his day, when he smeared scholars and teachers as communists. "The people who are doing the most damage to American democracy are men like Charles A. Beard," said a historian at Trinity College in Hartford, speaking at a high school on the subject of "Democracy and the Future," and warning against reading Beard's books—at a time when Nazis in Germany and Austria were burning "un-German" books in public squares. That did not exactly happen here, but in the 1930s four of five American superintendents of schools recommended assigning only those U.S. history textbooks which "omit any facts likely to arouse in the minds of the students question or doubt concerning the justice of our social order and government." Beard's books, God bless them, raised doubts.

Beard didn't back down. Nor did WPA muralists and artists, who were subject to the same attack. Instead, Beard took pains to point out that Americans liked to think of themselves as good talkers and good arguers, people with a particular kind of smarts. Not necessarily book learning, but street smarts—reasonableness, open-mindedness, level-headedness. "The kind of universal intellectual prostration required by Bolshevism and Fascism is decidedly foreign to American 'intelligence,'" Beard wrote. Possibly, he allowed, you could call this a stubborn independence of mind, or even mulishness. "Whatever the interpretation, our wisdom or ignorance stands in the way of our accepting the totalitarian assumption of Omniscience," he insisted. "And to this extent it contributes to the continuance of the arguing, debating, never-settling-anything-finally methods of political democracy." Maybe that was whistling in the dark, but sometimes a whistle is all you've got.

The more argument the better is what the North Carolina–born George V. Denny Jr. was banking on, anyway, after a neighbor of his, in Scarsdale, declared that he so strongly disagreed with FDR that he never listened to him. Denny, who helped run something called the League for Political Education, thought that was nuts. In 1935, he launched *America's Town Meeting of the Air*, an hour-long debate program, broadcast nationally on NBC's Blue Network. Each episode opened with a town crier ringing a bell and hollering, "Town meeting tonight! Town meeting tonight!" Then Denny moderated a debate, usually among three or four panelists, on a controversial subject (Does the U.S. have a truly free press? Should schools teach politics?), before opening the discussion up to questions from an audience of more than a thousand people. The debates were conducted at a lecture hall, usually in New York, and broadcast to listeners gathered in public libraries all over the country, so that they could hold their own debates once the show ended. "We are living today on the thin edge of history," Max

Lerner, the editor of *The Nation*, said in 1938, during a *Town Meeting of the Air* debate on the meaning of democracy. His panel included a communist, an exile from the Spanish Civil War, a conservative American political economist, and a Russian columnist. "We didn't expect to settle anything, and therefore we succeeded," the Spanish exile said at the end of the hour, offering this definition: "A democracy is a place where a 'Town Meeting of the Air' can take place."

No one expected anyone to come up with an undisputable definition of democracy, since the point was disputation. Asking people about the meaning and the future of democracy and listening to them argue it out was really only a way to get people to stretch their civic muscles. "Democracy can only be saved by democratic men and women," Dorothy Thompson once said. "The war against democracy begins by the destruction of the democratic temper, the democratic method and the democratic heart. If the democratic temper be exacerbated into wanton unreasonableness, which is the essence of the evil, then a victory has been won for the evil we despise and prepare to defend ourselves against, even though it's 3,000 miles away and has never moved."

The most ambitious plan to get Americans to show up in the same room and argue with one another in the 1930s came out of Des Moines, Iowa, from a one-eyed former bricklayer named John W. Studebaker, who had become the superintendent of the city's schools. Studebaker, who after the Second World War helped create the G.I. Bill, had the idea of opening those schools up at night, so that citizens could hold debates. In 1933, with a grant from the Carnegie Corporation and support from the American Association for Adult Education, he started a five-year experiment in civic education.

The meetings began at a quarter to eight, with a fifteen-minute news update, followed by a forty-five-minute lecture, and thirty minutes of debate. The idea was that "the people of the community of every political affiliation, creed, and economic view have an opportunity to participate freely." When Senator Guy Gillette, a Democrat from Iowa, talked about "Why I Support the New Deal," Senator Lester Dickinson, a Republican from Iowa, talked about "Why I Oppose the New Deal." Speakers defended fascism. They attacked capitalism. They attacked fascism. They defended capitalism. Within the first nine months of the program, thirteen thousand of Des Moines' seventy-six thousand adults had attended a forum. The program got so popular that in 1934 FDR appointed Studebaker the U.S. Commissioner of Education and, with the eventual help of Eleanor Roosevelt, the program became a part of the New Deal, and received federal funding. The federal forum program started out in ten test sites—from Orange County, California, to Sedgwick County, Kansas, and Pulaski County, Arkansas. It came to include almost five hundred forums in forty-three states and involved two and a half million Americans. Even people who had steadfastly predicted the demise of democracy participated. "It seems to me the only method by which we are going to achieve democracy in the United States," Du Bois wrote, in 1937.

The federal government paid for it, but everything else fell under local control, and ordinary people made it work, by showing up and participating. Usually, school districts found the speakers and decided on the topics after collecting ballots from the community. In some parts of the country, even in rural areas, meetings were held four and five times a week. They started in schools and spread to YMCAs and YWCAs, labor halls, libraries, settlement houses, and businesses, during lunch hours. Many of the meetings were broadcast by radio. People who went to those meetings debated all sorts of things:

Should the Power of the Supreme Court Be Altered?
Do Company Unions Help Labor?
Do Machines Oust Men?
Must the West Get Out of the East?
Can We Conquer Poverty?
Should Capital Punishment Be Abolished?
Is Propaganda a Menace?
Do We Need a New Constitution?
Should Women Work?
Is America a Good Neighbor?
Can It Happen Here?

These efforts don't always work. Still, trying them is better than talking about the weather, and waiting for someone to hand you an umbrella.

WHEN A TERRIBLE HURRICANE hit New England in 1938, Dr. Lorine Pruette, a Tennessee-born psychologist who had written an essay called "Why Women Fail," and who had urged FDR to name only women to his cabinet, found herself marooned at a farm in New Hampshire with a young neighbor, sixteen-year-old Alice Hooper, a high school sophomore. Waiting out the storm, they had nothing to do except listen to the news, which, needless to say, concerned the future of democracy. Alice asked Pruette a question: "What is it everyone on the radio is talking about—what is this democracy—what does it mean?" Somehow, in the end, NBC arranged a coast-to-coast broadcast, in which eight prominent thinkers—two ministers, three professors, a former ambassador, a poet, and a journalist—tried to explain to Alice the meaning of democracy. American democracy had found its "Yes, Virginia, there is a Santa Claus" moment, except that it was messier, and more interesting, because those eight people didn't agree on the answer. Democracy, Alice, is the darnedest thing.

That broadcast was made possible by the workers who brought electricity to rural New Hampshire; the legislators who signed the 1934 federal Communications Act, mandating public interest broadcasting; the executives at NBC who decided that it was important to run this program; the two ministers, the three professors, the former ambassador, the poet, and the journalist who gave their time, for free, to a public forum, and agreed to disagree without acting like asses; and a whole lot of Americans who took the time to listen, carefully, even though they had plenty of other things to do. Getting out of our current jam will likely require something different, but not entirely different. And it will be worth doing.

A decade-long debate about the future of democracy came to a close at the end of the 1930s—but not because it had been settled. In 1939, the World's Fair opened in Queens, with a main exhibit featuring the saga of democracy and a chipper motto: "The World of Tomorrow." The fairgrounds included a Court of Peace, with pavilions for every nation. By the time the fair opened, Czechoslovakia had fallen to Germany, though, and its pavilion couldn't open. Shortly afterward, Edvard Beneš, the exiled president of Czechoslovakia, delivered a series of lectures at the University of Chicago on, yes, the future of democracy, though he spoke less about the future than about the past, and especially about the terrible present, a time of violently unmoored traditions and laws and agreements, a time "of moral and intellectual crisis and chaos." Soon, more black bunting was brought to the World's Fair, to cover Poland, Belgium, Denmark, France, Luxembourg, and the Netherlands. By the time the World of Tomorrow closed, in 1940, half the European hall lay under a shroud of black.

The federal government stopped funding the forum program in 1941. Americans would take up their debate about the future of democracy, in a different form, only after the defeat of the Axis. For now, there was a war to fight. And there were still essays to publish, if not about the future, then about the present. In 1943, E. B. White got a letter in the mail, from the Writers' War Board, asking him to write a statement about "The Meaning of Democracy." He was a little weary of these pieces, but he knew how much they mattered. He wrote back, "Democracy is a request from a War Board, in the middle of a morning in the middle of a war, wanting to know what democracy is." It meant something once. And, the thing is, it still does.

—2020

YOU'RE FIRED

B IRD-EYED AARON BURR WAS WANTED FOR MUR-
der in two states when he presided over the impeachment
trial of Supreme Court Justice Samuel Chase in the Senate, in 1805.
The House had impeached Chase, a Marylander, on seven articles of
misconduct and one article of rudeness. Burr had been indicted in
New Jersey, where, according to the indictment, "not having the fear
of God before his eyes but being moved and seduced by the insti-
gation of the Devil," he'd killed Alexander Hamilton, the former
secretary of the treasury, in a duel. Because Hamilton, who was shot
in the belly, died in New York, Burr had been indicted there, too.
Still, the Senate met in Washington, and, until Burr's term expired,
he held the title of vice president of the United States.

The public loves an impeachment, until the public hates an
impeachment. For the occasion of Chase's impeachment trial, a
special gallery for lady spectators had been built at the back of the
Senate chamber. Burr, a Republican, presided over a Senate of
twenty-five Republicans and nine Federalists, who sat, to either
side of him, on two rows of crimson cloth-covered benches. They
faced three rows of green cloth-covered benches occupied by members of the House of Representatives, Supreme Court justices, and
President Thomas Jefferson's cabinet. The House managers (the
impeachment-trial equivalent of prosecutors), led by the Virginian
John Randolph, sat at a table covered with blue cloth; at another
blue table sat Chase and his lawyers, led by the red-faced Maryland
attorney general, Luther Martin, a man so steady of heart and clear
of mind that in 1787 he'd walked out of the Constitutional Convention, and refused to sign the Constitution, after objecting that
its countenancing of slavery was "inconsistent with the principles

of the Revolution and dishonorable to the American character." Luther (Brandybottle) Martin had a weakness for liquor. This did not impair him. As a wise historian once remarked, Martin "knew more law drunk than the managers did sober."

Impeachment is an ancient relic, a rusty legal instrument and political weapon first wielded by Parliament, in 1376, to wrest power from the king by charging his ministers with abuses of power, convicting them, removing them from office, and throwing them in prison. Some four hundred years later, impeachment had all but vanished from English practice when American delegates to the Constitutional Convention provided for it in Article II, Section 4: "The President, Vice President and all civil Officers of the United States, shall be removed from Office on Impeachment for, and Conviction of, Treason, Bribery, or other high Crimes and Misdemeanors."

It's one thing to know this power exists. It's another to use it. In one view, nicely expressed by an English solicitor general in 1691, "The power of impeachment ought to be, like Goliath's sword, kept in the temple, and not used but on great occasions." Yet in the autumn of 2019, in the third year of the presidency of Donald J. Trump, House Democrats have unsheathed that terrible, mighty sword. Has time dulled its blade?

IMPEACHMENT IS A TERRIBLE POWER because it was forged to counter a terrible power: the despot who deems himself to be above the law. The delegates to the Constitutional Convention included impeachment in the Constitution as a consequence of their knowledge of history, a study they believed to be a prerequisite for holding a position in government. From their study of English history, they learned what might be called the law of knavery: there aren't any good ways to get rid of a bad king. Really, there were only three ways and they were all horrible: civil war, revolution, or assassination. England had already endured the first and America the second, and no one could endorse the third. "What was the practice before this in cases where the chief Magistrate rendered himself obnoxious?" Benjamin Franklin asked at the convention. "Recourse was had to assassination, in which he was not only deprived of his life but of the opportunity of vindicating his character."

But the delegates knew that Parliament had come up with another way: clipping the king's wings by impeaching his ministers. The House of Commons couldn't attack the king directly because of the fiction that the king was infallible ("perfect," as Donald Trump would say), so, beginning in 1376, they impeached his favorites, accusing Lord William Latimer and Richard Lyons of acting "falsely in order to have advantages for their own use." Latimer, a peer, insisted that he be tried by his peers—that is, by the House of Lords, not the House of Commons—and it was his peers who convicted him and sent him to prison. That's why the House in 2019 prepared articles of impeachment against Trump, acting as his accusers, but it is the Senate that would judge his innocence or his guilt.

Parliament used impeachment to thwart monarchy's tendency toward absolutism, with mixed results. After conducting at least ten impeachments between 1376 and 1450, Parliament didn't impeach anyone for more than a hundred and seventy years, partly because Parliament met only when the king summoned it, and, if Parliament was going to impeach his ministers, he'd show them by never summoning it, unless he really had to, as when he needed to levy taxes. He, or she: during the forty-five years of Elizabeth I's reign, Parliament was in session for a total of three. Parliament had forged a sword. It just couldn't ever get into Westminster to take it out of its sheath.

The Englishman responsible for bringing the ancient practice of impeachment back into use was Edward Coke, an investor in the Virginia Company who became a Member of Parliament in 1589. Coke, a profoundly agile legal thinker, had served as Elizabeth I's attorney general and as chief justice under her successor, James I. In 1621—two years after the first Africans, slaves, landed in the Virginia colony and a year after the Pilgrims, dissenters, landed at a place they called Plymouth—Coke began to insist that Parliament could debate whatever it wanted to, and soon Parliament began arguing that it ought to meet regularly. To build a case for the supremacy of Parliament, Coke dug out of the archives Magna Carta of 1215, calling it England's "ancient constitution," and he resurrected, too, the ancient right of Parliament to impeach the king's ministers. Parliament promptly impeached Coke's chief adversary, Francis Bacon, the lord chancellor, for bribery; Bacon was convicted, removed from office, and reduced to penury. James then dissolved Parliament and locked up Coke in the Tower of London.

Something of a political death match followed between Parliament and James and his Stuart successors Charles I and Charles II, over the nature of rule. In 1626, the House of Commons impeached the Duke of Buckingham for "maladministration" and corruption, including failure to safeguard the seas. But the king, James's son, Charles I, forestalled a trial in the House of Lords by dismissing Parliament. After Buckingham died, Charles refused to summon Parliament for the next eleven years. In 1649, he was beheaded for treason. After the restoration of the monarchy, in 1660, under Charles II, Parliament occasionally impeached the king's ministers, but in 1716 stopped doing so altogether. Because Parliament had won. It had made the king into a flightless bird.

Why the Americans should have resurrected this practice in 1787 is something of a puzzle, until you remember that all but one of England's original thirteen American colonies had been founded before impeachment went out of style. Also, while Parliament had gained power relative to the king, the colonial assemblies remained virtually powerless, especially against the authority of colonial governors, who, in most colonies, were appointed by the king. To clip their governors' wings, colonial assemblies impeached the governors' men, only to find their convictions overturned by the Privy Council in London, which acted as an appellate court. Colonial lawyers pursuing these cases dedicated themselves to the study of the impeachments against the three Stuart kings. John Adams owned a copy of a law book that defined "impeachment" as "the Accusation and Prosecution of a Person for Treason, or other Crimes and Misdemeanors." Steeped in the lore of Parliament's seventeenth-century battles with the Stuarts, men like Adams considered the right of impeachment to be one of the fundamental rights of Englishmen. And when men like Adams came to write constitutions for the new states, in the 1770s and '80s, they made sure that impeachment was provided for. In Philadelphia in 1787, thirty-three of the convention's fifty-five delegates were trained as lawyers; ten were or had been judges. As Frank Bowman, a law professor at the University of Missouri, reports in *High Crimes and Misdemeanors: A History of Impeachment for the Age of Trump*, fourteen of the delegates had helped draft constitutions in their own states that provided for impeachment. In Philadelphia, they forged a new sword out of very old steel. They Americanized impeachment.

THIS NEW GOVERNMENT WOULD HAVE a president, not a king, but Americans agreed on the need for a provision to get rid of a bad one. All four of the original plans for a new constitution allowed for presidential impeachment. When the Constitutional Convention began, on May 25, 1787, impeachment appears to have been on nearly everyone's mind, not least because Parliament had opened its first impeachment investigation in more than fifty years, on April 3, against a colonial governor of India, and the member charged with heading the investigation was England's famed supporter of American independence, Edmund Burke. What with one thing and another, impeachment came up in the convention's very first week.

A president is not a king; his power would be checked by submitting himself to an election every four years, and by the separation of powers. But this did not provide "sufficient security," James Madison said. "He might pervert his administration into a scheme of peculation or oppression. He might betray his trust to foreign powers." Also, voters might make a bad decision, and regret it, well in advance of the next election. "Some mode of displacing an unfit magistrate is rendered indispensable by the fallibility of those who choose, as well as by the corruptibility of the man chosen," the Virginia delegate George Mason said.

How impeachment actually worked would be hammered out through cases like the impeachment of Samuel Chase, a Supreme Court justice, but, at the Constitutional Convention, nearly all discussion of impeachment concerned the presidency. ("Vice President and all civil Officers" was added only at the very last minute.) A nation that had cast off a king refused to anoint another. "No point is of more importance than that the right of impeachment should continue," Mason said. "Shall any man be above Justice? Above all shall that man be above it, who can commit the most extensive injustice?"

Most of the discussion involved the nature of the conduct for which a president could be impeached. Early on, the delegates had listed, as impeachable offenses, "mal-practice or neglect of duty," a list that got longer before a committee narrowed it down to "Treason & bribery." When Mason proposed adding "maladministration," Madison objected, on the ground that maladministration could mean just about anything. And, as the Pennsylvania delegate Gouverneur Morris put it, it would not be unreasonable to suppose that "an election of every four years will prevent maladministration." Mason therefore proposed substituting "other high crimes and misdemeanors against the State."

The "high" in "high crimes and misdemeanors" has its origins in phrases that include the "certain high treasons and offenses and misprisons" invoked in the impeachment of the Duke of Suffolk, in 1450. Parliament was the "high court," the men Parliament impeached were of the "highest rank"; offenses that Parliament described as "high" were public offenses with consequences for the nation. The phrase "high crimes and misdemeanors" first appeared in an impeachment in 1642, and then regularly, as a catchall for all manner of egregious wrongs, abuses of authority, and crimes against the state.

In 1787, the delegates in Philadelphia narrowed their list down to "Treason & bribery, or other high crimes & misdemeanors against the United States." In preparing the final draft of the Constitution, the Committee on Style deleted the phrase "against the United States," presumably because it is implied.

"What, then, is an impeachable offense?" Gerald Ford, the Michigan Republican and House minority leader, asked in 1970. "The only honest answer is that an impeachable offense is whatever a majority of the House of Representatives considers it to be at a given moment in history." That wasn't an honest answer; it was a depressingly cynical one. Ford had moved to impeach Supreme Court justice William O. Douglas, accusing him of embracing a "hippie-yippie-style revolution," indicting him for a decadent life style, and alleging financial improprieties, charges that appeared, to Ford's critics, to fall well short of impeachable offenses. In 2017, Nancy Pelosi claimed that a president cannot be impeached who has not committed a crime (a position she would not likely take today). According to *Impeachment: A Citizen's Guide*, by the legal scholar Cass Sunstein, who testified before Congress on the meaning of "high crimes and misdemeanors" during the impeachment of William Jefferson Clinton, both Ford and Pelosi were fundamentally wrong. "High crimes and misdemeanors" does have a meaning. An impeachable offense is an abuse of the power of the office that violates the public trust, runs counter to the national interest, and undermines the republic. To believe that words are meaningless is to give up on truth. To believe that presidents can do anything they like is to give up on self-government.

THE U.S. SENATE HAS HELD only eighteen impeachment trials in two hundred and thirty years, and only twice for a president. Because impeachment happens so infrequently, it's hard to draw conclusions about what it does, or even how it works, and, on each occasion, people spend a lot of time fighting over the meaning of the words and the nature of the crimes. Every impeachment is a political experiment.

The ordeal of Samuel Chase is arguably the most significant but least studied impeachment in American history. The Chase impeachment was only the third ever attempted. In 1797, the House had impeached the Tennessee senator William Blount, who stood accused of scheming to conspire with the British and to enlist the Creek and Cherokee Nations to attack the Spanish, all with the design of increasing the value of his highly speculative purchase of western lands. ("Whether the scheme was merely audacious or just plain crazy remains debatable," Bowman writes, darkly foreshadowing more recent shenanigans, involving the possible acquisition of Greenland.) The case rested on a letter allegedly written by Blount, describing this plan; after two senators said they recognized Blount's handwriting, the Senate expelled him in a vote of 25–1, and he slinked off to Tennessee. The House had voted to impeach, but Blount's lawyers argued that senators are not "civil officers," and so can't be impeached. ("#IMPEACHMITTROMNEY," Trump tweeted. The Blount precedent went some way toward establishing that this is an impossibility.) The motion to dismiss was read aloud in the Senate by Jefferson, who was vice president at the time.

Samuel Chase's troubles began when Congress passed the 1798 Sedition Act, aimed at suppressing Republican opposition to John Adams's Federalist administration. Chase, riding circuit, had presided over the most notorious persecutions of Republican printers on charges of sedition, including the conviction of the printer James Callender. The Sedition Act expired on March 3, 1801, the day before Jefferson's inauguration, but, through a series of midnight appointments, Adams had connived to insure that Jefferson inherited a Federalist Supreme Court. Chase had actively campaigned for Adams and spoke intemperately for the bench, denouncing Republicans. In an overheated charge to a grand jury in Baltimore, he attacked Republicanism, describing it as "mobocracy." Jefferson set an impeachment in motion when he wrote to House Republicans, "Ought this sedition and official attack on the principles of our Constitution . . . go unpunished?"

If the proceedings against Blount tested whether senators could be impeached, the proceedings against Chase tested a new theory of executive power—that Supreme Court justices serve at the pleasure of the president. This test came in the wake of *Marbury v. Madison*, in 1803, in which John Marshall's Supreme Court exercised a prerogative not specified in the Constitution: the Court had declared an act of Congress unconstitutional. A Republican leader of the Senate told the Massachusetts senator John Quincy Adams that he hoped to impeach the entire court. Judicial independence? Judicial review? No. "If the Judges of the Supreme Court should dare, AS THEY HAD DONE, to declare an act of Congress unconstitutional . . . it was the undoubted right of the House of Representatives to remove them, for giving such opinions," he said. "A removal by impeachment was nothing more than a declaration by Congress to this effect: You hold dangerous opinions, and if you are suffered to carry them into effect you will work the destruction of the nation."

John Randolph, a steadfast Republican but no lawyer, drafted the articles of impeachment against Chase, which broadly charged him with prostituting his high office to the low purpose of partisanship but, narrowly, rested on all manner of pettiness, including the charge that during Callender's trial Chase had used "unusual, rude, and contemptuous expressions toward the prisoner's counsel" and had engaged in "repeated and vexatious interruptions." Notwithstanding the weakness of the charges, not to say their vexatiousness, the House voted to impeach. The trial in the Senate opened on February 4, 1805.

An impeachment trial is a medieval play, with its mummers and its costumes and its many-colored cloth-covered tables. Chase's trial lasted a month. Burr ran a well-ordered court. He warned the senators not to eat apples and cake while in session. He censured them for leaving their seats. He hushed the spectators in the galleries.

The trial turned less on what Chase had done than on whether he could be impeached for having done those things. John Randolph, though, didn't really have a theory of impeachment. He had a theory of vengeance. His arguments, a distressed John Quincy Adams wrote in his diary, consisted "altogether of the most hackneyed commonplaces of popular declamation, mingled up with panegyrics and invectives." Randolph called eighteen witnesses, few of whom aided his case, and some of whom aided Chase's. "Saw nothing that struck me as remarkable," one witness, who had attended Callender's trial, said. As an observer put it, "I swear if they go on much farther, they will prove Judge Chase an angel."

Chase's defense called thirty-one witnesses, including some of Randolph's. Chase's attorneys said the charges were plainly silly, and they didn't much bother to refute them, especially since Randolph had done that job so well himself. Instead, they argued about the nature of impeachment. One of Chase's younger lawyers, Joseph Hopkin-son, insisted that "no judge can be impeached and removed from office for any act or offense for which he could not be indicted." In other words, an impeachable offense has to be an indictable offense: a crime. "High crimes and misdemeanors," Hopkinson argued, meant "high crimes" and "high misdemeanors."

The trial reached its climax on February 23, when a red-faced Luther Martin rose from behind the defense's table. He spoke for a day and a half, expounding on his own theory of impeachment. A judge could commit a crime, like hitting someone, for which he could not be impeached. He could even commit a high crime for which he could not be impeached. All that he could be impeached for were crimes "such as relate to his office, or which tend to cover the person, who committed them, with *turpitude* and *infamy*; such as show there can be no dependence on that integrity and honor which will secure the performance of his official duties." To be impeached, Martin said, a judge had to commit crimes that either derived from his judicial power or were so horrible, so grotesquely unethical, that they disqualified him from holding a position of public trust.

Republicans outnumbered Federalists in the Senate 25–9. On March 1, for each article, Burr asked of each senator, "Is Samuel Chase, Esq., guilty or not guilty of a high crime or misdemeanor in the article of impeachment just read?" A majority voted guilty for three articles. None earned the required two-thirds supermajority. Six Republicans broke ranks on all eight articles. By a vote of 19–15, the Senate came closest to convicting Chase on the article regarding his partisan zeal in his charge to the Baltimore grand jury. Burr stood up. "It becomes my duty to pronounce that Samuel Chase, Esq., is acquitted," he said. Then he bowed to Chase and left the chamber. As for Burr, he was never convicted of killing Alexander Hamilton. (Two years later, in an unrelated incident of amazing sneakiness, he was tried for treason, and acquitted.)

The acquittal of Samuel Chase established the independence of the judiciary. It also established another principle, as Bowman argues: "The price of the independence granted by life tenure is abstention from party politics." It did not, however, establish a lasting theory of impeachment. Brandybottle Martin had stated his case beautifully, and easily defeated the hapless John Randolph, but Martin's argument was wrong. Nothing in American history, from the founding of its earliest colonies, suggests that an impeachable offense has to be an indictable crime, not for the king's men, not for judges and justices, and not for the president of the United States. Presidents can be impeached for actions that are not crimes, not least because the criminal code was not written with presidents in mind. Most of us cannot commit such staggering outrages as to direct the FBI to spy on our enemies or enlist foreign powers to interfere in our elections. The president has powers that only a president can exercise, or abuse. Were these powers beyond the reach of the people's power, impeachment would be a dead letter.

If the House votes to impeach Donald Trump, it is by no means clear that the Senate will hold a trial. And, if the Senate does hold a trial, the likelihood that it will convict is small. Impeachment is a tall and rickety ladder; conviction is a tiny window, barely cracked open. It's difficult and dangerous to climb the ladder, and no one who has made it to the top has ever managed to crawl in through the window.

After the acquittal of Samuel Chase, in 1805, the House, in the next decades, impeached two more judges, one in 1830 and one in 1862; the Senate acquitted the first and convicted the second. The first real attempt to impeach a president came in 1843, when a Virginia congressman accused John Tyler of "corruption, malconduct, high crimes and misdemeanors," but the House voted down a motion to investigate, 127–83.

In 1868, "out of the midst of political gloom, impeachment, that dead corpse, rose up and walked forth again!" Mark Twain wrote. Republicans in the House impeached President Andrew Johnson by a vote of 126–47. They were desperate, as Brenda Wineapple chronicles in *The Impeachers: The Trial of Andrew Johnson and the Dream of a Just Nation*. Johnson, a Tennessee Democrat who didn't free his slaves until 1863, after the Emancipation Proclamation, had been Abraham Lincoln's improbable vice president, and had assumed the office of the presidency after his assassination, in 1865. Lincoln and congressional Republicans had one plan for Reconstruction: it involved welcoming the freedmen into the political community of the nation. Johnson, who believed that, "in the progress of nations, negroes have shown less capacity for government than any other race of people," betrayed that vision. "Slavery is not abolished until the black man has the ballot," Frederick Douglass declared. But granting the franchise to Black men was the last thing Johnson intended to allow. While Congress was out of session, he set in motion a Reconstruction plan that was completely at variance with what Congress had proposed: he intended to return power to the very people who had waged war against the Union, and he readmitted the former Confederate states to the Union. "No power but Congress had any right to say whether ever or when they should be admitted to the Union as States and entitled to the privileges of the Constitution," the Pennsylvania representative Thaddeus Stevens said during Johnson's impeachment proceedings. (Stevens, ailing, had to be carried into the Capitol on a chair.) "And yet Andrew Johnson, with unblushing hardihood, undertook to rule them by his own power alone." Johnson vetoed the 1866 Civil Rights Bill and nearly every other congressional attempt to reassert authority over the law of the United States. But the Republicans' strategy, to pass a law they expected Johnson to break, so that they could impeach him, backfired.

The Senate acquitted Johnson, falling short by a single vote of the two-thirds majority necessary to convict. Stevens died a couple of months later, "the bravest old ironclad in the Capitol," Twain wrote. The Republicans had tried to save the republic by burying the Confederacy for good. They failed.

EVERY IMPEACHMENT REINVENTS what impeachment is for, and what it means, a theory of government itself. Every impeachment also offers a chance to establish a new political settlement in an unruly nation. The impeachment of Samuel Chase steered the

United States toward judicial independence, and an accommodation with a party system that had not been anticipated by the framers. Chase's acquittal stabilized the republic and restored the balance of power between the executive and the judicial branches. The failed impeachment of Andrew Johnson steered the United States toward a regime of racial segregation: the era of Jim Crow, which would not be undone until the Civil Rights Act of 1964 and the Voting Rights Acts of 1965 were passed, a century later, in the administration of another Johnson. Johnson's acquittal undid the Union's victory in the Civil War, allowed the Confederacy to win the peace, and nearly destroyed the republic.

Johnson's acquittal also elevated the presidency by making impeachment seem doomed. Jefferson once lamented that impeachment had become a "mere scarecrow." That's how it worked for much of the twentieth century: propped up in a field, straw poking out from under its hat. A Republican congressman from Michigan called for the impeachment of FDR, after the president tried to pack the Court. Nothing but another scarecrow.

The impeachment of Richard Nixon, in 1974, which, although it never went to trial, succeeded in the sense that it drove Nixon from office, represented a use entirely consistent with the instrument's medieval origins: it attempted to puncture the swollen power of the presidency and to reassert the supremacy of the legislature. Nixon's presidency began to unravel only after the publication of the Pentagon Papers, in 1971—which indicted not Nixon but Lyndon Johnson, for deceiving the public about Vietnam—and the public anger that made impeachment possible had to do not only with Nixon's lies and abuses of power but also with Johnson's. But a new settlement, curtailing the powers of the president, never came. Instead, the nation became divided, and those divisions widened.

The wider those divisions, the duller the blade of impeachment. Only very rarely in American history has one party held more than two-thirds of the seats in the Senate (it hasn't happened since 1967), and the more partisan American politics the less likely it is that sixty-seven senators can be rounded up to convict anyone, of anything.

194 THE AMERICAN BEAST

And yet the wider those divisions the more willing Congress has been to call for impeachment. Since Ronald Reagan's inauguration in 1981, members of the House have introduced resolutions for impeachment during every presidency. And the people, too, have clamored. IMPEACH BUSH, the yard signs read. IMPEACH OBAMA.

Not every impeachment brings about a political settlement, good or bad. The failed impeachment of Bill Clinton, in 1999, for lying about his sexual relationship with Monica Lewinsky, settled less than nothing, except that it weakened Americans' faith in impeachment as anything other than a crudely wrought partisan hatchet, a prisoner's shiv.

Clinton's impeachment had one more consequence: it got Donald Trump, self-professed playboy, onto national television, as an authority on the sex lives of ego-mad men. "Paula Jones is a loser," Trump said on CNBC. "It's a terrible embarrassment." Also, "I think his lawyers . . . did a terrible job," Trump said. "I'm not even sure that he shouldn't have just gone in and taken the Fifth Amendment." Because why, after all, should any man have to answer for anything?

"Heaven forbid we should see another impeachment!" an exhausted Republican said at the end of the trial of Samuel Chase. The impeachment of an American president is certain to lead to no end of political mischief and almost certain to fail. Still, worse could happen. Heaven forbid this republic should become one man's kingdom.

—2019

Postscript: In 2019 and again in 2021, after the insurrection at the Capitol, the House voted to impeach Trump but the Senate acquitted him.

MISJUDGED

RUTH BADER GINSBURG BLINKED BEHIND GIANT, round eyeglasses. It was the first day of her confirmation hearings, in July of 1993, the year after the Year of the Woman, and Joe Biden, the chairman of the Senate Judiciary Committee, was very pleased to see her. Keen to do penance for the debacle of the Clarence Thomas hearings, just two years before—the year before the Year of the Woman—when an all-male committee, chaired by Biden, failed to credit what Anita Hill had to say about George H. W. Bush's Supreme Court nominee, he could hardly have been friendlier to Bill Clinton's nominee, a much respected and widely admired sixty-year-old appellate judge. She sat with the stillness of a watchful bird. "Judge Ginsburg, welcome," Biden said heartily. "And, believe me, you are welcome here this morning."

He had more reasons, too, to beam at Ginsburg. Only weeks earlier, Clinton had withdrawn his nomination of Lani Guinier as assistant attorney general, an abandonment that had followed the very new president's unsuccessful nominations of two female attorneys general, Kimba Wood and Zoë Baird. Clinton and Biden needed a successful, high-profile female appointment, one without a discussion of pubic hair or video porn or nannies. On the way to work on the first day of the Ginsburg hearings, Biden had read the *New York Times* on the train and found that there was no mention of Ginsburg on page 1, or page 2, or page 3, which, he told Ginsburg, "was the most wonderful thing that has happened to me since I have been chairman of this committee." He flashed his movie star grin.

During that first session, scheduled for two and a half hours, the committee members—sixteen men and two lately added women—did nearly all the talking, delivering opening statements. Not until the outset of the second session did Biden sidle up to a question. "The Constitution has to be read by justices in light of its broadest and most fundamental commitments, commitments to liberty, commitments to individual dignity, equality of opportunity," he said, putting on his glasses, and taking them off again. Ginsburg blinked and stared and waited.

Biden's question concerned a recent speech, the Madison Lecture, in which Ginsburg had said that in making decisions concerning rights not listed in the Constitution judges should be "moderate and restrained" and avoid stepping "boldly in front of the political process," as he reminded her. "But, Judge," Biden said, "in your work as an advocate in the seventies you spoke with a different voice. In the seventies, you pressed for immediate extension of the fullest constitutional protection for women under the Fourteenth Amendment, and you said the Court should grant such protection notwithstanding what the rest of society, including the legislative branch, thought about the matter. . . . Can you square those for me or point out their consistency to me?"

What Biden was getting at has been mostly lost in the years since, years during which Ruth Bader Ginsburg, a distinguished justice, became a pop-culture feminist icon, a comic-book superhero. In the past year alone, the woman known to her fans as the Notorious RBG was the subject of a *Saturday Night Live* skit; a fawning documentary; a biopic, *On the Basis of Sex* (from a screenplay written by Ginsburg's nephew); a CNN podcast, *RBG Beyond Notorious*; and a biography, *Ruth Bader Ginsburg: A Life,* by Jane Sherron De Hart, an emeritus history professor at the University of California, Santa Barbara.

Such lavish biographical attention to a living Supreme Court justice is unusual, and new, even if that change is easy to lose sight of amid the intense scrutiny of the high school and college years of the Trump nominee Brett Kavanaugh, accused of sexual assault. (He denied the allegations.) Unlike candidates for political office, most sitting justices have preferred to remain, if not anonymous, largely unknown. The position is unelected, the appointment is for life, and the justices are not supposed to place themselves in the public eye, for fear of making themselves beholden to public opinion: arguably, the less attention to their personal lives the better. Before the past tumultuous decade, few, if any, justices who hadn't previously held an elected office had been the subject of a full-dress biography while still serving on the Court.

Writing a biography of a sitting justice introduces all kinds of problems of perspective, authority, and obligation. At the time De Hart was writing, Ginsburg had not deposited her papers in any archive and, having refused calls to resign under Obama's watch, insisted that she had no plans to retire. De Hart, who worked on the project for fifteen years, relied on published material, public records, and, extensively, interviews. Her publisher describes the book as "written with the cooperation of Ruth Bader Ginsburg." It would have been impossible to write the book without that cooperation, but it comes at no small cost.

Making De Hart's problems worse was Ginsburg's unprecedented judicial celebrity. On Matt Groening's animated series *Futurama*, Ginsburg appeared as an artificially preserved head, and although Antonin Scalia's severed head made a cameo or two as well, it was the Ginsburg character's catchphrase—"You Ruth Bader believe it!"— that ended up on T-shirts and coffee mugs, and is the thing your teenager says to you at the dinner table. At eighty-five, Ginsburg did her daily workout with Stephen Colbert on *The Late Show*. "I'm a huge fan!" Colbert said. Thurgood Marshall never lifted weights with Johnny Carson. Three goats were brought to Montpelier to eat the poison ivy spreading throughout the Vermont state capital: they were named Ruth, Bader, and Ginsburg. To my knowledge, no flock of sheep were ever named Oliver, Wendell, and Holmes.

God bless Ruth Bader Ginsburg, goats, bobbleheads, and all. But trivialization—RBG's workout tips! her favorite lace collars!—is not tribute. Female heroes are in short supply not because women aren't brave but because female bravery is demeaned, no kind more than intellectual courage. *Isn't she cute?* Ginsburg was a scholar, an advocate, and a judge of formidable sophistication, complexity, and, not least, contradiction and limitation. It is no kindness to flatten her into a paper doll and sell her as partisan merch.

Doing so also obscures a certain irony. Ginsburg often waxed nostalgic about her confirmation hearings, as she did when, regretting the partisan furor over Brett Kavanaugh—even before Christine Blasey Ford came forward—she said, "The way it was was right; the way it is is wrong." The second of those statements is undeniably and painfully true, but the first flattens the past. What Biden was getting at, in 1993, was what the president himself had said, dismissing the idea of nominating Ginsburg when it was first suggested to him. "The women," Clinton said, "are against her."

RUTH BADER WAS BORN in Brooklyn in 1933. At thirteen, she wrote a newspaper editorial, a tribute to the Charter of the United Nations. Her mother, an admirer of Eleanor Roosevelt, died when she was seventeen. Bader went to Cornell, where she liked to say that she learned how to write from Vladimir Nabokov. At Cornell, she also met Martin Ginsburg, and fell in love. They married in 1954 and had a baby, Jane, in 1955. Brilliant and fiercely independent, Ginsburg was devoted to Marty, to Jane, and to the law. At Harvard Law School, which first admitted women in 1950, she was one of only nine women in a class of some five hundred. In one of the first scenes in *On the Basis of Sex*, Erwin Griswold, the dean of the law school, asks each of those nine women, during a dinner party at his house, why she is occupying a place that could have gone to a man. In the film, Ginsburg, played by Felicity Jones, gives the dean an answer to which he can have no objection: "My husband, Marty, is in the second-year class. I'm at Harvard to learn about his work. So that I might be a more patient and understanding wife." This, which is more or less what Ginsburg actually said, was a necessary lie. It was possible for a woman to attend law school—barely—but it was not possible for her to admit her ambition.

In 1957, Marty was diagnosed with testicular cancer. During his illness and treatment—surgery followed by radiation—Ruth not only cared for him, and for the baby, but also covered all of his classes and helped him with his papers. She kept up an almost inhuman schedule, often working through the night. After Marty graduated, he took a job in New York, and Ruth transferred to Columbia. She graduated first in her class. "That's my mommy," four-year-old Jane said, when Ginsburg crossed the stage to accept her diploma.

Looking for work, Ginsburg confronted the limits of the profession's willingness to take female lawyers seriously. Felix Frankfurter, the first Supreme Court justice to hire an African American clerk, in 1948, refused to hire a woman, even after he was reassured that Ginsburg never wore pants. Stymied, Ginsburg went to Sweden to undertake a comparative study of Swedish and American law. On her return, in 1963, she accepted a position at Rutgers, teaching civil procedure. A year and a half later, when she found herself pregnant—given her husband's medical history, this blessing was unexpected—Ginsburg delayed informing the university, for fear of losing her position.

Ginsburg, in other words, had plenty of experience of what would now be called—because she called it this—discrimination on the basis of sex. In 1969, Ginsburg was promoted to full professor and her son, James, entered nursery school, rites of passage that freed her to explore a new interest: she began volunteering for the ACLU. Working with and eventually heading the ACLU's Women's Rights Project, Ginsburg pursued a series of cases designed to convince the Supreme Court, first, that there is such a thing as sex discrimination and, second, that it violates the Constitution.

Influenced by the pioneering constitutional analysis of Pauli Murray and Dorothy Kenyon, Ginsburg borrowed, too, from the strategy of Thurgood Marshall, who, as head of the NAACP's Legal and Educational Defense Fund beginning in 1940, had pursued his agenda step by step, case by case, over fourteen years, all the way to *Brown v. Board of Education*, decided in 1954. Erwin Griswold, notwithstanding his resentment of women law students, eventually dubbed Ginsburg "the Thurgood Marshall of gender equality law."

She prepared herself for litigation by teaching courses on women and the law, a subject that had rarely been taught. An undisputed leader of an emerging field, she soon left Rutgers. ("Columbia Snares a Prize in the Quest for Women Professors," the *Times* reported.) Unlike Marshall, who was very often on the front lines of civil unrest and political protest, Ginsburg worked full time as a law school professor, which placed constraints on her time and kept her at some remove from protests taking place on the streets. And, as De Hart observes, several crucial features distinguish their strategies. Marshall relied on the equal protection clause—"No State shall . . . deny to any person within its jurisdiction the equal protection of the laws"— of the Fourteenth Amendment, which was adopted after the Civil War in order to stop the former Confederate states from denying former slaves equal rights. Ginsburg also invoked the equal protection clause, but was left to argue only by analogy, suggesting that discrimination on the basis of sex is the same sort of thing. Finally, while there were plenty of rifts within the civil rights movement, Marshall never had to battle African Americans opposed to the very notion of equality under the law; Ginsburg, by contrast, faced a phalanx of conservative women, led by Phyllis Schlafly, who objected to equal rights altogether.

In one of the earliest of Ginsburg's antidiscrimination cases, *Reed v. Reed* (1971), she established that an Idaho law that gave preference to men over women in the administration of estates violated the equal protection clause. Ginsburg called her victory in *Reed* "a small, guarded step." She next hoped to bring to the Supreme Court a case called *Struck v. Secretary of Defense*. When Captain Susan Struck became pregnant, she decided to have the baby, but air force policy meant that she would lose her job unless she had an abortion. Ginsburg prepared to argue Struck's case on equal protection grounds: since no air force policy barred men from having children, the government was discriminating against Struck on the basis of sex. In choosing a case that would advance a desperately needed argument about reproductive autonomy, Ginsburg had cleverly selected one in which the litigant had chosen to have a baby, rather than to end a pregnancy, so that the Court's attention would be focused on the equality claims of women (and not on the politics of abortion). But the air force changed its policy and, in 1972, at the urging of then solicitor general Erwin Griswold, the case was dismissed, a decision that had profound consequences: the following year, the Court ruled on *Roe v. Wade* instead, and struck down anti-abortion legislation not on the ground of equal protection but on the ground of a much weaker constitutional doctrine, the right to privacy.

If *Struck* was Ginsburg's next, carefully placed stepping stone across a wide river, *Roe* was a rickety wooden plank thrown down across the water and—Ginsburg thought—likely to rot. In a lecture she delivered in 1984, she noted the political significance of the fact that the Court had treated sex discrimination as a matter of equal protection but reproductive autonomy as a matter of privacy. When the Court overturned laws on the basis of sex discrimination, no great controversy ensued, she observed, but *Roe v. Wade* remained "a storm center." She went on, "*Roe v. Wade* sparked public opposition and academic criticism, in part, I believe, because the Court ventured too far in the change it ordered and presented an incomplete justification for its action."

There are more what-ifs than there are stars in the sky. But *Roe* helped conservatives defeat the Equal Rights Amendment, which had passed Congress and appeared well on its way to ratification until Schlafly warned, starting in 1974, that the "ERA means abortion." Following Ginsburg's logic, it's impossible not to wonder whether, if the Court had heard *Struck* instead of *Roe*, the ERA would have passed, after which reproductive rights would have been recognized by the courts as a matter of equal protection. And the nation would not have become so divided. If, if.

Asked by the ACLU to take on litigation relating to the defense of *Roe*, Ginsburg declined. Instead, she continued to pursue anti-discrimination cases, and first appeared before the Supreme Court in *Frontiero v. Richardson*, in 1973, advocating for Sharron Frontiero, an air force lieutenant who had been denied benefits for her husband which were granted to men for their wives. "I ask no favor for my sex," Ginsburg told the nine men on the bench, quoting the nineteenth-century women's rights advocate Sarah Grimké. "All I ask of our brethren is that they take their feet off our necks." Ginsburg won, though the Court's holding was narrow. As she proceeded to try to widen that holding, she continued teaching at Columbia and writing law review articles. In 1979, after Jimmy Carter signed legislation expanding the federal judiciary, Ginsburg began pursuing a judgeship.

Carter was determined to appoint women and asked Sarah Weddington, the lawyer who had argued *Roe*, to help him find them. By 1970, only three in a hundred lawyers and fewer than two hundred of the nation's ten thousand judges were women. In 1971, Chief Justice Warren Burger, on hearing that Richard Nixon was considering nominating a woman to the Court, drafted a letter of resignation. "Feminist Picked for U.S. Court of Appeals Here," the *Washington Post* announced in December of 1979, even before Carter had officially named Ginsburg to the DC Circuit.

Strom Thurmond, whose office dismissed the nominee as a "one-issue woman," cast the lone vote against her nomination in the Senate Judiciary Committee, and she took a seat on the notoriously fractious DC court. There she became known as a consensus builder who adhered closely to precedent, wrote narrowly tailored decisions, and refused to join intemperately written opinions. A 1987 study showed that she voted more often with Republican appointees than with Democratic appointees. In *Dronenburg v. Zech* (1984), she voted against rehearing a case involving a sailor's allegation that the navy had discriminated against him by discharging him for homosexual conduct. She generally agreed with conservatives in opposing expanded regulation of corporate conduct. She insisted on the importance of not getting ahead of the law. In *Women's Equity Action League v. Cavazos* (1990), she dismissed a two-decades-old suit, arguing that the litigant groups' claim that federal agencies had failed to comply with their own antidiscrimination statutes "lacks the requisite green light from the legislative branch."

Of the fifty-seven people she hired as law clerks, interns, or secretaries during her time on the DC bench, not one was African American. Ginsburg was asked about this when she appeared before the Senate Judiciary Committee, and she promised, "If you confirm me for this job, my attractiveness to Black candidates is going to improve." But in her quarter century on the Supreme Court she hired only one African American clerk (a record that, distressingly, does not distinguish her from most of the bench). And, as both judge and justice, she frequently sided with conservatives on questions concerning criminal justice reform. In *Samson v. California* (2006), she joined an opinion, written by Clarence Thomas, upholding warrantless searches of people on parole; in *Davis v. Ayala* (2015), she declined to join an opinion condemning solitary confinement.

De Hart describes Ginsburg's thirteen years on the circuit court as something like a decontamination chamber, in which Ginsburg was rinsed and scrubbed of the hazard of her thirteen years as an advocate for women's rights. By 1993, she had been sufficiently depolarized to be appointed to the Supreme Court.

ON MARCH 9, 1993, seven weeks after Bill Clinton's inauguration, Ginsburg delivered the James Madison Lecture on Constitutional Law, at New York University. She took as her subject the importance of collegiality in decision-making and moderation in style. The lecture can be read as an indictment, not just of judicial excess but of the changing character of American political discourse. She inveighed against "too frequent resort to separate opinions and the immoderate tone of statements." Ginsburg had no use for grandstanding, or the cheeky remark, or even the snippy footnote. She offered a list of phrases used by dissenters who disparaged majority opinions by calling them "outrageous," or "inexplicable" or "Orwellian" or a "blow against the People." As an example of the sort of screeds she wished federal judges would stop writing, she cited a dissent that began this way: "Running headlong from the questions briefed and argued before us, my colleagues seek refuge in a theory as novel as it is questionable."

One measure of how politics has descended into acrimony since then is that the Notorious RBG came to be celebrated for just this kind of blistering, contemptuous dissent, as if spitting had become a virtue. Consider a Bustle.com feature, "4 Epic Ginsburg Dissents That Prove She's a Badass," or the signature line of Kate McKinnon's RBG: "That's a Ginsburn!" In fact, there really aren't many Ginsburns to be found in the records of the Supreme Court. Ginsburg produced forcefully written dissents, especially as the Court moved to the right, but they are not themselves immoderate. Instead, they scold her colleagues for their immoderacy, as when, in 2013, objecting to the majority's decision to overturn much of the 1965 Voting Rights Act, she complained, "The Court's opinion can hardly be described as an exemplar of restrained and moderate decisionmaking."

Early in 1993, less than two weeks after Ginsburg delivered her Madison Lecture, Justice Byron White notified President Clinton of his intention to retire. The White House counsel, Bernard Nussbaum, gave the president a list of some forty possible nominees. No Democratic president had appointed a Supreme Court justice since Lyndon Johnson named Thurgood Marshall, in 1967. Clinton, as in so many things, proved indecisive; he was also distracted, and still staffing his Justice Department. He conferred with senators, but relied on seventy-five (unnamed) DC lawyers for advice. He contemplated Mario Cuomo and George J. Mitchell, the Senate majority leader. Most presidential selection processes—in the days before Trump's *Survivor*-style public charades—took place secretly, and quickly. Clinton's process was open, and interminable. The longer he took to make his decision the more interest groups were able to influence the process, not least because the White House invited them in. Over eighty-seven days and nights, Clinton asked all sorts of people their opinions. Kim Gandy, the executive vice president of the National Organization for Women, told the historian Richard Davis that her conduit to the president was the press: "We were frequently asked, 'What do you think about Bruce Babbitt for the Supreme Court?' and 'What do you think about Breyer?'" He just couldn't make up his mind.

Janet Reno, Clinton's very new attorney general, urged him to name a woman. But Ginsburg, for all that she had done to advance women's rights during the 1970s, was apparently not on the lists sent to the White House by women's groups. In her Madison Lecture,

Ginsburg cited *Roe* to illustrate a crucial problem in judicial decision-making—"doctrinal limbs too swiftly shaped, experience teaches, may prove unstable." It would have been better, she thought, if the Court had decided *Struck* instead. Saying this took courage. In 1993, Operation Rescue ("If you believe abortion is murder, act like it's murder") was protesting outside abortion clinics. Other feminists disagreed with the reasoning behind *Roe*—just as some feminists today lament the tactics of the #MeToo movement—but calling *Roe* into question in public when abortion clinics were being bombed seemed beyond the pale. Many also found Ginsburg's counterfactual implausible. "Coulda, woulda, shoulda," NOW's president, Patricia Ireland, said; pro-life activists "don't care about the legal theory—they care about stopping abortion and controlling women's lives."

And so when Clinton, eager to please, entertained names proposed by women's groups, he learned that some of them refused to support Ginsburg, because they were worried that she might be willing to overturn *Roe* (which is not what she had written, but one gathers that the Madison Lecture was more often invoked than read). At one point, Clinton asked Senator Daniel Patrick Moynihan to suggest a woman. "Ruth Bader Ginsburg," Moynihan answered. "The women are against her" was the president's reply. Moynihan called Martin Ginsburg and said, "You best take care of it."

Ginsburg, a prominent and well-connected tax lawyer, was already running a behind-the-scenes campaign, without his wife's knowledge. In February 1993, he'd organized a breakfast meeting with the president of a leading women's group in DC to seek her support for his plan to get his wife nominated as solicitor general. He did not succeed. He had the same experience at a meeting in New York. In April and May, he courted the press and solicited at least thirty-four letters of support, largely from the legal academy, where Ginsburg, an excellent scholar, was widely admired. Fourteen members of the faculty of NYU Law School—people who had been in the room when Ginsburg delivered the Madison Lecture—wrote a joint letter to say that they were "distressed that her remarks at NYU have been misconstrued as anti-choice and anti-women."

All spring, the Ginsburg family kept up the campaign, which involved bringing the lack of support among women's groups out into the open, so that it could be countered. The Brookings Institution fellow Stephen Hess, a cousin of Ginsburg's, warned reporters, including the *New York Times* columnist Anthony Lewis, that feminists were opposed to Ginsburg, and mailed them copies of the Madison Lecture. "I do not know Judge Ginsburg," Lewis wrote in his column on May 10. "I do not support or oppose her as a possible choice for the Supreme Court. I just find the knee-jerk arguments invoked against her—and against others who have been mentioned—depressing."

Nine days later, the heads of the National Women's Law Center, the Women's Legal Defense Fund, and NOW's Legal Defense and Education Fund (on whose board Ginsburg had served) sent Nussbaum a remarkable joint statement: "It has been reported that the women's movement would oppose the nomination of Judge Ruth Bader Ginsburg to the Supreme Court. We want to be certain there is no confusion about where our organizations stand: at this stage in the process, we have not taken any position in favor or in opposition to any candidate." It was hardly a ringing endorsement. Nussbaum faxed a copy of the letter to Marty Ginsburg, who later recalled, "I saw it as a pearl beyond price," since it would allow him to expose and embarrass the authors. He sent copies of the letter to members of the press. Eventually, key women's groups, which had been unwilling to oppose Ginsburg publicly, ceased opposing her privately, especially after May 29, when Clinton hired David Gergen as a senior adviser. Women's groups believed that Gergen was steering Clinton toward Bruce Babbitt and Stephen Breyer. "One minute there were all these female nominees," Kim Gandy said. "And then, as soon as David Gergen gets there, suddenly all the nominees look like David Gergen."

Summoned to the White House on Sunday, June 13, Ginsburg met with the president for ninety minutes. He made his decision later that day and, after watching a Chicago Bulls game that went into three overtimes, called her nearly at midnight. The *Wall Street Journal* posited a rule: "When Bill Clinton is doing the picking, it's better to be last than first." The *Washington Post* applauded Clinton for valuing "reputation rather than celebrity." The next day, in the Rose Garden, Clinton announced his nomination, and Ginsburg delivered a moving acceptance speech. Her daughter had written in her high school yearbook in 1973, under "Ambition": "To see her mother appointed to the Supreme Court. If necessary, Jane will appoint her." Ginsburg told the crowd, "Jane is so pleased, Mr. President, that you did it instead."

When Ginsburg finished, Brit Hume, then at ABC News, asked a question:

> The withdrawal of the Guinier nomination, sir, and your apparent focus on Judge Breyer, and your turn, late it seems, to Judge Ginsburg, may have created an impression, perhaps unfair, of a certain zigzag quality in the decision-making process here. I wonder, sir, if you could kind of walk us through it, perhaps disabuse us of any notion we might have along those lines. Thank you.

If you watch the footage today, the question comes across as gentlemanly, even Edwardian. But Clinton turned beet red and said:

> I have long since given up the thought that I could disabuse some of you of turning any substantive decision into anything but political process. How you could ask a question like that after the statement she just made is beyond me.

And then he took no more questions.

It was a month later, riding the train into the capital, that Biden was thrilled to discover no mention of Ginsburg's nomination hearings on the front pages of the *Times*. She was an excellent nominee. "My approach, I believe, is neither liberal nor conservative," Ginsburg told the committee. The Senate voted to confirm her 96–3, with one abstention. But the idea that her appointment was uncontroversial is almost entirely a myth.

Few justices have been better prepared to appear before the Senate Judiciary Committee than Ginsburg, who had made an academic study of the history of the process. As she had related in a law review article, it was in many respects surprising that the executive would play so great a role in shaping the judiciary. At the Constitutional Convention in 1787, the Senate was initially granted the exclusive power to appoint Supreme Court justices; that measure, proposed on June 13, was accepted without objection. A proposal made on July 18 for the president to name justices and for the Senate to provide advice and consent was defeated. Only on September 7, ten days before the final draft, did the convention revisit this question, and adopt the proposed sharing of power.

In 1988, taking stock of two hundred years of Supreme Court nominations, Ginsburg observed that more than a hundred men and one woman had served on the Court, and the Senate had rejected twenty-eight, of whom only five had been blocked in the twentieth century. No nominee was questioned before the Senate Judiciary Committee until 1925, when Harlan Stone made a brief appearance to answer questions specifically about the Teapot Dome scandal. The next nominee to appear before the committee was Felix Frankfurter, in 1939, who announced: "While I believe that a nominee's record should be thoroughly scrutinized by this committee, . . . I should think it not only bad taste but inconsistent with the duties of the office for which I have been nominated for me to attempt to supplement my past record by present declarations. That is all I have to say."

He relented, but largely for the purpose of denying that he was a communist. Only since 1955 have nominees routinely appeared before the committee. All followed some version of the Frankfurter rule, placing strict limits on what they would discuss, until Robert Bork, who said, on the first day of his confirmation hearings, "I welcome this opportunity to come before the committee and answer whatever questions the members might have." He quickly clarified that, although he said he was happy to discuss his "judicial philosophy," he would demur on specific cases—a distinction, as Ginsburg observed, that "blurred as the questions and answers wore on," not least because Bork, Nixon's former solicitor general and the last man standing after the Saturday Night Massacre in 1973, seemed delighted by the attention.

Bork's confirmation hearings were both the last episode of the Watergate scandal and the first episode of a new and enduring scandal, the blurring of the legislative and judicial branches of the federal government. Bork's nomination elicited paid television advertisements, as if he were running for an elected office. Since then, the distance between the judiciary and the political process has almost entirely eroded. With Merrick Garland, Senate Republicans, acting with breathtaking heedlessness, abandoned the constitutional principle that a Supreme Court nomination is meant to be insulated from public opinion, Mitch McConnell arguing that the American people, not the sitting American president, would name the next Supreme Court justice. "I wish I could wave a magic wand and have it go back to the way it was," Ginsburg said in September, after the first Kavanaugh hearings. Partisanship has corrupted the confirmation process. The legitimacy of the Court has declined. Women have yet to gain the equal protection of the law. And there is no wand.

IN THE SUMMER OF 1993, when Biden finally sidled up to his question, he was asking Ginsburg to explain the distance between her 1973 *Frontiero* brief and her 1993 Madison Lecture. How could she at one point say that the Court can move ahead of public opinion and at another point say that it shouldn't? The transcript reads:

> THE CHAIRMAN: Can you square those for me or point out their consistency to me?
> JUDGE GINSBURG: Yes.
> THE CHAIRMAN: That is a good answer. Now we will go on to the next question. [*Laughter*]

Biden pressed; Ginsburg evaded. "I saw my role in those days as an advocate," she said, talking about *Reed*, and those stepping stones.

"Judge, I don't mean to cut you off," Biden said. "I am trying to square, though, your—I understand your position as an advocate. Then you became an appellate court judge, and you gave a lecture this year called the Madison Lecture. . . ."

Biden found her charming. And she *was* charming, and she was smart, and she was much better prepared than he was. He could not nail her down. Ginsburg answered with a precision that was characteristic of her briefs, of her oral arguments, and of her opinions from the federal appellate court, but also with a self-control honed by decades of experience arguing with people who underestimated her.

"My time is up, Judge," Biden eventually said, wearily. "You have been very instructive about how things have moved, but you still haven't—and I will come back to it—squared for me the issue of whether or not the Court can or should move ahead of society." Ginsburg offered a short sermon about reticence:

> We cherish living in a democracy, and we also know that this Constitution did not create a tricameral system. Judges must be mindful of what their place is in this system and must always remember that we live in a democracy that can be destroyed if judges take it upon themselves to rule as Platonic guardians.

She never answered Biden's question. Instead, she established her own rule: the Ginsburg precedent, a rule of restraint. But there are very few rules left anymore, and even less restraint.

—2018

Postscript: Ruth Bader Ginsburg died in 2020.

BLOOD ON THE GREEN

PHILLIP LAFAYETTE GIBBS MET DALE ADAMS WHEN they were in high school, in Ripley, Mississippi, a town best known as the home of William Faulkner's great-grandfather, who ran a slave plantation, fought in the Mexican-American War, raised troops that joined the Confederate Army, wrote a best-selling mystery about a murder on a steamboat, shot a man to death and got away with it, and was elected to the Mississippi legislature. He was killed before he could take his seat, but that seat would have been two hundred miles away in the state capitol, in Jackson, a city named for Andrew Jackson, who ran a slave plantation, fought in the War of 1812, was famous for killing Indians, shot a man to death and got away with it, and was elected president of the United States. Phillip Gibbs's father and Dale Adams's father had both been sharecroppers: they came from families who had been held as slaves by families like the Jacksons and the Faulkners, by force of arms.

In 1967, after Gibbs and Adams started dating, he'd take her out to the movies in a car that he borrowed from his uncle, a car with no key; he had to jam a screwdriver into the ignition to start it up. After Dale got pregnant, they were married, at his sister's house. They named the baby Phillip Jr.; Gibbs called him his little man. Gibbs went to Jackson State, a historically Black college, and majored in political science. In 1970, his junior year, Gibbs decided that he'd like to study law at Howard when he graduated. He was opposed to the war in Vietnam, but he was also giving some thought to joining the air force, because that way, at least, he could provide his family with a decent apartment. "I really don't want to go to the air force but I want you and my man to be staying with me," he wrote to Dale, after she and the baby had moved back home to Ripley to save money.

The Jackson State campus was divided by a four-lane road called Lynch Street, named for Mississippi's first Black congressman, John Roy Lynch, who was elected during Reconstruction, in 1872, though a lot of people thought that the street honored another Lynch, the slaveholding judge whose name became a verb. It was on Lynch Street, just after midnight, on May 15, 1970, that policemen in riot gear shot and killed Phillip Gibbs. He was twenty-one. In a barrage—they fired more than a hundred and fifty rounds in twenty-eight seconds—they also fatally shot a seventeen-year-old high school student named James Earl Green, who was walking down the street on his way home from work. Buckshot and broken glass wounded a dozen more students, including women watching from the windows of their dormitory, Alexander Hall. Phillip Gibbs's sister lived in that dormitory.

That night, as the historian Nancy K. Bristow recounts in *Steeped in the Blood of Racism: Black Power, Law and Order, and the 1970 Shootings at Jackson State College*, students at Jackson State had been out on Lynch Street protesting, and young men from the neighborhood had been throwing rocks and setting a truck on fire, partly because of something that had happened ten days before and more than nine hundred miles away: at Kent State University, the Ohio National Guard had shot and killed four students and wounded nine more. They fired as many as sixty-seven shots in thirteen seconds. "Four dead in Ohio," Crosby, Stills, Nash & Young would sing, in a ballad that became an anthem. "Shot some more in Jackson," the Steve Miller Band sang, in 1970, in the "Jackson-Kent Blues." In the days between the shootings at Kent State and Jackson State, police in Augusta, Georgia, killed six unarmed Black men, shot in the back, during riots triggered by the death of a teenager who had been tortured while in police custody. At a march on May 19, protesters decorated coffins with signs: 2 KILLED IN JACKSON, 4 KILLED IN KENT, 6 KILLED IN AUGUSTA.

Two, plus four, plus six, plus more. In 1967, near Jackson State, police killed a twenty-two-year-old civil rights activist—shot him in the back and in the back of the head—after the Mississippi National

Guard had been called in to quell student demonstrations over concerns that ranged from police brutality to the Vietnam War. And in 1968, at South Carolina State, police fatally shot three students and wounded dozens more, in the first mass police shooting to take place on an American college campus. Four dead in Ohio? It's time for a new tally.

MAY 2020 MARKED THE FIFTIETH ANNIVERSARY of the Kent State shootings, an occasion explored in Derf Backderf's deeply researched and gut-wrenching graphic nonfiction novel, *Kent State: Four Dead in Ohio*. Backderf was ten years old in 1970, growing up outside Kent; the book opens with him riding in the passenger seat of his mother's car, reading *Mad*, and then watching Richard Nixon on television. *Kent State* reads, in the beginning, like a very clever college newspaper comic strip—not unlike early *Doonesbury*, which debuted that same year—featuring the ordinary lives of four undergraduates, Allison Krause, Jeff Miller, Sandy Scheuer, and Bill Schroeder, their roommate problems, their love lives, their stressy phone calls with their parents, and their fury about the war. As the violence intensifies, Backderf's drawings grow darker and more cinematic: the intimate, moody panels of smart, young, good people, muddling through the inanity and ferocity of American politics yield to black-backed panels of institutional buildings, with the people around them saying completely crazy things, then to explosive splash pages of soldiers, their guns locked and loaded, and, finally, to a two-page spread of those fateful thirteen seconds: *"BOOM!" "BANG!" "BANG! BANG! POW!"*

Backderf's publisher billed his book as telling "the untold story of the Kent State shootings," but the terrible story of what happened at Kent State on May 4, 1970, has been told many times before, including by an extraordinary fleet of reporters and writers who turned up on campus while the blood was still wet on the pavement. Joe Eszterhas and Michael Roberts, staff writers for the *Cleveland Plain Dealer*, both of whom had reported on Vietnam, reached campus within forty-five minutes of the first shot—they rushed in to cover the growing campus unrest—and stayed for three months to report *Thirteen Seconds: Confrontation at Kent State*, their swiftly published book. Eszterhas went on to become a prominent screenwriter. Philip Caputo, a twenty-eight-year-old *Chicago Tribune* reporter who later won a Pulitzer Prize and wrote a best-selling memoir about his service in Vietnam, was driving to Kent State, from the Cleveland airport, when the news about the shots came over the radio. "I remember stepping on the gas," he writes, in the introduction to *13 Seconds: A Look Back at the Kent State Shootings*, a series of reflections on his earlier reporting. "I entered the picture late," the best-selling novelist James A. Michener wrote. "I arrived by car in early August." He stayed for months. *Reader's Digest* had hired him to write *Kent State: What Happened and Why*, providing him with reams of research from on-the-spot reporters. The political commentator I. F. Stone cranked out a short book—really, a long essay—titled *The Killings at Kent State: How Murder Went Unpunished*. So many books were published about the shooting, so fast, that when NBC's *Today* show featured their authors the result was a screaming match. Before introducing them, the host, Hugh Downs, gave a grave, concise, newsman's account of the sequence of events:

On Thursday, April 30th, 1970, President Richard Nixon announced that American forces were moving into Cambodia. On Friday, May 1st, students at Kent State University in Kent, Ohio, expressed their displeasure at the President's announcement. That night, there was violence in the streets of Kent. On Saturday, May 2nd, the ROTC building was burned, National Guardsmen moved onto the campus. On Sunday, May 3rd, students and Guardsmen traded insults, rocks, and tear gas. On Monday, May 4th, the confrontations continued. There was marching and counter-marching. Students hurled rocks and Guardsmen chased students, firing tear gas. The Guardsmen pursued the students up an area called Blanket Hill. Some Guardsmen pointed their rifles menacingly. And suddenly, it happened.

Nearly all accounts of what happened at Kent State begin the way the *Today* show did, on April 30, 1970, when, in a televised address, Nixon announced that the United States had sent troops into Cambodia, even though, only ten days earlier, he had announced the withdrawal of a hundred and fifty thousand troops from Vietnam. Students on college campuses had been protesting the war since 1965, beginning with teach-ins at the University of Michigan. By 1970, it had seemed as though U.S. involvement in the war in Vietnam was finally winding down; now, with the news of the invasion of Cambodia, it was winding back up. Nixon, who had campaigned on a promise to restore law and order, warned Americans to brace for protest. "My fellow Americans, we live in an age of anarchy, both abroad and at home," he said. "Even here in the United States, great universities are being systematically destroyed."

Nixon's Cambodia speech led to antiwar protests at hundreds of colleges across the country. Campus leaders called for a National Student Strike. Borrowing from the Black Power movement, they used a Black fist as its symbol. The number of campuses involved grew by twenty a day. Most demonstrations were peaceful, but others were violent, even terrifying. In some places, including Kent, students rioted, smashing shop windows, pelting cars, setting fires, and throwing firebombs. In Ohio, the mayor of Kent asked the governor to send in the National Guard.

Nixon hated the student protesters as much in private as he did in public. "You see these bums, you know, blowing up the campuses," he said the day after the Cambodia speech. He had long urged a hard line on student protesters: antiwar protesters, civil rights activists, all of them. So had Ronald Reagan, who ran for governor of California in 1966 on a promise to bring law and order to Berkeley, a campus he described as "a rallying point for communists and a center for sexual misconduct." In 1969, he ordered the California Highway Patrol to clear out a vacant lot near the Berkeley campus which student and local volunteers had turned into a park. Police fired shots, killing one onlooker, and injuring dozens of people. Reagan called in the National Guard. Weeks before Nixon's Cambodia speech stirred up still more protest, Reagan, running for reelection, said that he was ready for a fight. "If it takes a bloodbath," he said, "let's get it over with."

MAY 4, 1970, THE DAY OF THAT BLOODBATH, fell on a Monday. The Guardsmen at Kent State started firing not long after noon, while students were crossing campus; there seems to be some chance that they mistook the students spilling out of buildings for an act of aggression, when, actually, they were leaving classes. Bill Schroeder, a sophomore, was an ROTC student. "He didn't like Vietnam and Cambodia but if he had to go to Vietnam," his roommate said later, "he would have gone." Schroeder was walking to class when he was shot in the back. Jeff Miller, a junior from Plainview, Long Island, hated the war, and went out to join the protest; he was shot in the mouth. Sandy Scheuer had been training to become a speech therapist. Shot in the neck, she bled to death. Allison Krause, a freshman honor student from outside Pittsburgh, was about to transfer. She'd refused to join groups like Students for a Democratic Society, which, by 1969, had become increasingly violent. (Her father told a reporter that she had called them "a bunch of finks.") But she became outraged when the National Guard occupied the campus. On a final exam, she had tried to answer the question "What is the point of history?" "Dates and facts are not enough to show what happened in the past," she wrote. "It is necessary to analyze and delve into the human side of history to come up with the truth." She had lost her naivete, she told her professor, in a reflection that she wrote at the end of the exam: "I don't take the books as 'the law' anymore." Her professor wrote back, "A happy thing—that." She had gone out to protest the invasion of Cambodia.

Thirteen seconds later, with four students on the ground, the shooting seemed likely to start up again, until Glenn Frank, a middle-aged geology professor, grabbed a megaphone. "Sit down, please!" he shouted at the students, his voice frantic, desperate. "I am begging you right now. If you don't disperse right now, they're going to move in, and it can only be a slaughter. Would you please listen to me? Jesus Christ, I don't want to be a part of this!" Finally, the students sat down.

Students elsewhere stood up. Campuses across the country erupted. Demonstrations took place in four out of every five colleges and universities. One in five simply shut down, including the entire University of California system, and sent their students home. Students marched on administration buildings, they burned more buildings, they firebombed, they threw Molotov cocktails. And they marched on Washington. *The New Yorker* declared it "the most critical week this nation has endured in more than a century."

BUT ONE OF THE MOST VIOLENT PROTESTS was a counterprotest, as David Paul Kuhn points out in his riveting book *The Hardhat Riot: Nixon, New York City, and the Dawn of the White Working-Class Revolution*. For all the talk of tragedy in the nation's newspapers and magazines, a majority of Americans blamed the students. They'd had it with those protests: the destruction of property, the squandering of an education. Hundreds of thousands of U.S. servicemen were fighting in Vietnam, young people who hadn't dodged the draft; most of them came from white, blue-collar families. Kent State students were shattering shop windows and burying the Constitution and telling National Guardsmen to go fuck themselves? Four dead in Ohio? Fifty thousand servicemen had already died in Vietnam, and more were dying every day. (It's worth noting that both Trump and Biden avoided the draft: Trump said he had bone spurs; Biden got five student deferments and later cited asthma.)

On May 7, three days after the shooting at Kent State, as many as five thousand students thronged the Manhattan funeral service of Jeff Miller. As the mourners marched through the city, scattered groups of construction workers, up on girders, threw beer cans at them. The mayor, John Lindsay, had declared May 8 a "day of reflection," and closed the city's public schools. A thousand college students turned up for an antiwar rally, hoping to shut down Wall Street: "One-two-three-four. We don't want your fuckin' war! Two-four-six-eight. We don't want your fascist state!" They were met by construction workers, many of whom had come down from the Twin Towers and not a few of whom had buried their soldier sons, or their neighbors' sons, in flag-draped coffins.

Joe Kelly, six feet four and from Staten Island, was working on building the elevators at the World Trade Center. He said he'd reached his "boiling point," and headed over to the protest during his lunch hour, joining hundreds of workers in yellow, red, and blue hard hats, some carrying American flags, many chanting, "Hey, hey, whaddya say? We support the USA!" and "Love it or leave it!" Kelly thought the students looked "un-American." The students called the hard hats "motherfucking fascists." Kelly punched a kid who, he said, swung at him and knocked the kid down. While police officers looked on, more or less approvingly, the workers attacked the protesters, clubbing them with tools, kicking them as they lay on the ground. Some of the policemen dragged hippies out of the fight by their hair. Even some Wall Street guys, in suits and ties, joined the hard hats. Lindsay had called for the flag at city hall to be lowered to half-mast. The construction workers swarmed the building and forced city workers to raise the flag back up. Other workers chased undergraduates from Pace University back to campus, breaking into a building on which students had draped a white banner that read VIETNAM? CAMBODIA? KENT STATE? WHAT NEXT? Pace was next. Students tried to barricade the buildings while construction workers broke windows and leaped inside, shouting, "Kill those long-haired bastards!"

Two weeks later, at the White House, Nixon received a memo from his aide Patrick Buchanan. "A group of construction workers came up Wall Street and beat the living hell out of some demonstrators who were desecrating the American flag," Buchanan reported. "The most insane suggestion I have heard about here in recent days was to the effect that we should somehow go prosecute the hard hats to win favor with the kiddies." He advised the opposite tack: abandon the kiddies, and court the hard hats. The day before, a hundred and fifty thousand New York construction workers, teamsters, and longshoremen marched through the streets of the city.

The *Daily News* called it a "Parade for Nixon." They were trying to make America great again. Nixon invited the march's leaders to the White House, where they gave hard hats as a gift. Nixon was well on his way to becoming the hero of the white working class, men and women, but especially men, who left the Democratic Party for the GOP. "These, quite candidly, are *our people now*," Buchanan told Nixon. They were Nixon's, and they were Reagan's, and they are Trump's.

ON MAY 7, the day of Jeff Miller's funeral in New York, signs were posted all over the Jackson State campus:

BE CONCERNED
MEET IN FRONT THE DINING HALL
AT 2:00 P.M. TODAY
TO DISCUSS CAMBODIA.

A small crowd showed up. Two days later, only about a dozen Jackson State students went to a rally in downtown Jackson. One student leader recalled, "The kids at Kent State had become second-class niggers, so they had to go." They had found out what he and his classmates had known their whole lives: what happens when the police think of you as Black.

It's not clear that Phillip Gibbs went to any of those rallies, but in high school, in Ripley, he'd joined sit-ins aiming to integrate the town swimming pool, an ice-cream shop, and the Dixie Theatre. In *Lynch Street: The May 1970 Slayings at Jackson State College*, published in 1988, Tim Spofford argued that Jackson State had never been a particularly political campus. But Jackson had in fact been very much in the fray of the civil rights, antiwar, and Black Power movements. In 1961, students at Mississippi's Tougaloo College—another historically Black school—had held a sit-in in an attempt to desegregate the Municipal Library, in nearby Jackson. After the Tougaloo students were arrested, students at Jackson State marched down Lynch Street, toward the jail where the Tougaloo protesters were being held; they were stopped by police with tear gas, billy clubs, and attack dogs. Two years later, the civil rights activist Medgar Evers was assassinated at his home in Jackson. The next year, his brother, Charles Evers, who had replaced Medgar as head of the state's NAACP, tried to calm campus protesters after a female student was nearly killed by a hit-and-run as she crossed Lynch Street. Police came and shot at the students, wounding three. The local press was not inclined to support the protesters. "Did you hear about the new NAACP doll?" a columnist for the *Jackson Daily News* had asked. "You wind it up and it screams, 'police brutality.'"

A lot of students at Jackson State couldn't afford to get involved. In the wake of the 1970 shootings, one student said, "Mothers are out scrubbing floors for white folks and sending these kids to Jackson State. 'You're doin' better than I ever did,' they tell the kids. 'You better stay outta that mess.'"

Still, by May 13, 1970, five days after the Hard Hat Riot in New York, there were plans, or at least rumors about plans, to burn the Jackson State ROTC building. That night, students threw rocks at cars driving down Lynch Street. "Havin' nigger trouble on Lynch Street?" one squad car asked over the police radio. When students started setting fires, the governor called in the Mississippi National Guard, but, before they could arrive, the all-white Mississippi Highway Patrol turned up. Jackson State's president, an alumnus, met with students the next morning; they told him that they were angry about Cambodia, the draft, and Kent State, and also about the curfew for students in the women's dormitory and the lack of a pedestrian bridge over Lynch Street. He called the police chief and asked him to close Lynch Street overnight; the police chief initially refused.

That night, a rumor spread that Charles Evers, who was now the mayor of Fayette, Mississippi, and who had a daughter at Jackson State, had been shot. As the National Guard had done at Kent State, the authorities at Jackson State insisted that the police and patrolmen had identified a sniper. (No evidence has ever corroborated these claims.) A few minutes after midnight, law enforcement officers began firing. In the morning, the college president closed the campus and sent the students home.

"So we'll film the show without an audience, and edit in the gasps of wonder later."

Time called what happened in Mississippi "Kent State II." After Phillip Gibbs's wife, Dale, learned that her husband had been killed, she found out she was pregnant, with her second child. This one, Demetrius, graduated from Jackson State in 1995, and has had a hard time explaining what happened to the father he never knew. "If I try to tell people about the shootings at Jackson State, they don't know about it," he has said. "They don't know until I say, 'Kent State.'"

In *Steeped in the Blood of Racism*, Bristow insists, "Jackson State was not another Kent State." Bristow blames white liberals for failing to understand the shootings at Jackson State as a legacy of the Jim Crow South's brutal regime of state violence, and for deciding, instead, that what happened at Jackson State was just like what happened at Kent State. She faults the Beach Boys, for instance, for a track on their 1971 album, *Surf's Up*; even though they had noted the specific racial nature of the events at Jackson State ("The violence spread down South to where Jackson State brothers / Learned not to say nasty things about Southern policemen's mothers"), these lines appeared in a song called "Student Demonstration Time," which, Bristow laments, "told listeners the Jackson State shootings belonged in a litany of crises on college campuses."

That was more or less the verdict of the President's Commission on Campus Unrest, appointed by Nixon in June 1970. It wasn't a bunch of whitewashers. The nine-person commission, chaired by William Scranton, the former Republican governor of Pennsylvania, included the president of Howard University; a Black member of the Harvard Society of Fellows studying the history of racism; and, as its only active military member, the first African American air force general, a former commander of the Tuskegee Airmen. After holding public hearings in Kent and Jackson, the Scranton Commission concluded that most campus unrest had been peaceful, that it was a response to racial inequality and the war in Vietnam, that it wasn't mayhem, and,

222 THE AMERICAN BEAST

also, that it wasn't unusual. "It is not so much the unrest of the past half-dozen years that is exceptional as it is the quiet of the 20 years which preceded them," the report asserted, noting that Americans who attended college from the 1940s to the early 1960s had formed a "silent generation." As far as the commission was concerned, the modern era of campus unrest began on February 1, 1960, when four students from North Carolina Agricultural and Technical College sat down at a "Whites Only" lunch counter in Greensboro. Nixon rejected the report.

It's this argument—that white and Black student protesters can be understood to have been involved in a single movement, for racial justice, free speech, and peace, led by the fight for civil rights—that Bristow, bizarrely, rejects as a white-liberal fantasy. If it was a fantasy, it was also Martin Luther King Jr.'s fantasy. In 1967, after King first spoke out against the war in Vietnam, people asked him why, saying, "Peace and civil rights don't mix." Their response saddened him, he said, because it suggested that "they do not know the world in which they live."

A QUESTION, LATELY, IS: Which world do Americans remember? The Scranton Commission concluded that the shootings at both Kent State and Jackson State had been unjustified. It did not, however, urge the prosecution of the shooters, something that a lot of people who wrote books about Kent State urged but that James Michener opposed. "It would be an exercise in futility," he said during his commencement address at Kent State, in December 1970. In his five-hundred-page *Kent State: What Happened and Why*, Michener blamed the protesters and, especially, outside radical agitators, who, like the snipers, seem to have been mostly an invention of the authorities. Joe Eszterhas and Michael Roberts called Michener's book "a Magical Mystery Tour of innuendo, half-truth, carefully-structured quotation and anonymous attribution." They concluded that the National Guardsmen, exhausted, poorly trained, and badly led, had committed murder. "There was death, but not murder," Michener insisted.

A week short of the first anniversary of the shootings at Kent State, Michener, Eszterhas, Roberts, and I. F. Stone appeared on that panel on the *Today* show. "Hugh—obviously, this will be a free-swinging affair," Downs's producer noted, in the show overview. By the end of the hour, the guests had nearly come to blows. "Jim, don't you believe in American justice?" Eszterhas asked, after Michener continued to insist that a federal grand jury investigation would be a waste of time, because no jury would convict the Guardsmen. "How do you know that?" Roberts asked. Michener: "Because it has been the history throughout our country. The law doesn't run its course." At this point, even Downs jumped in: "Aren't you in effect indicting the American system of justice?" Stone tried to read out loud from a statement by Kent students. Michener shouted him down: "I won't let you read that."

That spring, the *New York Times* ran a long investigative piece, "Jackson State a Year After," by Stephan Lesher, a legal affairs correspondent. Alexander Hall was still pockmarked with bullet holes. Lynch Street had been closed to traffic, but with a tall chain-link fence, which made the campus feel like a prison. "No one has been punished," Lesher wrote. "No one is going to be":

> No one—least of all Jackson's blacks—expected a different outcome. . . . Yet, there is a barely perceptible chance that the Jackson State violence will be remembered as more than simply another brutal chapter in Mississippi's disregard for Black humanity.

No one has been punished, and no one is going to be. Except everyone's been punished, the whole nation has suffered, and will keep on suffering, until the shooting stops. That will take a political settlement, a peace, that the nation has needed for a half century. And it will require a history that can account for Greensboro, and Berkeley, and Kent State, and the Hard Hats, and Jackson State, all at once. King made a prediction: "If we do not act, we shall surely be dragged down the long, dark, and shameful corridors of time reserved for those who possess power without compassion, might without morality, and strength without sight." It turns out that the corridor of time is longer than he could have known.

—2020

Postscript: The 2020 anniversary of Kent State was largely ignored. Three weeks later, George Floyd was killed in Minneapolis.

THE RIOT REPORT

O N FEBRUARY 14, 1965, BACK FROM A TRIP TO LOS Angeles, and a week before he was killed in New York, Malcolm X gave a speech in Detroit. "Brothers and sisters, let me tell you, I spend my time out there in the street with people, all kind of people, listening to what they have to say," he said. "And they're dissatisfied, they're disillusioned, they're fed up, they're getting to the point of frustration where they are beginning to feel: What do they have to lose?"

That summer, President Lyndon B. Johnson signed the Voting Rights Act. In a ceremony at the Capitol Rotunda attended by Martin Luther King Jr., Johnson invoked the arrival of enslaved Africans in Jamestown, in 1619: "They came in darkness and they came in chains. And today we strike away the last major shackles of those fierce and ancient bonds." Five days later, Watts was swept by violence and flames, following a protest against police brutality. The authorities eventually arrested nearly four thousand people; thirty-four people died. "How is it possible, after all we've accomplished?" Johnson asked. "How could it be? Is the world topsy-turvy?"

Two years later, after thousands of police officers and National Guard troops blocked off fourteen square miles of Newark and nearly five thousand troops from the 82nd and the 101st Airborne were deployed to Detroit, where seven thousand people were arrested, Johnson convened a National Advisory Commission on Civil Disorders, chaired by Illinois's governor, Otto Kerner Jr., and charged it with answering three questions: "What happened? Why did it happen? What can be done to prevent it from happening again and again?" Johnson wanted to know why Black people were still protesting, after Congress had finally passed landmark legislation, not only the Voting Rights Act but also the Civil Rights Act of 1964, and a raft of anti-poverty programs. Or maybe he really didn't want to know why. When the Kerner Commission submitted its report, the president refused to acknowledge it.

There's a limit to the relevance of the so-called race riots of the 1960s to the protests of the Black Lives Matter movement. But the tragedy is: they're not irrelevant. Nor is the history that came before. The language changes, from "insurrection" to "uprising" to the bureaucratic "civil disorder," terms used to describe everything from organized resistance to mayhem. But, nearly always, they leave a bloody trail in the historical record, in the form of government reports. The Kerner Report followed centuries of official and generally hysterical government inquiries into Black rebellion, from the unhinged *A Journal of the proceedings in the Detection of the Conspiracy formed by some White People, in conjunction with Negro and other Slaves, for burning the City of New-York in America, and murdering the Inhabitants,* in 1744, to the largely fabricated *Official Report of the Trials of Sundry Negroes, charged with an attempt to raise an insurrection in the state of South-Carolina,* in 1822. The white editor of the as-told-to (and highly dubious) "The Confessions of Nat Turner, the Leader of the Late Insurrection in Southampton, Va. . . . also, An Authentic Account of the Whole Insurrection, with Lists of the Whites Who Were Murdered . . . ," in 1831, wrote, "Public curiosity has been on the stretch to understand the origin and progress of this dreadful conspiracy, and the motives which influences its diabolical actors." What happened? Why did it happen? What can be done to prevent it from happening again and again?

AFTER RECONSTRUCTION, IDA B. WELLS, in *Southern Horrors: Lynch Law in All Its Phases,* which appeared in 1892, turned the genre on its head, offering a report on white mobs attacking Black men, a litany of lynchings. "Somebody must show that the Afro-American race is more sinned against than sinning, and it seems to have fallen upon me to do so," Wells wrote in the book's preface, after a mob burned the offices of her newspaper, the *Free Speech.*

White mob violence against Black people and their homes and businesses was the far more common variety of race riot, from the first rising of the KKK, after the Civil War, through the second, in 1915. And so the earliest twentieth-century commissions charged with investigating "race riots" reported on the riots of white mobs, beginning with the massacre in East St. Louis, Illinois, in 1917, in which, following labor unrest, as many as three thousand white men roamed the city, attacking, killing, and lynching Black people, and burning their homes. Wells wrote that as many as a hundred and fifty men were killed, while police officers and National Guardsmen either looked on or joined in. Similar riots took place in 1919, in twenty-six cities, and the governor of Illinois appointed an interracial commission to investigate. "This is a tribunal constituted to get the facts and interpret them and to find a way out," he said.

The Chicago Commission on Race Relations, composed of six whites and six Blacks, who engaged the work of as many as twenty-two whites and fifteen Blacks, heard nearly two hundred witnesses and, in 1922, published a seven-hundred-page report, with photographs, maps, and color plates: *The Negro in Chicago: A Study of Race Relations and a Race Riot*. It paid particular attention to racial antipathy: "Many white Americans, while technically recognizing Negroes as citizens, cannot bring themselves to feel that they should participate in government as freely as other citizens." Much of the report traces how the Great Migration brought large numbers of blacks from the Jim Crow South to Chicago, where they faced discrimination in housing and employment, and persecution at the hands of local police and the criminal justice system:

> The testimony of court officials before the Commission and its investigations indicate that Negroes are more commonly arrested, subjected to police identification, and convicted than white offenders, that on similar evidence they are generally held and convicted on more serious charges, and that they are given longer sentences. . . . These practices and tendencies are not only unfair to Negroes, but weaken the machinery of justice and, when taken

with the greater inability of Negroes to pay fines in addition to or in lieu of terms in jail, produce misleading statistics of Negro crime.

Very little came of the report. In 1935, following riots in Harlem, yet another hardworking commission weighed in:

This sudden breach of the public order was the result of a highly emotional situation among the colored people of Harlem, due in large part to the nervous strain of years of unemployment and inse-curity. To this must be added their deep sense of wrong through discrimination against their employment in stores which live chiefly upon their purchases, discrimination against them in the school system and by the police, and all the evils due to dreadful overcrowding, unfair rentals and inadequate institutional care. It is probable that their justifiable pent-up feeling, that they were and are the victims of gross injustice and prejudice, would sooner or later have brought about an explosion.

Who was to blame?

The blame belongs to a society that tolerates inadequate and often wretched housing, inadequate and inefficient schools and other public facilities, unemployment, unduly high rents, the lack of recreation grounds, discrimination in industry and public utilities against colored people, brutality and lack of courtesy of the police.

In Detroit in 1943, after a riot left twenty-five blacks and nine whites dead and led to the arrest of nearly two thousand people, Michigan's governor appointed the commissioner of police and the attorney general to a panel that concluded, without conducting much of an investigation, that responsibility for the riots lay with Black leaders, and defended the police, whom many had blamed for the violence. A separate, independent commission, led by Thurgood Marshall, then chief counsel for the NAACP, conducted interviews, hired private detectives, and produced a report titled "The Gestapo in Detroit." The group called for a grand jury, arguing that "much of the blood spilled in the Detroit riot is on the hands of the Detroit police department." No further investigation took place, and no material reforms were implemented.

That's what usually happens. In a 1977 study, "Commission Politics: The Processing of Racial Crisis in America," Michael Lipsky and David J. Olson reported that, between 1917 and 1943, at least twenty-one commissions were appointed to investigate race riots, and, however sincerely their members might have been interested in structural change, none of the commissions led to any. The point of a race-riot commission, Lipsky and Olson argue, is for the government that appoints it to appear to be doing something, while actually doing nothing.

THE CONVULSIONS THAT LED to the Kerner Commission began in Los Angeles, in 1965. Between 1960 and 1964, the nation enjoyed unrivaled prosperity, but in Watts, among the poorest neighborhoods of LA, one in three men had no work. In Los Angeles, as Mike Davis and Jon Wiener write in Set the Night on Fire: L.A. in the Sixties, "the LAPD operated the nation's most successful negative employment scheme." Police stopped Black men for little or no reason, and, if they talked back, they got arrested; left with an arrest record, they became unemployable.

On August 11, 1965, a Wednesday, a motorcycle cop pulled over a car with a driver and a passenger, two brothers, Ronald and Marquette Frye, about a block from their house, near 116th Street. Their mother, Rena, all of five feet tall, came over. Marquette resisted handcuffs—he would strike those fierce and ancient shackles. The motorcycle cop called for backup; twenty-six police vehicles raced to the scene, sirens screaming. "Does it take all these people to arrest three people?" an onlooker asked. When Rena Frye tried to stop the police from beating her sons with billy clubs, they pinned her to the hood of a patrol car and, after a crowd had gathered, arrested another of her sons and dragged her away. "Goddam! They'd never treat a white woman like that!" someone called out. The crowd protested, and grew, and protested, and grew. What came to be known as the Watts riot lasted for six days and spread across nearly fifty square miles. On Friday night, a man said:

> I was standing in a phone booth watching. A little kid came by carrying a lamp he had taken out of a store. Maybe he was about twelve. He was with his mother. I remember him saying: "Don't run Mommy. They said we could take the stuff because they're going to burn the store anyway." Then, suddenly, about five police cars stopped. There were about 20 cops in them and they all got out. One came up to the booth I was standing in. The cop hit me on the leg with his club. "Get out of here, nigger," he yelled at me. I got out of the booth. Another cop ran up to the boy and hit him in the head with the butt of a shotgun. The kid dropped like a stone. The lamp crashed on the sidewalk. I ran out of the phone booth and grabbed the cop by the arm. I was trying to stop him from beating the boy. Two cops jumped on my back. Others struck the boy with their clubs. They beat that little kid's face to a bloody pulp. His mother and some others took him away. That's when I thought, white people are animals.

Johnson could barely speak about what was happening in Watts. An aide said, "He refused to look at the cable from Los Angeles describing the situation. He refused to take the calls from the generals who were requesting government planes to fly in the National Guard. . . . We needed decisions from him. But he simply wouldn't respond."

The same Friday, the National Guard arrived. "More Americans died fighting in Watts Saturday night than in Vietnam that day," an observer wrote. On Sunday, fifteen police officers fired eleven shotgun rounds into Aubrey Griffith, inside his own house, where he and his wife had been in bed while their son, on leave from the air force, was watching TV. The officers banged on the door, and Griffith told his wife to call the police. An inquest ruled his death—and every other death at the hands of the National Guard or the police during the days of protest—a justifiable homicide.

Martin Luther King Jr. arrived on Tuesday. "All we want is jobs," a man said to him, at a community meeting in Watts. "We get jobs, we don't bother nobody. We don't get no jobs, we'll tear up Los Angeles, period." Later, King recalled that one man told him, "We won!" King had replied, "What do you mean, 'We won'? Thirty-some people dead, all but two are Negroes. You've destroyed your own. What do you mean, 'We won'?" The man said, "We made them pay attention to us."

Paying attention, at that point, only ever really took this form: the governor appointed a commission, this time headed by John A. McCone, a lavishly wealthy and well-connected California industri-alist who, in 1961, had been made director of the CIA by President Kennedy but had resigned in April 1965, in part because he objected to Johnson's reluctance to engage in a wider war in Vietnam. The McCone Commission report, titled "Violence in the City," cele-brated the City of Angels: "A Negro in Los Angeles has long been able to sit where he wants in a bus or a movie house, to shop where he wishes, to vote, and to use public facilities without discrimina-tion. The opportunity to succeed is probably unequaled in any other major American city." It called for the creation of fifty thousand new jobs, but, first, "attitudinal training." It blamed the riots on outside agitators and civil rights activists: "Although the commis-sion received much thoughtful and constructive testimony from Negro witnesses, we also heard statements of the most extreme and emotional nature. For the most part our study fails to support—and indeed the evidence disproves—most of the statements made by the extremists." Fundamental to the McCone thesis was the claim that peaceful demonstrations produce violent riots, and should therefore be discouraged. In a devastating rebuttal, Bayard Rustin laid this argument to waste:

It would be hard to frame a more insidiously equivocal statement of the Negro grievance concerning law enforcement during a period that included the release of the suspects in the murder of the three civil rights workers in Mississippi, the failure to obtain convictions against the suspected murderers of Medgar Evers and Mrs. Violet Liuzzo . . . and the police violence in Selma, Alabama. . . . And surely it would have been more to the point to mention that throughout the nation Negro demonstrations have almost invariably been non-violent, and that the major influence on the Negro community of the civil-rights movement has been the strategy of discipline and dignity.

By the summer of 1967, amid the protests in Newark and Detroit, Johnson was facing a conservative backlash against his Great Society programs, and especially against the Fair Housing Act, which was introduced in Congress in 1966. He'd also been trying to gain passage of a Rat Extermination Act, to get rid of urban infestations; Republicans called it the Civil Rats Bill. Johnson had long since lost the right; now he was losing the left. By April, King had come out against the war in Vietnam. Beleaguered and defensive, Johnson launched an "Optimism Campaign," in an effort to convince the public that the U.S. was winning the war in Vietnam. George Romney, the Republican governor of Michigan, who was expected to run against Johnson in 1968, asked for federal troops to be sent to Detroit, which would be the first time since FDR sent them in 1943. Johnson wavered. "I'm concerned about the charge that we cannot kill enough people in Vietnam so we go out and shoot civilians in Detroit," he said. In the end, he decided to authorize the troops, and to blame Romney, announcing, on television, that there was "undisputed evidence that Governor Romney of Michigan and the local officials in Detroit have been unable to bring the situation under control." Twenty-seven hundred army paratroopers were deployed to Detroit, with Huey helicopters that most Americans had seen only in TV coverage of the war in Vietnam.

On July 27, 1967, Johnson gave a televised speech on "civil disorders," announcing his decision to form a national commission to investigate race riots. Protests had taken place, and turned violent, in more than a hundred and fifty cities that summer, and they were being televised. Were they part of a conspiracy? Johnson suspected so, even though his advisers told him that he was wrong. "I don't want to foreclose the conspiracy theory now," he said. "Keep that door open."

Johnson loved presidential commissions: people called him, not affectionately, "the great commissioner." In the first decade after the Second World War, U.S. presidents appointed an average of one and a half commissions a year. Johnson appointed twenty. In *Separate and Unequal: The Kerner Commission and the Unraveling of American Liberalism*, Steven M. Gillon observes that "commissions became a convenient way for presidents to fill the gap between what they could deliver and what was expected of them." To his new commission, Johnson appointed a Noah's ark of commissioners, two by two: two congressmen, one Republican, one Democrat; one business leader, one labor leader. Roy Wilkins, the executive director of the NAACP, was, with Edward Brooke, a Republican senator from Massachusetts, one of two African Americans. The commission included no political radicals, no protesters, and no young people. The president expected the commission to defend his legislative accomplishments and agenda, and to endorse his decision to send the National Guard to Detroit. When he called Fred Harris, the thirty-six-year-old Oklahoma senator, to discuss the appointment, he told Harris to remember that he was a "Johnson man." Otherwise, Johnson said, "I'll take out my pocket knife and cut your peter off." Nearly as soon as he convened the commission, Johnson regretted it, and pulled its funding.

OTTO KERNER, BORN IN CHICAGO in 1908, went to Brown and then Northwestern, for law school, and, in the 1930s and into the Second World War, served in the Illinois National Guard for twenty years, retiring in 1954 with the rank of major general. Under his leadership, as Bill Barnhart and Gene Schlickman report in their biography, *Kerner: The Conflict of Intangible Rights*, the Illinois guard had the nation's highest percentage of African Americans. A former district attorney, later elected to a county judgeship, Kerner had a reputation for strict personal integrity, earning him the nickname Mr. Clean. He was elected governor of Illinois in 1960, and it is possible that his coattails delivered the state to John F. Kennedy, in one of the closest presidential races in American history. He had a strong record on civil rights, and was an adamant supporter of fair housing, declaring, in 1968, "Civil disorders will still be the order of the day unless we create a society of equal justice."

After Kerner got the call from Johnson, he announced, "Tomorrow, I go to Washington to help organize this group of citizens for the saddest mission that any of us in our careers have been asked to pursue—why one American assaults another, why violence is inflicted on people of our cities, why the march to an ideal America has been interrupted by bloodshed and destruction. We are being asked, in a broad sense, to probe into the soul of America."

Kerner wanted open hearings. "My concern all the time about this commission has been that at the conclusion our greatest problem is going to be to educate the whites, rather than the Negro," he said. Kerner did not prevail on this point. J. Edgar Hoover testified on the first day, to say that the FBI had found no evidence of a conspiracy behind the riots, and that he thought one good remedy for violence would be better gun laws. "You have to license your dog," he said. Why not your gun? Martin Luther King Jr. told the commission, "People who are completely devoid of hope don't riot."

Maybe the most painful testimony came from Kenneth B. Clark, the African American psychologist, at the City College of New York, whose research on inequality had been pivotal to the Supreme Court's decision in *Brown v. Board of Education*. He told the commission:

> I read that report . . . of the 1919 riot in Chicago, and it is as if I were reading the report of the investigating committee on the Harlem riot of '35, the report of the investigating committee on the Harlem riot of '43, the report of the McCone Commission on the Watts riot. I must again in candor say to you members of this Commission—it is a kind of Alice in Wonderland—with the same moving picture re-shown over and over again, the same analysis, the same recommendations, and the same inaction.

The historical trail is blood spilled in a deeply rutted road.

John V. Lindsay, the handsome liberal mayor of New York who served as vice-chair of the commission, got most of the media attention. But Kerner did his work. When the commission traveled, Kerner went out on the street to talk to people. He went for a walk in Newark, and talked to a group of people who told him they had three concerns: police brutality, unemployment, and the lack of a relocation program for displaced workers. One man told the governor that he hadn't had a job in eight years.

After months of hearings and meetings, the commission began assembling its report. Kerner wanted it to be moving, and beautifully written. John Hersey was asked to write it, perhaps in the style of *Hiroshima*; Hersey said no. (Instead, much of the report was drafted by the commission's executive director, David Ginsburg, who later helped write Hubert Humphrey's campaign platform.) Toward the end of the commission's deliberations, Roy Wilkins offered emotional personal testimony that greatly informed a draft by Lindsay, describing "two societies, one black, one white." Another draft contained a passage that was later stricken: "Past efforts have not carried the commitment, will or resources needed to eliminate the attitudes and practices that have maintained racism as a major force in our society. Only the dedication of every citizen can generate a single American identity and a single American community." Every word of the report was read aloud, and every word was unanimously agreed on. The final draft did include this passage: "Race prejudice has shaped our history decisively; it now threatens to affect our future. White racism is essentially responsible for the explosive mixture which has been accumulating in our cities since the end of World War II." In the final report, as the historian Julian Zelizer writes in an introduction to a 2016 edition, "no institution received more scrutiny than the police." That's been true of every one of these reports since 1917.

Johnson, when he got the report, was so mad that he refused to sign the letters thanking the commissioners for their service. "I'd be a hypocrite," he said. "Just file them . . . or get rid of them."

THE KERNER REPORT WAS PUBLISHED on March 1, 1968, but first it was leaked (probably by Ginsburg) to the *Washington Post*, which ran a story with the headline "Chief Blame for Riots Put on White Racism." It became an overnight bestseller. It sold more copies than the Warren Commission report, three-quarters of a million copies in the first two weeks alone. Released in a paperback edition by Bantam, it was said to be the fastest-selling book since *Valley of the Dolls*.

Civil rights activists, expecting a whitewash, were stunned. "It's the first time whites have said, 'We're racists,'" the head of CORE declared. Republicans rejected it. "One of the major weaknesses of the president's commission is that it, in effect, blames everybody for the riots except the perpetrators of the riots," Nixon said from the campaign trail. "I think this talk . . . tends to divide people, to build a wall in between people." Conservatives deemed it absurd. "What caused the riots," William F. Buckley Jr. wrote, "isn't segregation or poverty or frustration. What caused them is a psychological disorder which is tearing at the ethos of our society as a result of boredom, self-hatred, and the arrogant contention that all our shortcomings are the result of other people's aggressions upon us."

Johnson came up with his own explanation for what had happened in America during his presidency: "I've moved the Negro from D+ to C−. He's still nowhere. He knows it. And that's why he's out in the streets. Hell, I'd be there, too." In 1969, Harry McPherson, Johnson's chief speechwriter, tried to explain what had so bothered Johnson about the Kerner Report. "It hurt his pride," McPherson said, because it made it clear that Johnson had not, somehow, saved the Negro. But there was a bigger, sounder reason, he believed: "The only thing that held any hope for the Negro was the continuation of the coalition between labor, Negroes, intellectuals, . . . big city bosses and political machines and some of the urban poor. . . . In other words, it required keeping the Polacks who work on the line at River Rouge in the ball park and supporting Walter Reuther and the government as they try to spend a lot of money for the blacks." Middle-class whites didn't give a damn, he thought, but blacks needed poor and working-class whites on their side. "Then a Presidential commission is formed and goes out and comes back, and what does it say? Who's responsible for the riots? 'The other members of the coalition. They did it. Those racists.' And thereupon, the coalition says . . . 'we'll go out and find ourselves a guy like George Wallace, or Richard Nixon.'"

That spring, Martin Luther King Jr. was killed, and then Robert F. Kennedy. In July, five months after the release of the report, Kerner wrote his own reflections, looking back at the response to the maelstrom that had followed King's assassination, and arguing against the militarization of the police: "Armored vehicles, automatic weapons and armor-piercing machine guns are for use against an enemy, and not a lawbreaker. . . . If you come out with a show of force, you in a sense challenge the other side to meet you. Force begets force."

Still, Johnson fulfilled Kerner's wish to be appointed to the federal bench. During Kerner's confirmation hearings, he was questioned by Strom Thurmond about the conclusions of the report that bore his name:

> *THURMOND:* Why do you say "white racism" caused these riots?
> *KERNER:* I beg your pardon.
> *THURMOND:* Why do you want to blame the white people . . . for this trouble?
> *KERNER:* Because we say this has developed over a period of time, and the people in the Negro ghettos indicated that the rebellion was against the white establishment. . . .
> *THURMOND:* . . . What does that term mean? What did you think it meant when you put it in this report or approved of it?
> *KERNER:* I thought it meant this—that over a period of years the Negro was kept within a certain area economically and geographically and he was not allowed to come out of it.

In 1971, Kerner became involved in a scandal connected with his ownership of stock in a racetrack; he was eventually charged and convicted of mail fraud. Sentenced to three years in prison, he went to the Federal Correctional Institution, a minimum security prison in Fayette County, Kentucky, on July 29, 1974, two weeks before Nixon resigned. He insisted that his conviction was one of Nixon's "dirty tricks." "I have reason to believe I was one of the victims of this overall plan," he wrote. He suspected Nixon of punishing him for his role in Kennedy's victory in 1960. In his cell, Kerner kept a journal. "So frequently I sit here alone," he wrote, thinking thoughts that inmates have thought since the beginning of prisons:

> I wonder of what use is our prison system—as I have often wondered when I was seeking an alternative to this inhuman manner of restraining those who have violated the law. The waste of man power—both by the restrainers and the one restrained. Removing the individual from the outside world really accomplishes nothing of a positive nature. The restraint builds up frustrations and a smothering of the will. It kills motivation and completely removes decision ability.

With an ailing heart and what was soon discovered to be lung cancer, Kerner was paroled after serving seven months. He spent what time he had left urging prison reform. He died in 1976. Not long before his death, asked about the Kerner Report, he said, "The basis for the report, I think, is as valid today as the day we sent it to the government printing office."

ON JUNE 1, 2020, IN WASHINGTON, DC, police in riot gear cleared Lafayette Square of peaceful protesters by force. ("Take off the riot gear, I don't see no riot here," protesters chanted.) The purpose was to allow President Trump to stride to St. John's Church, accompanied by the attorney general and the chairman of the Joint Chiefs of Staff, and be photographed holding a Bible. The next day, Ohio's Republican senator, Rob Portman, called for a national commission on race relations. "It would not be a commission to restate the problem but to focus on solutions and send a strong moral message that America must live up to the ideal that God created all of us as equal," Portman said. He suggested that it might be co-chaired by former presidents Barack Obama and George W. Bush.

The United States does not need one more commission, or one more report. A strong moral message? That message is being delivered by protesters every day, on street after street after street across the nation. *Stop killing us.* One day, these reports will lie archived, forgotten, irrelevant. Meanwhile, they pile up, an indictment, the stacked evidence of inertia. In the summer of 1968, the civil rights leader Whitney Young published an essay titled "The Report That Died," writing, "The report is still there, it still reads well, but practically nothing is being done to follow its recommendations." It was as it had ever been. It is time for it to be something else.

—2020

THE TRUMP PAPERS

D ONALD TRUMP IS NOT MUCH OF A NOTE-TAKER, and he does not like his staff to take notes. During his presidency, he had a habit of tearing up documents at the close of meetings. (Records analysts, armed with Scotch tape, have tried to put the pieces back together.) No real record exists for five meetings Trump had with Vladimir Putin during the first two years of his presidency. Members of his staff routinely used apps that automatically erase text messages, and, before he was banned from Twitter, Trump often deleted his own tweets, notwithstanding a warning from the National Archives and Records Administration that doing so contravenes the Presidential Records Act.

Trump cannot abide documentation for fear of disclosure, and cannot abide disclosure for fear of disparagement. For decades, in private life, he required people who worked with him, and with the Trump Organization, to sign nondisclosure agreements, pledging never to say a bad word about him, his family, or his businesses. He also extracted nondisclosure agreements from women with whom he had or is alleged to have had sex, including both of his ex-wives. In 2015 and 2016, he required these contracts from people involved in his campaign, including a distributor of his MAKE AMERICA GREAT AGAIN hats. (Hillary Clinton's 2016 campaign required NDAs from some employees, too. In 2020, Joe Biden called on Michael Bloomberg to release his former employees from such agreements.) In 2017, Trump, unable to distinguish between private life and public service, carried his practice of requiring nondisclosure agreements into the presidency, demanding that senior White House staff sign NDAs. According to the *Washington Post*, at least one of them, in draft form, included this language: "I understand that the United

242 THE AMERICAN BEAST

States Government or, upon completion of the term(s) of Mr. Donald J. Trump, an authorized representative of Mr. Trump, may seek
any remedy available to enforce this Agreement including, but not
limited to, application for a court order prohibiting disclosure of
information in breach of this Agreement." Aides warned him that,
for White House employees, such agreements are likely not legally
enforceable. The White House counsel, Don McGahn, refused to
distribute them; eventually, he relented, and the chief of staff, Reince
Priebus, pressured employees to sign them.

Those NDAs haven't stopped a small village's worth of ex-Trump
cabinet members and staffers from blabbing about him, much to the
president's dismay. "When people are chosen by a man to go into
government at high levels and then they leave government and they
write a book about a man and say a lot of things that were really
guarded and personal, I don't like that," he told the *Washington Post*.
In 2019, he tweeted, "I am currently suing various people for violating their confidentiality agreements." That year, a former campaign worker filed a class action lawsuit that, if successful, would
render void all campaign NDAs. Trump has only stepped up the
fight. Earlier suits were filed by Trump personally, or by his campaign, but in 2020 the Department of Justice filed suit against Steph-
anie Winston Wolkoff for publishing a book, *Melania and Me*, about
her time volunteering for the First Lady, arguing, astonishingly, that
Wolkoff's NDA is "a contract with the United States and therefore
enforceable by the United States." (Unlike the suit against Trump's
former national security adviser John Bolton, relating to the publication of his book *The Room Where It Happened*, there is no claim that
anything in Wolkoff's book is or was ever classified. The suit was
later dropped.) And Trump hasn't stopped: during the pandemic,
he required doctors and staff who treated him at the Walter Reed
National Military Medical Center to sign NDAs.

Hardly a day of his presidency passed that Trump did not attempt
to suppress evidence, as if all the world were in violation of an
NDA never to speak ill of him. He sought to discredit publications
and broadcasts that question him, investigations that expose him,

crowds that protest him, polls that failed to favor him, and, well past the bitter end, ballots cast against him. None of this boded well for the historical record and for the scheduled transfer of materials from the White House to the National Archives, on January 20, 2021. That morning, even as President-elect Joseph R. Biden Jr. is ascending the steps of the Capitol, staffers from the archives were in the White House, unlocking doors, opening desks, packing boxes, and removing hard drives. What was missing, that day, from file drawers and computer servers at 1600 Pennsylvania Avenue would take months to determine. But records that were never kept, were later destroyed, or were taken, illegally, chronicle the day-to-day doings of one of the most consequential presidencies in American history and might well include evidence of crimes, violations of the Constitution, and human rights abuses. It took a very long time to establish rules governing the fate of presidential records. Trump does not mind breaking rules and, in the course of a long life, has regularly done so with impunity. The Presidential Records Act isn't easily enforceable. The Trump presidency nearly destroyed the United States. Will what went on in the darker corners of his White House ever be known?

"THE TRUTH BEHIND A PRESIDENT'S ACTIONS can be found only in his official papers," Harry S. Truman said in 1949, "and every Presidential paper is official." Truman became an advocate of archival preservation after learning about the fate of his predecessors' papers. When George Washington left office, in 1797, he brought his papers back to Mount Vernon, but, loaned out, they were "extensively mutilated by rats and otherwise injured by damp"; eventually, they were carried by the historian Jared Sparks to Massachusetts, where Sparks threw out anything he didn't like, scrapped what he found worthless, gave away much of the rest, and, beginning in 1837, published what he liked best as *The Writings of George Washington*.

For many years, there was no alternative for a departing president but to take his papers home with him; there wasn't really any place to put them. Thomas Jefferson, "having no confidence that the office of the private secretary of the President of the U.S. will ever be a regular and safe deposit for public papers," took pains to deposit many of his papers with his cabinet departments. In 1810, Congress established a Committee on Ancient Public Records and Archives of the United States. It reported that the records of the federal government were "in a state of great disorder and exposure; and in a situation neither safe nor convenient nor honorable to the nation." Congress took little action. In 1814, the congressional library burned to the ground.

Most of the papers of William Henry Harrison, the log-cabin candidate, succumbed to flames when that log cabin burned down. Those of both John Tyler and Zachary Taylor were largely destroyed during the Civil War. In 1853, when Millard Fillmore left the White House, he had his papers shipped to a mansion in Buffalo. He died in 1874, having made no provisions for the papers. When Fillmore's only son died, in 1889, his will ordered his executors to "burn or otherwise effectively destroy all correspondence or letters to or from my father." Only by the merest miracle were forty-four volumes of Fillmore's presidential letter books found in an attic of a house, in 1908, and only because it was on the verge of being demolished.

Chester Arthur's son had most of his father's presidential papers burned in three garbage cans. "The only place I ever found in my life to put a paper so as to find it again was either a side coat-pocket or the hands of a clerk," Ulysses S. Grant once said. For years after Grant's administration, scholars were able to locate hardly any of his presidential papers. In 1888, Congress urged the Library of Congress to collect the papers of the presidents. In the 1890s, the library established a Manuscript Division, and a historian who later became its chief began lobbying for the establishment of a National Archives; meanwhile, the American Historical Association formed a Public Archives Commission. In 1910, after the commission reported that "many of the records of the Government have in the past been lost or destroyed," the AHA petitioned Congress to build a depository. Congress authorized the funds, but no plan was undertaken until after the close of the First World War.

Grover Cleveland, during his two terms, preferred to communicate in person, leaving no paper trail. He insisted that the records of his presidency were his personal property and, in 1886, refused to turn over papers that the Senate had demanded: "if I saw fit to destroy them no one could complain." (That is what, during the presidency of Dwight D. Eisenhower, came to be called "executive privilege.") Cleveland's contention became a convention: the president's papers belong to the president, who can deny requests for disclosure not only from the public but from other branches of the federal government. William McKinley was assassinated in 1901; his secretary held on to his papers until 1935, when he donated them to the Library of Congress, where they remained under his, and later his son's, tight control until 1954. In 1924, a raft of papers from the Taft, Wilson, and Harding administrations were found in the attic of the White House. Warren Harding's presidency was riven by scandal; after his death, his wife told the chief of the Manuscript Division of the Library of Congress that she had destroyed all his papers, although she had burned only those she thought "would harm his memory." Most of the rest she left to the Harding Memorial Association. The Library of Congress acquired a cache of those and other papers in 1972, on the condition that they be closed to the public until 2014. (They turned out to include a thousand pages of love letters between Harding and his mistress. "Won't you please destroy?" he wrote her in one letter. She did not destroy.) Calvin Coolidge instructed his private secretary to destroy all his personal files; on Coolidge's death, the secretary said, "There would have been nothing preserved if I had not taken some things out on my own responsibility."

In 1933, Herbert Hoover laid the cornerstone of the National Archives Building. "This temple of our history will appropriately be one of the most beautiful buildings in America, an expression of the American soul," he said. A granite, marble, and limestone monument with two forty-foot bronze doors behind seventy-two Corinthian columns, it was built at the height of the Depression, a massive public works project. In 1941, with Hitler in power in Germany and Mussolini in Italy, Franklin Delano Roosevelt spoke at its dedication:

To bring together the records of the past and to house them in buildings where they will be preserved for the use of men and women living in the future, a Nation must believe in three things. It must believe in the past. It must believe in the future. It must, above all, believe in the capacity of its own people so to learn from the past that they can gain in judgements in creating their own future.

Americans used to believe in those three things. Do they still?

ARCHIVES ARE ANCIENT, but national archives, the official repositories of the records of a nation-state, date to the French Revolution: France established its Archives Nationales in 1790. Britain established what became a pillar of its National Archives in 1838. Newly independent nations have established national archives as part of the project of declaring independence: Argentina established what would become its national archive in 1821, Mexico in 1823, Brazil in 1838.

National archives uphold a particular vision of a nation and of its power, and, during transitions of power in nations that are not democratic, archives are not infrequently attacked. Most attacks involve the destruction of the evidence of atrocity. Brazil abolished slavery in 1888. Two years later, after a military coup, a minister of the new republic ordered the destruction of every document in any archive in the country which related to its history of slavery.

Richard Ovenden's *Burning the Books: A History of the Deliberate Destruction of Knowledge*, is a litany of this sort of tragedy. "The preservation of information continues to be a key tool in the defense of open societies," Ovenden, who runs the Bodleian Libraries, at Oxford, writes. UNESCO's report "Lost Memory" is an inventory of inventories: a list of libraries and archives that were destroyed in the twentieth century, including the widespread devastation of the First and Second World Wars, the burning of some of the collections in the National Library in Phnom Penh by the Khmer Rouge, and the destruction of the National and University Library in Sarajevo,

by the Bosnian Serb army, in 1992. Libraries house books: copies.
Archives store documents: originals. Archives cannot be replaced. As
UNESCO's report puts it, "The loss of archives is as serious as the
loss of memory in a human being."

All is not always lost. Officials of the British Empire set fire to entire
archives as they left the colonies. In 1961, in Uganda, the objectives of
what came to be known as Operation Legacy included the elimina-
tion of all documents that might "embarrass" Her Majesty's government. Decades later, some three hundred boxes from Kenya and nearly
nine thousand files from more than thirty other former British colonies, including Malta, Malaya, and the Bahamas, were discovered in a
top secret government fortress north of London. In 1992, guards from
the former Soviet republic of Georgia burned to the ground the State
Archive of Abkhazia. But many of its documents had been micro-
filmed or photocopied, and these records were stored in other buildings. In 2005, Guatemalan officials conducting a safety inspection of
a munitions depot came across the long-hidden records of the brutal
force that was the National Police—an estimated eighty million pages,
described by my Harvard colleague Kirsten Weld as "papers spilling
forth from rusted file cabinets, heaped on dirt floors, in trash bags and
grain sacks, shoved into every conceivable nook and cranny, moldy
and rotting." People have spent more than a decade preserving and
organizing them.

Governments that commit atrocities against their own citizens
regularly destroy their own archives. After the end of apartheid,
South Africa's new government organized a Truth and Reconcil-
iation Commission because, as its report stated, "the former government deliberately and systematically destroyed a huge body of
state records and documentation in an attempt to remove incrimi-
nating evidence and thereby sanitise the history of oppressive rule."
Unfortunately, the records of the commission have fared little better: the archive was restricted and shipped to the National Archives
in Pretoria, where it remains to this day, largely uncatalogued and
unprocessed; for ordinary South Africans, it's almost entirely unus-
able. In the aftermath of the Trump administration, the most elusive

records won't be those in the White House. If they exist, they'll be far away, in and around detention centers, and will involve the least powerful: the families separated at the border, whose suffering federal officials inflicted, and proved so brutally indifferent to that they have lost track of what children belong to which parents, and how to find them.

IN 1950, Truman signed the Federal Records Act, which required federal agencies to preserve their records. It did not require presidents to save their papers, which remained, as ever, their personal property. In 1955, Congress passed the Presidential Libraries Act, encouraging presidents to deposit their papers in privately erected institutions—something that every president has done since FDR, who was also the first president to install a tape recorder in the White House, a method of record-keeping that was used by every president down to Richard M. Nixon.

The presidential libraries are overseen by the National Archives and Records Administration. They were intended to be research centers, and include museums; and they serve, too, as monuments. The Barack Obama Presidential Library is the first presidential library whose collections will be entirely digital—they will be available to anyone, anywhere, anytime. But the presidential library, which started with FDR, may well end with Obama.

Donald Trump, if he decides that he wants a presidential library, is far more likely to build a presidential museum, or even a theme park, and would most likely build it in Florida. "I have a lot of locations, actually," Trump said on NBC in 2019. In 2020, an anonymous group from New York published its own plans for a Trump library at djtrumplibrary.com. Its exhibits include a Criminal Records Room and a COVID Memorial, just off the Alt-Right Auditorium. But, long before Trump gets around to designing an actual Trump Library, he is likely to run afoul of a struggle over presidential records that began with Watergate and Nixon's tapes.

In 1974, a special prosecutor subpoenaed the Nixon administration for the Watergate tapes. The White House refused to comply.

The case went to the Supreme Court. In *United States v. Nixon*, the Court devised a balancing test that measured the argument for executive privilege against the judiciary's interest in criminal justice, and ordered Nixon to turn over the tapes on July 24, 1974. Fifteen days later, Nixon resigned, and proceeded to sign an agreement with the General Services Administration that would have allowed him to destroy the records of his presidency. Congress then passed the Presidential Recordings and Materials Preservation Act, which prohibited Nixon from destroying the tapes. Nixon sued but, in 1977, in *Nixon v. Administrator of General Services*, he lost. Still, his legal battles continued into the 1990s.

To avoid all this happening all over again with another president, Congress in 1978 passed the Presidential Records Act. It puts presidential records in the public domain; the public can see those records five years after the president leaves office, though a president can ask to extend those five years to twelve for material deemed sensitive. No longer are presidential papers the private property of the president. The act also directs every White House to "take all such steps as may be necessary to assure that the activities, deliberations, decisions, and policies that reflect the performance of the President's constitutional, statutory, or other official or ceremonial duties are adequately documented and that such records are preserved and maintained as Presidential records." What counts as "such records" has been much contested. The archivist of the United States is appointed by the president; the archivist cannot tell the president what to do or what to save but can only provide advice, which the president can simply ignore.

The Presidential Records Act was scheduled to go into effect on January 20, 1981, with the inauguration of the next president, who turned out to be Ronald Reagan. Reagan's attorney general, Edwin Meese III, decided to help Nixon, who was still fighting in court for control of the archives of his presidency. The Reagan administration aided the efforts of Nixon's lawyers, who argued that the archivist of the United States has no discretion in evaluating claims of executive privilege but must, instead, defer to them without review. In 1988, in *Public Citizen v. Burke*, the DC Circuit Court ruled against Nixon and the administration. The next year, Reagan left office, and his staff packed up his papers.

Reagan's was the first administration to use email. Preparing to leave the White House, people in the administration tried to erase the computer tapes that stored its electronic mail. The correspondence in question included records of the Iran-contra arms deal, which was, at the time, under criminal investigation. On the last day of Reagan's presidency, the journalist Scott Armstrong (formerly of the *Washington Post*), along with the American Historical Association, the National Security Archive (a nonprofit that Armstrong founded, in 1985), and other organizations, sued Reagan, George H. W. Bush, the National Security Council, and the archivist of the United States. That lawsuit remained unresolved four years later, in 1992, when C. Boyden Gray, a lawyer for the departing president, George H. W. Bush, advised him that destroying things like telephone logs was not a violation of the Presidential Records Act, because, he asserted, the act does not cover " 'non-record' materials like scratch pads, unimportant notes to one's secretary, phone and visitor logs or informal notes (of meetings, etc.) used only by the staff member."

Non-record records that the administration sought to destroy also included the White House's digital archive of email, a body of evidence that was the subject of yet another congressional investigation, this time into whether Bush had ordered the State Department to search Bill Clinton's passport records as part of an effort to discredit him during the campaign. A federal judge placed a ten-day restraining order on the Bush White House, banning the destruction of any computer records. "History is full of instances where the outgoing President has decided to erase, burn or destroy all or substantially all Presidential or Executive Office of the President records before the end of his term," the judge declared. But on January 19, 1993, the night before Clinton's inauguration, the Bush administration deleted those computer files, in defiance of the court order. Near midnight, the office of the archivist of the United States, Don W. Wilson, a Reagan appointee, made an agreement with Bush, granting him control over all "Presidential information and all derivative information in whatever form" after leaving office.

Critics of the Presidential Records Act say that, along with the creation of independent counsels, it contributes to endless investigations and the politics of scandal. Lloyd Cutler served as counsel to both Jimmy Carter and Bill Clinton. "Now every congressional committee asks for every scrap of paper under the sun," Cutler said in an oral history conducted in 1999. "Independent counsels ask for every piece of paper under the sun. In this Administration, I would guess ten, fifteen lawyers are kept busy all the time digging up documents by the thousands, literally by the thousands. . . . It stops people from writing memos. Many people came to me and said, 'Can they really look in my diary?' I said, 'I hope you don't keep a diary. Sure, they can look at your diary.'" And so they stopped keeping diaries. And some of them started conducting government business using private email accounts.

In some matters of secrecy, the Clinton administration took its cue from the outgoing Bush administration but promised to archive its emails properly. (A system was eventually set up so that if you tried to delete an email you'd get a message that doing so was in violation of the Presidential Records Act.) Clinton claimed executive privilege again and again, to protect himself from congressional investigation; his staff argued that congressional Republicans were on a mission to destroy him, and so was Kenneth Starr, the independent counsel of the Whitewater investigation. Evading the Presidential Records Act became just another move in the partisan chess game.

Post-Watergate presidential papers are seemingly more formal, more bureaucratic, less intimate, and less candid, as if the less control presidents have over their archives, the less interesting those archives have become. "This is horseshit" is the sort of thing LBJ might scrawl on a memo (or any of us in a self-destructing text). You don't see that as much anymore. Don Wilson, after leaving office, argued that the Presidential Records Act compromised the records of the presidency. Records whose preservation was intended to aid historical research had become, instead, ammunition for prosecutors, creating "a climate for avoiding documentation or perhaps even destroying it." Wilson told me, "Vice President Cheney once said, when I asked him for his papers as chief of staff, 'I didn't keep any.'" And, as Columbia Law School's David Pozen has argued, transparency does not always advance good government: it can interfere with the deliberative process, make deal-making impossible, and promote a culture of suspicion and mistrust.

Early in George W. Bush's first term, his administration disabled the automated email archive system. Nearly all senior officials in the Bush White House used a private email server run by the Republican National Committee. Then, between 2003 and 2009, they claimed to have lost, and later found, some twenty-two million email messages. Nor has this practice been limited to the White House. Hillary Clinton's use of a personal email account on a private email server to conduct official correspondence while serving as Obama's secretary of state violated the Federal Records Act, which allows the use of a personal account only so long as all emails are archived with the relevant agency or department; Clinton's were not. "The American people are sick and tired of hearing about your damn emails," Bernie Sanders said to Clinton in 2015, during a primary debate, all Larry David–like. But, closer to Election Day, renewed attention on Clinton's emails diminished her chances of defeating Trump.

The evidentiary shell game has been carried over from one administration to the next. Reagan tried to protect Nixon's executive privilege; Bush tried to protect Reagan's. That so many staff members who served in earlier Republican administrations serve again under later presidents has made their commitment to defying the Presidential Records Act even more ardent. This was something keenly felt by George W. Bush, who, after all, was also concerned about protecting his father's legacy (which is yet another argument against political dynasties).

In 2001, when the twelve-year restriction on the Reagan papers expired, they did not all become available to the public, because George W. Bush signed an executive order that had been drafted by his young associate counsel, Brett M. Kavanaugh. During the Clinton presidency, Kavanaugh had served as an aide to Ken Starr.

In that capacity, he had argued against executive privilege. But, in the second Bush presidency, Kavanaugh favored executive privilege. Executive Order No. 13233, Further Implementation of the Presidential Records Act, tried to extend executive privilege, in effect, indefinitely. Specifically, it granted to the current president the right to review the declassification of the records of his predecessors before their release to the public: "Concurrent with or after the former President's review of the records, the incumbent President or his designee may also review the records in question, or may utilize whatever other procedures the incumbent President deems appropriate to decide whether to concur in the former President's decision to request withholding of or authorize access to the records." This, of course, allowed Bush to withhold from public view anything in his father's papers that he did not wish to see enter the public record, including documents drafted by members of his own administration who had served in his father's administration or in the Reagan administration. As the archivist Bruce Montgomery observed, "In brief, the Bush order expanded executive privilege beyond the incumbent president to past presidents, their heirs, and even to vice presidents, seemingly in perpetuity."

Historians got angry. At a forum co-sponsored by the PEN American Center, Lyndon Johnson's biographer Robert Caro pointed out, "If you want to challenge the executive order, the historian must ask for specific, detailed things. The Johnson Library has thirty-four million pieces of paper. Unless you've been through it, you can't possibly know what's in there." This raises another delicate point. An archive that holds everything is useless unless you can find your way around it, and that requires money. The entire budget of the National Archives is about the cost of a single C-17 military transport plane. In 2018, when Trump nominated Kavanaugh to the Supreme Court, the National Archives, with its limited resources, processed twenty thousand pages of documents relating to his service in the independent counsel's office during the Clinton administration but was unable to get through all the requested documents from his work in the Bush administration in time for the Senate to review them. In any case, Kavanaugh's collection was vast: his records included more than six hundred thousand emails alone.

Barack Obama revoked Executive Order No. 13233 on his second day in office. His administration settled a suit filed by the National Security Archive against the Bush administration, for its failure to release visitor logs. Obama's White House published the logs of more than six million visitors, including the head of the National Security Archive. (Shaking his hand, Obama said, "You know, there's gonna be a record of this.") His administration did not require corporate-style NDAs. Nor had any president until Trump. Months before Trump left office, I asked Don Wilson what he expected of the Trump papers, and he said, "What kind of record will we have other than what he dictates will be a record?"

WHEN I VISITED THE OFFICE of the archivist of the United States, David Ferriero, he had three copies of letters that he wrote, as a kid in the 1960s, framed on his office wall. One is to Eisenhower, asking for a photograph. The second is to John F. Kennedy, inquiring about the Peace Corps. The third is to Johnson: "Mr. President, I wish to congratulate you and our country for passing John F. Kennedy's Civil Rights Bill." The originals of those letters ended up in the National Archives, preserved, long before the passage of the Presidential Records Act.

Ferriero, an Obama appointee, says that the PRA operates, essentially, as an honor system. He wishes that it had teeth. Instead, it's all gums. Kel McClanahan, a national security lawyer, told me, "If the president wanted to, he could pull together all of the pieces of paper that he has in his office and have a bonfire with them. He doesn't view the archivist as an impediment to anything, because the archivist is not an impediment to anything."

After Trump's inauguration, in January 2017, the National Archives and Records Administration conferred with the White House to establish rules for record-keeping, and, given the novelty of Trump's favored form of communication, advised Trump to save all his tweets, including deleted ones. Trump hasn't stopped deleting his tweets; instead, the White House set up a system to capture them, before they vanish. On February 22, the White House counsel Don McGahn sent a memo on the subject of Presidential Records Act Obligations to everyone working in the Executive Office of the President, with detailed instructions about how to save and synch email. McGahn's memo also included instructions about texting apps:

> You should not use instant messaging systems, social networks, or other internet-based means of electronic communication to conduct official business without the approval of the Office of the White House Counsel. If you ever generate or receive Presidential records on such platforms, you must preserve them by sending them to your EOP email account via a screenshot or other means. After preserving the communications, you must delete them from the non-EOP platform.

It appears that plenty of people in the White House ignored McGahn's memo. Ivanka Trump used a personal email for official communications. Jared Kushner used WhatsApp to communicate with the Saudi crown prince. The press secretary Sean Spicer held a meeting to warn staff not to use encrypted texting apps, though his chief concern appears to have been that White House personnel were using these apps to leak information to the press.

Ethically, if not legally, what records must be preserved by the White House and deposited with the National Archives at the close of Trump's presidency is subject to more dictates than those of the Presidential Records Act. In 2016, the International Council on Archives, founded with support from UNESCO in 1948, published a working document called "Basic Principles on the Role of Archivists and Records Managers in Support of Human Rights." Essentially an archivists' elaboration of the principles of the 1948 Universal Declaration of Human Rights, it urges governments to preserve archives that contain evidence of violation of human rights.

The rules about record-keeping, like so much about American government, weren't set up with someone like Trump in mind. It's not impossible that his White House will destroy records not so much to cover its own tracks but to sabotage the Biden administration. This would be a crime, of course, but Trump could issue blanket pardons. Yet, as with any administration, there's a limit to what can be lost. Probably not much is on paper, and it's harder to destroy electronic records than most people think. Chances are, a lot of documents that people in the White House might wish did not exist can't really be purged, because they've already been duplicated. Some will have been copied by other offices, as a matter of routine. And some will have been deliberately captured. "I can imagine that at State, Treasury, DOD, the career people have been quietly copying important stuff all the way along, precisely with this in mind," the historian Fredrik Logevall, the author of a biography of Kennedy, told me, in the last months of Trump's presidency.

Other attempts to preserve the record appear to have been less successful. The White House's PRA guidelines, as worked out with the National Archives, forbade the use of smartphone apps that can automatically erase or encrypt text messages. It's possible that the White House has complied with those guidelines, but there's nothing that the National Archives could have done, or could do now, if it hasn't. Watchdog groups sued, concerned about the use of such apps, but the Justice Department successfully argued that "courts cannot review the president's compliance with the Presidential Records Act." In 2019, the National Security Archive joined with two other organizations in a suit against Trump that led to a court's ordering the administration to preserve not only "all records reflecting Defendants' meetings, phone calls, and other communications with foreign leaders" but records having to do with the administration's record-keeping practices. In 2020, the judge in that case dismissed the lawsuit: "The Court is bound by Circuit precedent to find that it lacks authority to oversee the President's day-to-day compliance with the statutory provisions involved in this case."

"I'm very worried," Austin Evers, the executive director of the watchdog group American Oversight, told me, after Trump lost the election. "There are a lot of senior officials in the Trump administration who have been relying on impunity to sleep well at night, and I think it will dawn on them over the coming days and weeks that the records they leave behind will be in the hands of people they do not trust, including career public servants." But, if Jared Kushner set a bonfire in the Rose Garden, Evers thinks that there would be repercussions. "The PRA gets a bad rap," he says. It's difficult to enforce, but it's not unenforceable. And if evidence of document destruction comes out, Evers says, American Oversight is poised to file suit: "We have litigation in the can."

A WEEK AFTER ELECTION DAY, the House Oversight Committee sent strenuously worded letters to the White House and to dozens of federal agencies, warning them not to destroy or remove records during the transition. The letters were signed by the chairs of twenty other House committees. "That letter is the lifeguard whistle from the tower," Tom Blanton, who runs the National Security Archive, told me. " 'Watch out, there are records drowning out there!' "

Trudy Peterson, who served as the acting archivist of the United States under Clinton, helped oversee the packing up of the Ford White House on the day of Carter's inauguration. Crowds were lining the streets, she recalled, while, inside, "people were packing up the president's morning briefing. You have literally the hottest of the hot foreign policy materials in your hands." A convoy of trucks, under military escort, drove from Washington to Michigan. "We lost track of one of the trucks," she told me. "For a matter of moments. But it stopped your heart." Phillip Brady, who served under both Reagan and George H. W. Bush, once recalled what it was like to pack up. People from the White House counsel's office, he said, "would again remind everyone that these are presidential documents; you're not permitted to walk out of the White House with them; these are things that become part of the permanent record." Brady visited the archives at the Bush Library and rummaged through boxes with his name on them. "Some of the messages were a little more candid than you like to recall they were," he said in an interview later. "Because of the hustle of the day, many times you're writing notes to someone: 'I think that's a stupid idea.' . . . An awful lot more is preserved than you would imagine." That's how it's supposed to happen, anyway.

The memo that Don McGahn sent to executive office personnel in February 2017 came with a warning about leaving the White House:

> At all times, please keep in mind that presidential records are the property of the United States. You may not dispose of presidential records. When you leave EOP employment, you may not take any presidential records with you. You also may not take copies of any presidential records without prior authorization from the Counsel's office. The willful destruction or concealment of federal records is a federal crime punishable by fines and imprisonment.

Custody of the records of the Trump White House was to be formally transferred to the National Archives at noon on January 20, 2021, the minute that Biden took his oath of office on the steps of the Capitol. Trump, defying tradition, did not attend that ceremony. It was difficult, even, to picture him there. Maybe, earlier, he was in the Oval Office, yanking at the drawers of Resolute, the presidential desk, barking out orders, cornered, frantic, panicked. The obligation, the sober duty, to save the record of this administration fell largely to the people who work under him. It required many small acts of defiance.

The truth will not come from the ex-president. It was clear, even before that day, that, out of a job and burdened by debt, he'd want to make money, billions. He'd need, crave, hunger to be seen, looked at, followed, loved, hated; he'd take anything but being ignored. Would he sell secrets to American adversaries, in the guise of advice and expertise? It wasn't impossible.

"Will you shut up, man?" an exasperated Biden said to Trump during their presidential debate. Donald J. Trump cannot shut up. Aside from the prospect of silencing former White House staffers, shredding papers, deleting files, and burying evidence, another danger, when the sun set on the twentieth of January, wouldn't be what's left unsaid, unrecorded, and unsaved but what Trump would be willing to say, still. And to steal.

—2020

Postscript: It was later discovered that Trump had taken thousands of documents from the White House, in likely violation of the Presidential Records Act, and including a great deal of classified material. As of 2022, a Justice Department investigation is ongoing.

THE SIXTH OF JANUARY

"**B**IG PROTEST IN D.C. ON JANUARY 6TH," DONALD Trump tweeted before Christmas. "Be there, will be wild!" On New Year's Day, he tweeted again: "The BIG Protest Rally in Washington, D.C. will take place at 11:00 A.M. on January 6th." On January 5th: "I will be speaking at the SAVE AMERICA RALLY tomorrow on the Ellipse at 11AM Eastern. Arrive early—doors open at 7AM Eastern. BIG CROWDS!" The posters called it the "Save America March." What happened that day was big, and it was wild. If it began as a protest and a rally and a march, it ended as something altogether different. But what? Sedition, treason, a failed revolution, an attempted coup? And what will it be called, looking back? A day of anarchy? The end of America?

Trump called the people who violently attacked and briefly seized the U.S. Capitol building in order to overturn a Presidential election "patriots"; President-elect Joe Biden called them "terrorists." In a section of "Leviathan" called "Inconstant Names," Thomas Hobbes, in 1651, remarked that the names of things are variable, "For one man calleth Wisdome, what another calleth Feare; and one Cruelty, what another Justice." On the other hand, sometimes one man is right (those people *were* terrorists). And, sometimes, what to call a thing seems plain. "This is what the President has caused today, this insurrection," Mitt Romney, fleeing the Senate chamber, told a *Times* reporter.

By any reasonable definition of the word (including the Oxford English Dictionary's: "The action of rising in arms or open resistance against established authority"), what happened on January 6th was an insurrection. An insurrection is, generally, damnable: calling a political action an insurrection is a way of denouncing what its participants mean to be a revolution. "There hath been in Rome strange insurrections," Shakespeare wrote, in "Coriolanus." "The people against the senators, patricians, and nobles." Insurrection, in Shakespeare, is "foul," "base and bloody." In the United States, the language of insurrection has a vexed racial history. "Insurrection" was the term favored by slaveowners for the political actions taken by people held in human bondage seeking their freedom. Thomas Jefferson, in the Declaration of Independence, charged the king with having "excited domestic insurrections amongst us." The English lexicographer Samuel Johnson, an opponent of slavery, once offered a toast "To the next insurrection of the negroes in the West Indies." And Benjamin Franklin, wryly objecting to Southern politicians' conception of human beings as animals, offered this rule to tell the difference between them: "sheep will never make any insurrections."

The term's racial inflection lasted well beyond the end of slavery. In the nineteen-sixties, law-and-order Republicans used that language to demean civil-rights protests, to describe a political movement as rampant criminality. "We have seen the gathering hate, we have heard the threats to burn and bomb and destroy," Richard Nixon said, in 1968. "In Watts and Harlem and Detroit and Newark, we have had a foretaste of what the organizations of insurrection are planning for the summer ahead." In that era, though, "riot" replaced "insurrection" as the go-to racial code word: "riots" were Black, "protests" were white, as Elizabeth Hinton argues in an essential, forthcoming book, "America on Fire: The Untold History of Police Violence and Black Rebellion Since the 1960s." "Yet historically," Hinton observes, "most instances of mass criminality have been perpetrated by white vigilantes hostile to integration and who joined together into roving mobs that took 'justice' in their own hands." This remains an apt description of what happened on January 6th.

One possibility, then, is to call the Sixth of January a "race riot." Its participants were overwhelmingly white; many were avowedly white supremacists. A lot of journalists described the attack on the legislature as a "storming" of the Capitol, language that white-supremacist groups must have found thrilling. Hitler's paramilitary called itself the *Sturmabteilung*, the Storm detachment; Nazis published a newspaper called *Der Stürmer*, the stormer. QAnon awaits a "Storm" in which the satanic cabal that controls the United States will be finally defeated. So one good idea would be never, ever to call the Sixth of January "the Storming of the Capitol."

What words will historians use in textbooks? Any formulation is a non-starter if it diminishes the culpability of people in positions of power who perpetrated the lie that the election was stolen. It's not a coup d'etat because it didn't succeed. It's not even a failed coup, because a coup involves the military. And, as Naunihal Singh, the author of "Seizing Power: The Strategic Logic of Military Coups," told *Foreign Policy*, the word "coup" lets too many people off the hook. "The people who you want to point fingers at are the president, the party leaders, and the street thugs," Singh said. "And we lose that if we start talking about a coup; it gives a pass to all of the Republican politicians who have been endorsing what Trump's saying."

In truth, the language of the coop seems more appropriate than the language of the coup. I mean chickens. "Coming home to roost" quite aptly describes the arrival of armed terrorists in the hall where, moments before, Senator Ted Cruz had summoned that very flock as he stood on the floor and urged the legislature to overturn the election. Derrick Evans, the West Virginia Republican lawmaker who joined the mob and, as he breached the doors of the Capitol, cried out, "We're in! We're in!" acted with more honesty and consistency than the hundred and forty-seven members of the House and Senate who, later that night, voted to overturn the results of the election after having hidden, for hours, from the very people they'd been inciting for months and even years.

"Sedition" is too weak. Noah Webster, in his American Dictionary of the English Language, from 1828, offered this handy way to distinguish "sedition" from "insurrection": "sedition expresses a less extensive rising of citizens." In any case, sedition in the sense of a political rebellion, is obsolete. "Treason," an attempt to overthrow the government, seems fair, though it almost risks elevating what looked to be a shambles: a shabby, clownish, idiotic, and aimless act of mass vandalism. If I were picking the words, I'd want to steer very clear of ennobling it, so I'd be inclined to call it something blandly descriptive, like "The Attack on the U.S. Capitol," or "The Sixth of January."

"Remember this day forever!" Trump tweeted at one minute past six on Wednesday night. There's no danger that anyone will forget it, by whatever name. The harder question is not what to call the events of that day, but what to make of the maddening four years and more that led up to it: the long, slow rot of the Republican Party; the perfidy of Republicans in the House and Senate since January, 2017; the wantonness of a conservative media willing to incite violence; the fecklessness of Twitter and Facebook; and, not least, the venality, criminality, and derangement of the President. Whether that story belongs under a chapter titled "The Rise and Fall of Donald J. Trump" or "The End of America" awaits the outcome of events.

—2021

THE AMERICAN BEAST

Trump is going to do some crazy shit.
—Steve Bannon, October 31, 2020

THE GOVERNMENT PUBLISHING OFFICE'S 845-PAGE
report of the Select Committee to Investigate the January
6th Attack on the United States Capitol is divided into eight chapters, makes eleven recommendations, attaches four appendices, and
includes 4,285 endnotes. Its executive summary, which at nearly two
hundred pages can hardly be called a summary, provides a numbered
list of seventeen key findings, the first eleven of which have, as the
subject of the predicate, the forty-fifth president of the United States:

1. Donald Trump purposely disseminated false allegations
   of fraud. . . .
2. Donald Trump refused to accept the lawful result of the
   2020 election. . . .
3. Donald Trump corruptly pressured Vice President Mike
   Pence to refuse to count electoral votes. . . .
4. Donald Trump sought to corrupt the U.S. Department
   of Justice. . . .
5. Donald Trump unlawfully pressured State officials and
   legislators. . . .
6. Donald Trump oversaw an effort to transmit false electoral certificates. . . .
7. Donald Trump pressured Members of Congress to
   object to valid slates of electors. . . .
8. Donald Trump purposely verified false information
   filed in Federal court. . . .
9. Donald Trump summoned tens of thousands of supporters to Washington for January 6th. . . .

10.   Donald Trump purposely sent a social media message publicly condemning Vice President Pence. . . .

11.   Donald Trump refused repeated requests over a multiple hour period that he instruct his violent supporters to disperse and leave the Capitol. . . .

In a foreword to the report, Bennie G. Thompson, the committee's chairman, stresses the importance of "accountability at all levels," but although the word "conspiracy" appears both in finding No. 12—"Each of these actions by Donald Trump was taken in support of a multi-part conspiracy to overturn the lawful results of the 2020 Presidential election"—and more than a hundred times elsewhere in the document, the report is less an account of a conspiracy than a very long bill of indictment against a single man.

Two years ago, the president of the United States attempted to overturn an election for no reason other than that he had lost. A mere handful of Republican officeholders denounced him; for months, nationally prominent members of the GOP refused to acknowledge that Joseph Biden had won the presidency. On January 6, 2021, at Trump's urging, thousands of his supporters staged an armed, lethal, and yet somehow also inane insurrection at the Capitol, aimed at preventing a joint session of Congress from certifying the results of the election. They failed. Unless you count being temporarily banned from Twitter as punishment, the former president has suffered no consequences for his actions; Republicans have refused to hold him to account, not least because many party leaders have been implicated in the attempted overthrow of the United States government. Days after the insurrection, the House voted to impeach the president, but the Senate then failed to convict him. Months later, the House voted to establish an independent, 9/11-style commission to investigate the insurrection, but the Senate blocked that by way of the filibuster. The House soon voted to hold its own investigation, under the aegis of a select committee composed of seven Democrats and six Republicans. Then Nancy Pelosi, the Democratic Speaker of the House, refused to seat on the committee two Republicans who had supported the insurrection, whereupon Kevin McCarthy, the Republican minority leader, denounced the committee and pulled his members from it, after which the GOP, declaring the attack on the Capitol to have been "legitimate political discourse," censured the two Republicans who did serve on the committee, Liz Cheney and Adam Kinzinger, both of whom left office this month. (Cheney lost her bid for reelection, and Kinzinger declined to run.)

Congress established the January 6th Committee on June 30, 2021. The committee's report is the fullest record yet of the conspiracy to overturn the results of the 2020 presidential election, much of it deriving from the dauntless work of earlier reporters, much of it newly gathered by the committee itself. In the course of eighteen months, the committee reviewed thousands of pages of evidence and presented testimony from more than seventy witnesses during ten televised hearings produced with the aid of the former president of ABC News and illustrated with taped video interviews, Facebook posts, text messages, YouTube clips, and surveillance footage, all of it easily snipped and posted on social media. The hearings made for great television and, probably more important, great memes, the TikTokification of testimony. "Like our hearings, this report is designed to deliver our findings in detail in a format that is accessible for all Americans," Liz Cheney, the committee's vice-chair, writes in a foreword to the written report. But the report, unlike the hearings, is dreary, repetitive, and exhausting. In that sense, it's like Trump himself. It's also surprisingly scanty in the key elements of storytelling—setting, character, and plot. It's as if the committee found itself unable to surmount Trump's madness and senselessness, trapped in his very plotlessness.

The report doesn't lack for details, which consist mainly of running down and debunking bogus claims about dead voters, shredded ballots, dumped votes, voting machines linked to Hugo Chávez, a faked water-main rupture, suitcases full of ballots, USB drives, truckloads of ballots in garbage bins, unmarked vans, a Dominion voting machine connected to China by way of a smart thermostat, and some guy meddling with the election from inside a prison in

Italy. There are inconsequential but *Veep*-worthy revelations: an Oath Keeper calling followers of QAnon "Q-tards," and Lieutenant General Michael Flynn, at the rally at the Ellipse on January 6, asked whether he would march to the Capitol, answering, "Hell, no. It's freezing." Antics abound: Rudy Giuliani (who is now facing disbarment) holding a press conference at Four Seasons Total Landscaping; Ivanka and Jared fretting, uselessly; a Proud Boys subcommittee calling itself the Ministry of Self-Defense entertaining a proposal from South Florida cryptocurrency investors that refers to the planned attack on the Capitol as operation Storm the Winter Palace, a reference to the 1917 Bolshevik Revolution (leading the report's authors to huff, "No historical event has been less American"). At one point, Trump supporters in Michigan plan to hide out in the state's capitol overnight, so that, in the morning, they can sign an elector certificate that, by law, has to be signed in that building. Not for nothing did William Barr, the attorney general at the time, refer to Trump's legal team as the "clown car." It's all so madcap and vaudevillian that, if the stakes weren't so high, and the matter at hand not so grave, it would be the Marx Brothers in *Night at the White House*.

But the stakes *are* high; they tower. Trump might get reelected. Or he might get indicted. Both could happen. Even if he were to die tomorrow, the attempt to overturn the election would require an accounting of its deeper roots in American political behavior and discourse, of the anti-government takeover of the GOP, and of the role played by the 147 Republicans who, in the early morning of January 7, 2021, only hours after the Capitol had been cleared of rioters, voted against certifying the results of the election. The siege of the building is, in the end, the least of it. The Department of Justice has so far filed criminal charges against more than nine hundred people who participated in the insurrection, of whom nearly five hundred have either pleaded guilty or been convicted. The January 6th Report makes eight criminal referrals, recommending that the Department of Justice prosecute the former president (and in some cases other people) for crimes that include obstruction of an official proceeding, conspiracy to defraud the United States, and incitement or assistance of insurrection, the charge for which Trump was impeached in January 2021. Much turns on the reception of this report. As a brief for the prosecution, it's a start. As a book, it's essential if miserable reading. As history, it's a shambles.

INVESTIGATORY COMMITTEES AND COMMISSIONS began to multiply about a century ago, with the rise of the administrative state and the extension of executive power. Their purpose is chiefly to hold bureaucrats and elected officials and, especially, the executive branch accountable for wrongdoing. It wasn't clear, at first, whether these commissions were constitutional. That question was resolved in 1927, when, in *McGrain v. Daugherty*, the U.S. Supreme Court upheld a conviction for contempt of the brother of the attorney general, who had refused to appear before a Senate committee investigating the Teapot Dome scandal. The investigatory commission proliferated during the Progressive Era, and has origins in "race riot" commissions like the Chicago Commission on Race Relations, established in 1919 by the governor of Illinois "to get the facts and interpret them and to find a way out," or, as Lyndon B. Johnson put it, when charging the Kerner Commission with investigating "civil disorders" half a century later, "What happened? Why did it happen? What can be done to prevent it from happening again and again?"

These same questions animate the January 6th investigation, and a case can be made that the insurrection was, among other things, a race riot—a white race riot. But the committee has not taken as its model the race-riot report. Instead, the report is indebted to earlier investigations into attacks on the United States, a kinship suggested by the committee's preference for the word "attack" over the word "insurrection," as if it came from without. "I don't know if you want to use the word 'insurrection,' 'coup,' whatever," a White House staffer told the committee. The committee knew which word it wanted to use.

Congress ordered the select committee to "investigate and report upon the facts, circumstances, and causes" of the attack on the Capitol. The charge borrows its language from investigations into earlier attacks on the United States. On December 18, 1941, eleven days after the Japanese bombing of Pearl Harbor, FDR appointed a commission "to ascertain and report the facts relating to the attack." In 1963, after John F. Kennedy was assassinated, Lyndon B. Johnson directed the Warren Commission "to evaluate all the facts and circumstances surrounding the assassination," which, at the time, many suspected to have been a covert operation coordinated by the KGB, given that Lee Harvey Oswald had defected to the Soviet Union in 1959. In 2002, Congress charged the 9/11 Commission with determining the "facts and circumstances relating to the terrorist attacks of September 11, 2001." Each investigated failures within the federal government, especially failures of intelligence, but each looked, too, to foreign actors.

If you're going to report on the facts, circumstances, and causes of an event, the natural way to do it is to write a story that is both painstakingly researched and kept kissing-close to the evidence—a story, in other words, that is also a history. A history has to be true, to the best of your knowledge at the time of the writing, and it ought to be riveting. The Warren Commission Report (1964) reads like a mystery novel: "In the corner house itself, Mrs. Barbara Jeanette Davis and her sister-in-law, Mrs. Virginia Davis, heard the shots and rushed to the door in time to see the man walk rapidly across the lawn shaking a revolver as if he were emptying it of cartridge cases." The Starr Report (1998), an investigation of a real estate deal that ended up exposing Bill Clinton's relationship with Monica Lewinsky, often reads like porn: "In the course of flirting with him, she raised her jacket in the back and showed him the straps of her thong underwear, which extended above her pants." The 9/11 Commission Report (2004) reads like an international thriller: "Tuesday, September 11, 2001, dawned temperate and nearly cloudless in the eastern United States. . . . In Sarasota, Florida, President George W. Bush went for an early morning run. For those heading to an airport, weather conditions could not have been better for a safe and pleasant journey. Among the travelers were Mohamed Atta and Abdul Aziz al Omari, who arrived at the airport in Portland, Maine." The January 6th Report reads like a prosecuting attorney's statement to a jury: "President Trump's decision to declare victory falsely on election night and, unlawfully, to call for the vote counting to stop, was not a spontaneous decision. It was premeditated." A page-turner it is not.

The reports of earlier investigatory commissions have been mixed successes. The Warren Report, which concluded that Oswald acted alone, is notorious, since it did little to halt the flowering of conspiracy theories involving everything from the Mafia to Martians. "We are looking to you, not to approve our own notions, but to guide us and to guide the country through a thicket of tension, conflicting evidence, and extreme opinion," LBJ told the Kerner Commission. But, when the report came in, the president refused even to accept a copy. The Starr Report is just plain embarrassing.

Reports of investigatory commissions don't age well: as is the case with all historical analysis, more evidence always comes out later. Still, some reports are better than others. The 9/11 Commission Report was a finalist for the National Book Award. In an "authorized" edition published by W. W. Norton, the report was also an unexpected bestseller. As with the January 6th Report, which is available from several different publishers as a book, you could get the 9/11 report free online, but people bought it anyway. *Time* described it as "one of the most riveting, disturbing and revealing accounts of crime, espionage and the inner workings of government ever written." The *Times Book Review* called it "an improbable literary triumph."

Families of the victims, not members of Congress, had demanded the formation of the 9/11 Commission, which consisted of five Democrats and five Republicans (none of whom were current members of Congress). The architects of the report were two professors of history—the commission's executive director, Philip D. Zelikow, and a senior adviser, Ernest R. May—who had taught courses together and had also collaborated on a book, *The Kennedy Tapes*. May, a Harvard professor (and a colleague of mine until his death, in 2009), wanted to reinvent the genre. "Typically, government reports focus on 'findings' and array the evidence accordingly," he explained. "None, to our knowledge, had ever attempted simply to produce professional-quality narrative history." This is what May set out to do—he wanted to create "enduringly readable history"—and it's not only the report's narrative structure but also its sense of historical time that endows it with both immediacy and lastingness.

The historical narrative is the first eleven chapters of a thirteen-chapter report. There is no two-hundred-page executive summary. There is no executive summary at all, or any list of findings. There is, instead, a taut, three-page preface, and then the story begins, the "story of eccentric and violent ideas sprouting in the fertile ground of political and social turmoil."

The 9/11 report has plenty of flaws, as May was the first to admit. "For one thing, the report skirts the question of whether American policies and actions fed the anger that manifested itself on September 11," he wrote in the *New Republic* in 2005. For another, because some members of the commission and its staff had worked at national security agencies, "collective drafting led to the introduction of passages that offset criticism of an agency with words of praise. Not all these words were deserved." Both Bill Clinton and George W. Bush got off even easier than the CIA, the FBI, and the NSA. What May was hinting at is illustrated in a thirty-one-page document declassified only this fall, a "memorandum for the record" of a meeting between Bush and the commissioners in which the commissioners repeatedly pressed Bush on whether he knew, in the summer of 2001, about the threat posed by Al Qaeda. Bush said he'd been briefed only about "threats overseas." This was a lie. He'd been warned about specific threats to the United States. Nowhere in the commission's final report—released in July 2004, less than four months before a presidential election—is the president implicated. If he had been, he might not have been reelected. "Our aim has not been to assign individual blame," reads the preface, written by the bipartisan commission's co-chairs. Instead, they hoped to provide an explanation.

May wanted the 9/11 report to "transcend the passions of the moment," and it did. He hoped it might serve as a model for future reports. "In these perilous times, there will surely be other events that will require the principles of historiography allied to the resources of government, so that urgency will sometimes become the friend of truth." This is the bar that was set for members of the January 6th Committee. Their report does not clear that bar. Not because the report isn't accurate but because it hasn't achieved escape velocity from the leaden passions of the present.

HERE, RADICALLY REDUCED—forty gallons of sap to one gallon of maple syrup—is a very un-executive summary of the report. Donald Trump never said he'd abide by the outcome of the election. In May of 2020, fearing that Biden might win in November, he tweeted, "It will be the greatest Rigged Election in history!" He understood that he would likely lose but that, owing to an effect known as the Red Mirage, it would look, for a while, as if he had won: more Democrats than Republicans would vote by mail and, since mail-in ballots are often the last to be counted, early counting would favor Republicans. "When that happens," Roger Stone advised him, "the key thing to do is to claim victory. . . . No, we won. Fuck you, Sorry. Over."

That was Plan A. In September, the *Atlantic* published a bombshell article by Barton Gellman reporting that the Trump campaign had a scheme "to bypass election results and appoint loyal electors in battleground states where Republicans hold the legislative majority." That was Plan B. Plan A ("Fuck you") was more Trump's style. "He's gonna declare victory," Steve Bannon said. "But that doesn't mean he's the winner. He's just gonna say he's a winner." On Election Night, November 3, Trump wanted to do just that, but his campaign team persuaded him not to. His patience didn't last long. "This is a fraud on the American public," Trump said on November 4. "We were getting ready to win this election. Frankly, we did win this election." The next day, he tweeted, "*STOP THE COUNT!*" On November 7, CNN, NBC, MSNBC, ABC, the Associated Press, and Fox News all declared that Joseph Biden had won. The election was not close. Counting the votes just took a while.

After Biden won, Trump continued to insist that widespread fraud had been committed. Bill Stepien, Trump's campaign manager, told the January 6th Committee that the campaign became a "truth tell-ing squad," chasing allegations, discovering them to be unfounded, and telling the president, "Yeah, that wasn't true." The Department of Homeland Security looked into allegations, most of which popped up online, and announced, "There is no evidence that any voting system deleted or lost votes, changed votes, or was in any way com-promised." The Justice Department, too, investigated charges of fraud, but, as Barr informed the committee, he was left telling the president, repeatedly, "They're not panning out."

For Plan C, the president turned to Rudy Giuliani and a group of lawyers that included Sidney Powell. They filed sixty-two law-suits challenging election results, and lost all but one of these suits (and that one involved neither allegations of fraud nor any signif-icant number of votes). Twenty-two of the judges who decided these cases had been appointed by Republicans, and ten had been appointed by Trump.

On December 11, the Supreme Court rejected a suit that had challenged the results in Pennsylvania, Georgia, Michigan, and Wis-consin. Trump had had every right to challenge the results of state elections, but at this point he had exhausted his legal options. He decided to fall back on Plan B, the fake-electors plan, which required hundreds of legislators across the country to set aside the popular vote in states won by Biden, claiming that the results were fraud-ulent, and appointing their own slate of electors, who would cast their Electoral College votes for Trump on December 14. Accord-ing to Cassidy Hutchinson, an aide to Trump's chief of staff, Mark Meadows, the White House counsel determined that, since none of the fraud allegations had been upheld by any court, the fake-electors plan was illegal. But one deputy assistant to the president told Trump that it didn't matter whether there had been fraud or not, because "state legislators 'have the constitutional right to substitute their judgment for a certified majority of their constituents' if that prevents socialism."

Plan B required Trump to put pressure on a lot of people. The com-mittee counted at least two hundred attempts he made to influence state or local officials by phone, text, posts, or public remarks. Instructing Trump supporters to join in, Giuliani said, "Sometimes it even requires being threatened." A Trump campaign spreadsheet documents efforts to contact more than 190 Republican state legislators in Arizona, Georgia, and Michigan alone.

Barr resigned. "I didn't want to be part of it," he told the committee. Plenty of other people were happy to be part of it, though. Ronna McDaniel, the RNC chair, participated and provided Trump with the assistance of RNC staffers. On December 14, certified electors met in every state. In seven states that Biden had won—Arizona, Georgia, Michigan, Nevada, New Mexico, Pennsylvania, and Wisconsin—fake electors also met and produced counterfeit Electoral College certificates for Trump. Five of these certificates were sent to Washington but were rejected because they lacked the required state seal; two arrived after the deadline. None were accepted.

Trump then launched Plan D, which was not so much a plan as a pig's breakfast of a conspiracy, a coup, and a putsch. Everything turned on January 6, the day a joint session of Congress was to certify the results of the Electoral College vote. To stop that from happening, Trump recruited members of Congress into a conspiracy to overturn the election by rejecting the certified votes and accepting the counterfeits; he asked the vice president to participate in a coup by simply declaring him the winner; and he incited his supporters to take over the Capitol by force, in a poorly planned putsch, which he intended to lead. On December 17, Kayleigh McEnany said on Fox News, "There has been an alternate slate of electors voted upon that Congress will decide in January." Two days later, Trump tweeted, "Big protest in D.C. On January 6th. Be there, will be wild." The legal architect of the Pence part of the pig's breakfast—"a coup in search of a legal theory," as one federal judge called it—was a lawyer named John Eastman. The Trump lawyer Eric Herschmann recalled a conversation he had with Eastman:

You're saying you believe the Vice President, acting as President of the Senate, can be the sole decisionmaker as to, under your theory, who becomes the next President of the United States? And he said, yes. And I said, are you out of your F'ing mind?

Trump pressed the acting attorney general, Jeffrey Rosen, and other members of the Department of Justice to aid the conspiracy by declaring some of the voting to have been fraudulent. Rosen refused. "The DOJ can't and won't snap its fingers and change the outcome of the election," he told Trump. Trump replied, "I don't expect you to do that. Just say the election was corrupt and leave the rest to me and the Republican congressmen." Trump tried to replace Rosen with a lackey named Jeffrey Clark, but, in a tense meeting at the White House on January 3, Rosen and others made clear to him that, if he did so, much of the department would resign. Trump and Eastman met repeatedly with Pence in the Oval Office and tried to recruit him into the conspiracy. Pence refused. At 11:20 *a.m.* on January 6, Trump called Pence and again asked him, and again Pence refused, after which, according to Ivanka, the president called the vice president a pussy.

Trump was slated to speak at his be-wild rally at the Ellipse at noon, but when he arrived he was unhappy about the size of the crowd. The Secret Service had set up magnetometers, known as mags, to screen for weapons. Twenty-eight thousand people went through the mags, from whom the Secret Service collected, among other banned items, "269 knives or blades, 242 cannisters of pepper spray, 18 brass knuckles, 18 tasers, 6 pieces of body armor, 3 gas masks, 30 batons or blunt instruments." Some people had ditched their bags, and presumably their weapons, in trees or cars. In a crowd that included members of white-supremacist and far-right, anti-government extremist groups—including the Proud Boys, the Oath Keepers, America First, and QAnon—another twenty-five thousand people simply refused to go through the mags. "I don't fucking care that they have weapons," Trump shouted. "They're not here to hurt *me*. Take the fucking mags away." The mags stayed. Trump took to the podium and fired up his followers for the march to the Capitol until 1:10 *p.m.*, and then he walked to his motorcade, climbed into the presidential SUV, which is known as the Beast, and demanded to be driven to the Capitol. Secret Service agents persuaded him to return to the White House.

Just before the joint session was to begin, at one o'clock, Pence released a written statement: "I do not believe that the Founders of our country intended to invest the Vice President with unilateral authority to decide which electoral votes should be counted during the Joint Session of Congress." The voting began. By 1:21, Trump had been informed that the Capitol was under attack. He spent the rest of the day watching it on television. For hours, his staff and his advisers begged him to order the mob to disperse or to call for military assistance; he refused. At 1:46, Representative Paul Gosar objected to the count from Arizona, after which Senator Ted Cruz endorsed that objection. Pence was evacuated at 2:12. Seconds later, Proud Boys achieved the first breach of the Capitol, smashing a window in the Senate wing. Eleven minutes later, the mob broke through the doors to the East Rotunda, and Trump tweeted, "Mike Pence didn't have the courage to do what should have been done." The mob chanted, "Hang Mike Pence." Meadows told a colleague, "He thinks Mike deserves it." Kevin McCarthy called the president. "They literally just came through my office windows," he said. "You need to call them off." Trump said, "Well, Kevin, I guess they're just more upset about the election theft than you are." At 4:17 *p.m.*, the president released a video message in which he asked the insurrectionists to go home, and told them that he loved them.

And that, in brief, is the report, which concludes that "the central cause of January 6th was one man, former President Donald Trump." And that, in brief, is the problem: chasing Trump, never quite untethering itself from him, fluttering in the biting wind of his violent derangement, like a ribbon pinned to the tail of a kite during a tornado, and failing, entirely, to see the tornado.

IN THE JANUARY 6TH REPORT, Donald Trump acted alone and came out of nowhere. He has no past. Neither does the nation. The rest of the country doesn't even exist. No one dies of COVID, no one loses a job, no one sinks to her knees in grief upon hearing on the radio the news that Americans—*Americans*—are staging an armed invasion of the Capitol. Among the many reasons this investigation ought to have been conducted by a body independent from the federal government is that there is very little suffering in Congress's January 6th Report, except that of members of Congress running for their lives that day.

The report is organized around the idea of the "Big Lie," which is the title of the report's first chapter. "The Big Lie" is what Democratic politicians and many journalists call Trump's claim that he had won the election. (It is also an expression first notably used by Adolf Hitler.) It is an inept phrase: it turns an attempted coup d'état into something that sounds like a children's book written by Margaret Wise Brown. "The Big Lie" is so ham-handed that, unsurprisingly, it's an expression that Trump adores. "The Fraudulent Presidential Election of 2020 will be, from this day forth, known as *THE BIG LIE!*" he announced at one point. Playing "You lie!" "No, you lie!" with Donald Trump is a fool's game.

"The Big Lie" is not a big lie. It is an elaborate fiction, an artful story, with heroes and villains, exotic locales, and a sinister plot. *The election was stolen by a cabal of Democrats, socialists, immigrants, criminals, Black people, and spies.* This story is vicious and idiotic, and none of it is true, but it is not a Big Lie devised by an orange-haired supervillain born rich in 1946: it is the latest chapter in a fictive counterhistory of the United States that has been told by the far right for decades and decades and wretched decades. In 2020, it gained so much speed so fast that it acted something like a stampede. Unfortunately, reading the report is like being in the stampede. "The stolen election narrative has proven to be remarkably durable precisely because it is a matter of belief—not evidence, or reason," the report states. It does not ask why this should be. Why believe? Two in five Americans and three in five Republicans *still* believe. Republicans who most fiercely believe hold the party by the throat. The 9/11 Commission Report asked, "How did Bin Ladin—with his call for indiscriminate killing of Americans—win thousands of followers and some degree of approval from millions more?" The January 6th Committee Report, for all its weight and consequence, never asks why anyone believed Donald Trump, which is why it is unlikely to persuade anyone not to.

WHY BELIEVE? Answering that question would have required a historical vantage on the decay of the party system, the celebration of political intolerance by both the right and the left, the contribution of social media to political extremism, and the predicament of American journalism. Calling the system rigged when you're losing is an old trick. At the end of the Cold War, American zealots turned their most ruthless ideological weapons on one another, Manicheans all. In 1992, Newt Gingrich told Republican candidates to get the message out that the Democrats were going to rig the presidential election. It didn't matter to Gingrich that this wasn't true. "They're going to buy registrations, they're going to buy votes," he warned. "They're going to turn out votes, they're going to steal votes, they're going to do anything they can." After the contested Bush v. Gore election of 2000, sowing doubt about elections became common practice for outsiders in both parties. "The system is rigged" was the watchword of Bernie Sanders's 2016 campaign: primaries rigged against challengers, the economy rigged against working people. Suspecting that things like elections might be rigged, even when that's not true, isn't a crazy conspiracy theory; it is a political product routinely sold to voters in every city and state in the country.

Why believe? In the past two decades, public approval of Congress has fallen from 80 percent to 20 percent. Might it be that Congress has lost any real grip on the American experience, and no longer speaks for a nation and a people that Richard Hofstadter once called a "huge, inarticulate beast"? The report lacks not only a sense of the past but also a meaningful sense of the present. A chronicle that runs from April 2020 to January 2021, it is a story told out of time. The "facts, circumstances, and causes" relating to the insurrection that it fails to investigate and, in most cases, even to note, include COVID-19 deaths, masks, lockdowns, joblessness, farm closures, guns and mass shootings, a national mental health crisis, daily reports of devastating storms and fires, George Floyd, Black Lives Matter, and partisan, and especially congressional, eye-gouging over each and every one of the items in this list. Why believe? Was the election stolen? No. But was 2020 painful? Yes.

Why believe? Nowhere acknowledged in the report is the fact that November 3, 2020, really was a weird Election Day. In the middle of a pandemic, unprecedented numbers of people voted by mail and by absentee ballot, and, even if you trudged out to the polls, you were met with the general misery of masks and loneliness and loss and, for many people, a sense of impending doom. For the entire stretch of time chronicled in this report, it felt to many Americans, not always for the same reasons, as though a great deal was being stolen from them: their jobs, their coworkers, a sense of justice and fairness in the world, predictable weather, the idea of America, the people they love, human touch. The January 6th Report offers no shuddering sense, not even a little shiver, of the national mood of vulnerability, fear, and sorrow. "The assassination of John Fitzgerald Kennedy on November 22, 1963, was a cruel and shocking act of violence directed against a man, a family, a nation, and against all mankind," the Warren Commission Report opens. Nothing in the January 6th report is stated so squarely.

Why believe? During the pandemic, more people spent more time online than ever before. The report fails to examine the way in which Facebook and Twitter profited by spreading misinformation about the election, providing the organizational architecture for the insurrection, and making possible the doxing and harassment of courageous and dedicated public servants who refused to participate in the conspiracy. When Trump staffers tell him that allegations of fraud are unfounded, he replies, "You guys may not be following the internet the way I do." Nor did the committee.

Why believe? Every single television and news outlet that reported live on Election Day, 2020, knew about the Red Mirage, and although some news anchors regularly pointed out that the outcome would not be known for days, they were nevertheless complicit in promoting the fiction of a Trump victory: simply by reporting, second by second, on November 3, 2020, they endorsed the idea that the outcome could be known that night even though they knew it to be untrue. The committee does not remark on this. Nor does it indict the media-run polls and horse-race coverage—vastly greater in number, speed, and influence than ever before—or the growing partisanship of the press. Nor does it inquire into the consequences of an educated national elite of politicians, journalists, and academics increasingly living their lives in a Met Gala to Davos to White House Correspondents' Dinner world, or the degree to which so many of them appear to have so wholly given themselves over to Twitter—knowing the world through it, reporting from it, being ruled by it.

Why believe? The answer to that question—the knowledge of what has happened to America—will have to wait for another day. From beneath the Capitol dome, the January 6th Committee has issued its report. It blames Trump. It explains very little. Outside, the whirling wind heaves and twists and roars.

—2023

Acknowledgments

Heartfelt thanks to Henry Finder at *The New Yorker* and to Bob Weil. I remain forever indebted to David Remnick. At Liveright, thanks to Janet Byrne, Don Rifkin, Steve Attardo, and Haley Bracken. Thanks, as ever, to Tina Bennett. Very special thanks to the many amazing librarians and archivists who helped me research the essays in this book and to all the fact-checkers who checked facts. I've drawn here on material from too many collections to name but they include those of the BBC, the Beinecke Library, and Houghton Library, and historical collections at the Harvard Business School Library, Special Collections at the Harvard Law School, the Library of Congress Manuscripts Division, the Massachusetts Historical Society, the National Archives, the Manuscripts and Archives Division of the New York Public Library, the Schlesinger Library at Radcliffe Institute for Advanced Study, and Manuscripts and Archives at Yale University. To Adrianna Alty, Dan Balz, Elise Broach, Gaby Calvocoressi, Jelani Cobb, Nancy Cott, Sophie Crane, Phil Deloria, Zachary Elkins, Deb Favreau, Benjamin Filene, Beverly Gage, Jamal Greene, Stephen Greenblatt, Elizabeth Hinton, Maya Jasanoff, Jane Kamensky, Elis and Josh Kanner, Lisa Lovett, Ken Mack, Luke Menand, Adelaide Mandeville, Liz McNerney, Benjamin Naddaff-Hafrey, Latif Nasser, Evan Osnos, Dan Penrice, Leah Price, Julie Reuben, Bruce Schulman, Rachel Seidman, Reva Siegel, Ramie Targoff, Sue Vargo, Denise Webb, to the late and much-missed Tony Horwitz, and to all the rest of my friends, colleagues, and family who talked me through essay after essay, love and thanks, always.